GW00580133

Identity, Home and Writing Elsewhere in Contemporary Chinese Diaspora Poetry

Identity, Home and Writing Elsewhere in Contemporary Chinese Diaspora Poetry

Jennifer Wong

BLOOMSBURY ACADEMIC
LONDON • NEW YORK • OXFORD • NEW DELHI • SYDNEY

BLOOMSBURY ACADEMIC
Bloomsbury Publishing Plc
50 Bedford Square, London, WC1B 3DP, UK
1385 Broadway, New York, NY 10018, USA
29 Earlsfort Terrace, Dublin 2, Ireland

BLOOMSBURY, BLOOMSBURY ACADEMIC and the Diana logo are
trademarks of Bloomsbury Publishing Plc

First published in Great Britain 2023

Copyright © Jennifer Wong, 2023

Jennifer Wong has asserted her right under the Copyright,
Designs and Patents Act, 1988, to be identified as Author of this work.

For legal purposes the Acknowledgements on p. viii constitute
an extension of this copyright page.

Cover design: Rebecca Heselton
Cover image © Alison Marras/ unsplash

All rights reserved. No part of this publication may be reproduced or transmitted
in any form or by any means, electronic or mechanical, including photocopying,
recording, or any information storage or retrieval system, without prior
permission in writing from the publishers.

Bloomsbury Publishing Plc does not have any control over, or responsibility for,
any third-party websites referred to or in this book. All internet addresses given
in this book were correct at the time of going to press. The author and publisher
regret any inconvenience caused if addresses have changed or sites have
ceased to exist, but can accept no responsibility for any such changes.

A catalogue record for this book is available from the British Library.

Library of Congress Cataloging-in-Publication Data
Names: Wong, Jennifer, 1978- author.
Title: Identity, home and writing elsewhere in contemporary Chinese diaspora
poetry / Jennifer Wong.
Description: London ; New York : Bloomsbury Academic, 2023. |
Includes bibliographical references and index.
Identifiers: LCCN 2022018433 | ISBN 9781350250338 (hardback) | ISBN 9781350250376
(paperback) | ISBN 9781350250345 (ebook) | ISBN 9781350250352 (epub) |
ISBN 9781350250369
Subjects: LCSH: American poetry–Chinese American authors–History and criticism. |
English poetry–Chinese authors–History and criticism. | Identity (Philosophical concept) in
literature. | Home in literature. | Chinese diaspora in literature. | LCGFT: Literary criticism.
Classification: LCC PS153.C45 W66 2022 | DDC 821/.91098951–dc23/eng/20220822
LC record available at https://lccn.loc.gov/2022018433

ISBN: HB: 978-1-3502-5033-8
          ePDF: 978-1-3502-5034-5
          eBook: 978-1-3502-5035-2

Typeset by Integra Software Services Pvt. Ltd.

To find out more about our authors and books visit www.bloomsbury.com
and sign up for our newsletters.

Contents

Illustrations

Acknowledgements

I am very grateful to a number of people who have supported me in writing this book: Niall Munro, Robert Hampson, Shirley Lim, Robin Schofield, Alex Goody, Sandeep Parmar, Simon Kovesi, Susheila Nasta, Rey Chow, Margaret Hillenbrand, Dorothy Wang, Katherine Baxter, Eddie Tay, Antony Huen, Agnes Lam, Mary Cooper and others for their inspiration, advice, sharing of ideas and friendship. Thank you to authors for interviews and scholars for my project, including Marilyn Chin, Li-Young Lee, Sarah Howe, Mary Jean Chan, Theophilus Kwek, Agnes Lam, Will Harris, Jane Yeh, Hannah Lowe, Sean Wai Keung, Jee Leong Koh, Xichuan, Eleanor Goodman, Cynthia Miller, Jennifer Lee Tsai, Sean Wai Keung, Nicholas Wong, Tammy Ho, Nina Mingya Powles, Jinhao Xie, L Kiew. Thank you to Alex Couto Alves and my family, my friends for their constant support and faith in my work including Wendy Law, Melissa Evans, Matt Bryden for your feedbacks.

I am grateful to Swire Trust for their generous scholarship for me to move from Hong Kong to England to pursue English literature at University College, Oxford, which formed the beginning of my interest in researching home, language and diasporic identities. I am thankful to Oxford Brookes for my PhD scholarship. Thanks also to Oxford TORCH for hosting my visiting fellowship in 2022 to deepen my understanding of 'home', so special thanks to Jennifer Altehenger, Wes Williams and Holly Knights for generous support.

Thank you to *Wasafiri*, Institute of English Studies and Oxford Brookes Poetry Centre, poets and moderators for launching the Poetics of Home Festival in 2020, in the midst of lockdowns, which deepened our thoughts on identity and home across the communities. Thank you Malachi McIntosh, Elizabeth Robertson and Susheila Nasta for your support.

I also thank the library staff at Oxford Brookes and Oxford University (Bodleian Libraries) for being so helpful in supporting my research work.

Due acknowledgement to *English: Journal of the English Association* (Oxford University Press) for publishing my article 'Hannah Lowe and Sarah Howe: Multicultural Heritage and Questions of Identity'.*

* *English: Journal of the English Association*, Volume 69, Issue 266, Autumn 2020, 246–269, <https://doi.org/10.1093/english/efaa015>.

Preface

Shirley Geok-lin Lim

Professor Emerita, University of California, Santa Barbara

Having agreed to write the preface for a yet unread monograph on Chinese diaspora poetry through the critical lens of a younger generation, Hong Kong-born, United Kingdom-based-and-trained poet-scholar, I crossed my fingers on what kind of project I was going to be pitched into. I was informed briefly that the readings spanned continents, generations and languages. Was the study to be theoretically dense, as such time and space expansions also necessitate compressions? Will the readings be close, specifically acute, yet historically contextualized? Will the wide-ranging chapters cohere in a thesis not yet promulgated in previous dissertations on the fascinatingly nuanced intersectionality of postcolonial, transnational, race, class, gender – i.e. the ever-increasing catalogue of identities – that cultural studies scholars have discovered in diverse closets and that are now discursively enlivening universities, societies and politics?

Jennifer Wong's study fulfils all these expectations, often with an original twist. Her bibliography is thick and rich, both in its theoretical layers, on pilings of feminist and gender performative concepts, Orientalist and subaltern alterity critiques, psychoanalytical and psycholinguistic approaches to human development and utterance, and more. But it is her selection of 'Chinese diasporic poets' that is new to me, often also considered a 'Chinese diasporic poet-scholar', albeit one across the Atlantic Pond, straddling both centuries, and for most of my adult life, grounded (rather as a lifeboat is grounded) on US territory and nation. Jokes may be made of the vanishing distances between these two Anglophone nation-states, increasingly shortened by submarine cable wires, satellite signals and air flights from Heathrow to John F. Kennedy Airport. But Wong's study makes emphatic deep historical and cultural divisions that differentiate communities departing from the same lands but landing on opposing Atlantic shores.

The book itself, *Identity, Home and Writing Elsewhere in Contemporary Chinese Diaspora Poetry*, is composed of two parts. The first is a conventional monograph of eight chapters, organized chronologically and geographically. The second, in a series of appendices, is in different critical and narrative voices, structured by Wong's questions to Chinese diaspora poets she has identified as such, and their polyvocal, dialogical responses, usually extensive, autobiographical and clarifying of their poetic praxes.

The chapters cover a surprising spectrum of poets, not simply set in time and space, but chiefly in language choices. The first six chapters focus on individual poets, the last seventh and eighth on a sweep of younger poets based in the UK and in Hong Kong. Interestingly, the term 'Anglophone' is deployed as a definitive marker only in these chapters on younger UK and US poets of Chinese ancestry. Yet, except for the first poet, Bei Dao, the five single-poet studies are also Anglophone, publishing in English-language presses, speaking and residing in English-language territories.

The decision to begin the study with Bei Dao, a Sinophone poet who would not have viewed himself as a diasporic Chinese or his works as those belonging in a canon of Chinese diaspora literature, prepares us for a more slippery understanding of the term 'diaspora' than has been theoretically formulated. Certain discursive repetitions explain the study's remit, both originally bold yet open to interrogation. One is the approving phrase 'creative tension', the other is the dependence on the generative Imaginary of the fixed polar stars of Home and Identity. This repeated thematic of 'creative tension' suggests that the study views the generative energy of composition as rising from conflictual impulses, actions, agents or sentiments in need of active reconciliation, or at least unpacking, to make a meaningful order, a poesis. Then, in her readings of these Chinese diaspora poets, Wong views 'diaspora', the dispersal from an original homeland with its accompanying losses, sorrows, yearnings, and present precarities and angst-ridden visions of the future, as central themes. These thematics indeed have prevailed in immigrant literatures through centuries and with myriad peoples.

Of the six poets singled for individual chapters, the well-known Bei Dao is an intriguing Sinophone outlier. He left in exile in 1989 for the United States and Europe, but after seventeen years shuttling abroad, he returned to China in 2006. The choice of Bei Dao to open the study immediately blurs the customary sharp distinctions between exile, usually framed as temporary, and diaspora, whose sense of dispersal embraces a different temporal – permanent – loss. Two poets are based in the United States – Li-Young Lee (who was born in Indonesia) and Marilyn Chin – and three in the UK. Out of the five Anglophone poets, four are women, and three of the women are Hong Kong-born (Marilyn Chin, Sarah Howe, who is also mixed-race, and Mary Jean Chan), underlining the importance of Hong Kong as a significant site of arrivals cum departures that the monograph's eighth chapter treats at greater length. Only Hannah Lowe, the second mixed-race 'Chinese diaspora poet' included, is UK-born. While Howe's father is white, Lowe can also pass for white, as her West-Indian-Chinese father has assimilated in the UK, an assimilation that the final chapter conclusively narrates.

Jennifer Wong's analyses are embedded in a Sinophone civilizational worldview, even when the poets themselves may disavow this orientation. Li-Young Lee's disdain for an ethnic-poetic identity is paradoxically contradicted in Wong's teasing of Confucianist pieties that infuse Lee's filial homage to a father whose elite Mandarin roots in China nourish Lee's transcendental lyricism.

And where the reader may expect national belonging to trace commonalities, at least with Lee and Marilyn Chin, the two American poets, among the dozens of monograph critiques, are representative chiefly in their polar differences – in gender, natal origins (Indonesia, Hong Kong), home languages (Mandarin, Cantonese), claimed socio-political positions (universalist, feminist) and poetic genres (lyrical, satirical).

This range of poets of Chinese ethnicity, born and growing up in different locations, is analysed for their poems that engage strongly with the idea of home. The inevitable, predictable hinging of home and identity raises the spectre of a restrictive approach, but the interviews organized as an illuminating series of appendixes afford the poets a perspectival subjective voice that pushes against any such restrictiveness.

My gratitude on this American side of the Atlantic rises from Wong's introduction of UK-based Chinese diaspora poets whom I had never heard of, despite their award-winning status in Britain and what Wong persuasively presents as a transformed cultural receptiveness to their bilingual poetics in the home of Tennysonian lyricism and Ted Hughes' muscular laureateship.

In totality, the emphasis on women poets, full-ethnic Chinese, Hong Kong-born, UK-based, also reflects the interrogator's, Jennifer Wong's, authorial positioning. My second debt to Wong comes from how her research is intrinsically grounded on her bilingual positionality, a not so common critical capacity that enlarges and deepens my apprehension of poetic voices, praxis and stylistics that large numbers of Anglophone diasporic Chinese poets like myself can only intuit. Wong's acute standpoint epistemology is remarkable in the ways her readings light up both the poems analysed and her own poetic practice. She writes, 'Bei Dao's metaphorical and surreal language captures the universal through the personal, a poetic language that has influenced my own writing .... I am influenced by the subtlety with which he assimilates Chinese and European poetics in the use of symbolism.' Only a fully fluent bilingual reader and poet can write thus. In 1998, Werner Sollors argued in a seminal edited collection, *Multilingual America: Transnationalism, Ethnicity, and the Languages of American Literature*, that US literature can only be fully understood as a canon of works in the multiple languages of its diverse immigrant communities. Even earlier, in 1987, Gloria Anzaldua in *Borderlands/La Frontera* included entire Spanish passages in her pioneering feminist Chicana work, while Louis Erdrich has experimented with including untranslated Ojibway (the language of her Chippewa people) passages in her fiction. Walter K. Lew's *Premonitions* (1995), an anthology of *New Asian North American Poetry*, includes only one such bilingually playful poet, Ho Hon Leung, whose poems I finally could decode with the assistance of my Taiwanese graduate students while I was a Visiting Professor at the National Sun Yat-sen University in Kaohsiung in 2008. Jennifer Wong's study offers a ream of such 'Anglophone' poetry, with Mandarin calligraphy, Cantonese tones, Hokkien and other dialect slippages, whose writers astound with their expectations that their books will find readers, will be lauded in Britain with mainstream publishers, awards and recognition for whom they are – UK-based Chinese diaspora poets.

The seventh chapter takes up six of these UK-based multicultural poets, one is tempted to term Anglo-Sinophone, diasporic poets whose complex engaged plays with the in-between meanings rising from switchbacks in two such radically different languages as English and Chinese generate a sense of an emerging tradition. But the poets themselves are so divergent as to make these commonalities challenging to grasp. Of the six, three women (Cynthia Miller, Nina Mingya Powles and L. Kiew) with Malaysian-Chinese ancestry are wholly different in class and family backgrounds. Sean Wai Keung appears to be of mixed-race, with a mother from Hong Kong, a city and culture he visits as a self-identified Cantonese Hong Konger, despite his white father, birth and residence in Glasgow. Jennifer Lee Tsai, UK-born, grew up in Liverpool; yet, her poems work chiefly with Chinese images, contexts and gestures. Finally, Natalie Linh Bolderston, also UK-born, insists on using Vietnamese and Chinese characters in her Anglophone poems, as a way, Wong observes, to represent her history and language even if – as a second generation – tongues can be (quoting Bolderston) 'unyielding': 'Names given up/because home did not rest easily/on unyielding tongues.'

That is, all six UK-based poets, whether first- or second-generation British, whether possessing fluency in Mandarin or a dialect like Hokkien or Cantonese, and whether having to learn Chinese as an adult, articulate their self-hood as pre-eminently Chinese, as if geneological descent is the uttermost of authentic identity, even as their poems, albeit half-consciously, struggle with retrieving traces out of erasures, asserting holistic histories out of fragments and, yes, imagining fantasies rather than writing memories. Nina Mingya Powles' poetry book title is both in English and in Chinese calligraphy, *Magnolia*, 木蘭. Born to a cosmopolitan family of diplomats, in Wellington, New Zealand, where she was raised as well as in New York and Shanghai, she moved to London to be with her partner in 2018, a few years ago. 'Powles' Sinophone identity is borne out of a keen longing and motivated by her desire to identify with family elders, but chiefly, as she says, 'I want to enter new realms of language and incorporate this unknown part of myself into my poetry'. Her 'bilingual' poems express a strange nostalgia for what had never been, a yearning of the erased Sino Other that the poet imagines as poetic traces. That is, as seen in the passage below, the speaker is making a familiar memory out of an *unheimlich*, a haunting uncanny, in order 'to embrace a culture that belongs to, and eludes, her'. Arguably, a descent genealogy cannot in reality place her in a culture that she has not experienced. She can imagine the cultural particulars,

> I was almost born in the lunar month of padded clothing
> almost spent a girlhood watching sandstorms
> tearing through the almost golden sunlight

but these are imaginaries, 'I was almost' suggests an authentic yearning for what never really was. These civilization signs ('padded clothing' and 'sandstorms'), to quote Wong citing Homi Bhabha's theory of the Third Space, are 'appropriated, translated, rehistoricized, and read anew'.

In her final chapter, Wong returns to her personal Chinese diasporic space, Hong Kong. She does not write of her own poems, although Hong Kong editors claim her as one of their own Anglophone tribe, a second generation to the elders the chapter opens with – Leung Ping Kwan, Louise Ho, Agnes Lam and myself. Wong's chapter hinges on the transition between poets born after the Second World War and those who followed after them, now barely in their thirties. This city-state, compressed between colonial British literary traditions and the postcolonial handover of Hong Kong to the People's Republic of China in 1997, was from its inception a site that was, as Wong argues, citing Douglas Kerr,

> a city of exiles, populated by people who had come, for the most part, from the mainland of China … and the wind that had blown them to the colony might

just as easily carry them further in due course, to other cities in Southeast Asia, to Australia or North America. Hong Kong was a transit camp of the Chinese diaspora, a city of sojourners, economic migrants and refugees, and not a place to develop sentimental ties.[1]

In short, Hong Kong is the global exemplar for the re-migrants. Many of the poets read here as Hong Kong-oriented are factually from elsewhere (Leung Ping Kwan from Guangdong, Shirley Geok-lin Lim from Malaysia and the United States, Eddie Tay from Singapore, Jason Eng Hun Lee, born in the UK), headed elsewhere (Louise Ho to Australia, for example) and/or had spent formative periods elsewhere (Agnes Lam in Singapore). Leung Ping-Kwan, the only Mainland-born poet, is also the only poet who is not Anglophone. While almost all his books have been translated from Chinese to English, and he has himself translated a few of his poems, it is his Cantonese orality (the home language spoken by 88.9 per cent of Hong Kong's population) that declares his pre-eminence as Hong Kong's iconic poet. The local-born poets, such as Tammy Ho and Nicholas Wong, look for their aesthetic stances from Western poets such as W. H. Auden and American-language poets. A quick run through of even younger Anglophone Hong Kong poets, Tim Tim Cheng, Felix Chow, Nicolette Wong, Florence Ng and Louise Leung, who have published chiefly in literary journals and anthologies, concludes the chapter, and the monograph, on a future promised in their more grounded identities, politically engaged, and as matching their city-state, composing poems 'always in transition and in flux within the wider Chinese diaspora [interrogating] the coherence of their location and identity'.

Indeed, despite its stated subject – Anglophone-Chinese diasporic poetry – Wong's capacious readings cover a generous spectrum sliding all the way from Sinophone poetry in English translation (Bei Dao and Leung Ping Kwan) to Anglo-Sinophone poetry to wholly Anglophone poetics. The poets also shift their territories as re-migrants, their Chinese descent vividly recalled or mythologized through Time's, and concurrently, their poetry shifts positionalities, modalities, traditions and voicings, composing a rich canon for a global twenty-first-century reader.

Note

1   Douglas Kerr's 'Afterword' in *Incense Tree: Collected Poems of Louise Ho* (Hong Kong: Hong Kong University Press, 2010) by Louise Ho, 155.

Introduction: Understanding concepts of home, identity and diaspora

In this introduction, my aims are twofold. First, I am going to map out the interconnected concepts of 'home', 'diaspora' and 'identity' in appreciating contemporary Anglophone Chinese diaspora poetry, which are becoming more significant than ever in the context of increased globalization, the popular use of virtual space and virtual communication, as well as the onset of the global pandemic situation where many individuals were unable to visit their families abroad. Secondly, I will map out the scope of the emerging field of contemporary Anglophone Chinese diaspora poetry its relevance in understanding the concepts of 'home', 'diaspora' and 'identity'.

The unhealable rift

As Edward Said defines in his seminal work *Orientalism*, exile for those who are displaced is experienced as an 'unhealable rift forced between a human being and a native place, between the self and its true home'.[1] But what, then, is a true home? For many who have moved away from their homeland, this sense of an 'unhealable rift' between the self and one's native place becomes part of their existence. Even if one's departure from home is not an enforced situation, it is often difficult to escape from the longing for a 'true home'. Home is a place of origin where personal history and longings begin. No matter where one is located, there revisiting or re-imagining, as one travels from one place to another, an individual's new knowledge and encounters transform his or her or their perception of and engagement with the world.

Philip Gleason's 'Identifying Identity: A Semantic History' provides an excellent overview on the definition of the term 'identity', tracing it to the Latin root *idem*, meaning sameness, a term in use since the sixteenth century, and the 'perennial mind-body problem in philosophy since the time of John Locke'.[2] This definition highlights the possible sameness in an individual who straddles different places, homes or cultures. According to Erikson, identity comprises both the core of an individual's being and their communal culture.[3] Building on his definition, identity is a process in which the self is constantly interpreting and re-interpreting itself within and beyond a communal culture, longing to be different yet accepted.[4] In *On Not Speaking Chinese*, Ien Ang argues that 'any identity is always mistaken'.[5] Ang's statement boldly asserts that there is no such thing as a correct or single authentic identity. Any attempt to present identity as 'correct' is to lose sight of its fluid and negotiated nature.

Derived from the Greek word *ethnikós* which means gentile, foreign or heathen, ethnicity denotes nationality or place of origin, and usually refers to one's status or membership arising from 'common descent, or having a common national or cultural tradition'.[6] According to Werner Sollors, the significance of ethnicity lies in the construction of contrast, naming or name-calling.[7] The term therefore implies being seen as the other or the exotic outside one's shared group of solidarity. In addition to the ways in which they are perceived, an individual also interprets his or her position with reference to generation(s). According to Sigrid Weigel, ethnicity is a term 'at the threshold between emergence and continuation [...] between origin and memory, where "the representative of a generation is a 'witness of history'".[8] In doing so, I highlight the tension between home and identity as an inevitable condition of cultural hybridity and migration, whether experienced first-hand or as embraced as part of one's family history.

With the increased impact of globalization and more frequent border-crossing movements between nations, identity is often articulated in terms of identity crises – in the context of migration, the identity of an immigrant arising from 'membership in groups that have suffered oppression on the basis of gender, race, class, or sexual preference is a major area of investigation'.[9] My interest lies in investigating how the specificity of life experience such as migration – one's encounter with or attempt to assimilate a different culture – will impact on the writer and his or her or their work.

In discussing the cohesiveness of the 'routes and roots' contained within a diaspora, James Clifford refers to identity formation as a 'matrix of experiences' within which individuals traverse different territories.[10] Clifford's approach towards understanding diasporic identity in terms of bidirectional journeys offers a creative, interactive paradigm to locate oneself in relation to personal, social and historical encounters. Moreover, following from C. Wright Mills' argument that 'neither the life of an individual nor the history of society can be understood without understanding both', it is crucial to reflect on the bilateral interaction between the writer and the writer's world, for the cultures of place(s) are also constantly revised by the individuals who engage with these places.[11] In understanding identity, Tölölyan remarks that diasporas are 'the exemplary communities of the transnational moment'.[12] Such transnational experience is not only articulated through the shift in locations but through inhabiting different temporal realities through imagination, creating a community that is at once both imaginary and real, both temporal and spatial, both local and transnational.

The prevalence of migration in recent decades has created an increased need to understand the nature, aspirations, the everyday experiences of transnational, (re-)imagined communities, while readers are becoming increasingly curious about literatures that arise from this diasporic imagination. The condition of transnationalism, according to Appardurai, is characterized by 'the growing disjuncture between territory, subjectivity and collective social movement' or 'a collision of historical space and imagination'.[13] Vertovec remarks that 'sustained real time and intensive practices of transnational communication, affiliation and exchange' cause the migrants to 'maintain and act upon particularly strong senses of connection to people, places and senses of belonging associated with their places of origin'.[14] Moreover, as Morley argues, 'traditional ideas of home, homeland, and nation have been destabilised, both by new patterns of physical mobility and migration and by new communication technologies, which routinely transgress the symbolic boundaries'.[15] The widespread use of technology, digital and social media has allowed these imagined communities to become interactive and to resemble more of an actual, local community, while on the other hand virtual reality and the presence of a networked society make the perception of distance more unreal than ever before.

According to the *Oxford English Dictionary*, 'diaspora' refers to 'people who have spread or been dispersed from their homeland', with the words 'diasperiein', 'disperse', coming from 'dia' (across) and speirein (scatter). This definition, which traces its origin to the Jewish Diaspora, i.e. the body of Jews living outside the land of Israel, or the dispersion of the Jewish people beyond the land of Israel, has also been extended to mean 'any group of people who have spread or become dispersed beyond their traditional homeland or point of origin; the dispersion or spread of a group of people in this way'.[16]

In his introduction to *Diasporas*, Stéphane Dufoix highlights the term's reference to displacement, its function in relation to the 'maintenance of a connection with a real or imagined homeland', and the issues raised about 'voluntary or involuntary migration of people to their spatially free floating existence'.[17] In other words, Dufoix equates the diasporic experience of immigrants with that of exiles and refugees. He also points out an important aspect of diaspora: the word cannot be the same each time it is used, because there is simply no word to express the individual-specific diaspora. I will argue for a dual understanding of diaspora, as the diasporic individual shares affinity with a real or imagined community in terms of their origin, rituals, cultural practices, values and/or experiences in border-crossing. In other words, an individual is a member to a real community from which he derives his descent, a place of origin where he and his family comes from, but at the same time he forms part of an imagined community – which may be located away from him and may include memories of or fantasies about the place that he identifies with. So while the individual reflects on his origin or communal culture, one also understands the untranslatable specificity of his or her own diasporic journey, feelings of belongingness or displacement straddling the places.

Diaspora is characterized by distance, especially the distance from one's home and the longing for home in some form. The *Oxford Dictionary*'s definitions of 'home' convey the multiple dimensions of home that go beyond a fixed residence, encompassing one's heritage and feelings of belonging to one's family or place of origin.[18] Therefore, the definition of home highlights the fact that home does not only refer to a physical location of where one lives, but captures certain affiliations or belonging, or a powerful configuration of personal experiences and memories that impact on one's identity.[19] Avtah Brah's idea that home is 'a mythic place of desire in the diasporic imagination' suggests the semi-fictional quality of home for the diasporic individual.[20] In her definition, Brah captures home as an emotional need, which reverberates and transcends the physical location. Moreover, she points out that diaspora is an active and collective process of repetition and (re)construction, 'a confluence of narratives as it is lived and re-lived, produced, reproduced and transformed through individual as well as collective memory and re-memory'.[21] Building on her argument, I emphasize that the diasporic poet has a need to articulate, rework and respond creatively to the diasporic state – be it a first-hand experience or that of one's family – in order to locate oneself.

Moreover, since David Damrosch defines world literature in terms of its access and circulation: '[a] work enters into world literature by a double process: first, by being read as a literature; second, by circulating out into a broader world beyond its linguistic and cultural point of origin. A given world can enter into world literature and then fall out of it again if it shifts beyond a threshold point along either axis, the literary or the world'.[22] Hence, a writer's recreation of diasporic experience can enter and circulate in another part of the world, away from the writer's origin, and influence other writers on a local or transnational scale. This implies that writers of the same or similar ethnicity may be more readily influenced by works by other writers of that ethnicity as they attempt to seek meaning in their diasporic experience from those with whom they identify a real or imagined sense of affinity.[23]

On a linguistic level, Agnes Heller's powerful description of home as a place where 'no footnotes are needed' sheds light on the idea of home as a common language.[24] 'Going home' should mean: returning to that firm position which we know, to which we are accustomed, 'where we find safe and where our emotional relationships are the most intense'.[25] In other words, home is experienced both inside and outside oneself, it is both spoken and unsaid, both possessed personally and shared. In the Chinese language, home also means family, and there is a common belief one's family relationships reveal the individual's integrity or ability to interact socially and politically.[26] This correspondence between the meaning of home and family can be traced back to the sayings of Mencius (*c.* 371–289 BC) and Mozi (*c.* 470–391 BC). Understanding this helps us appreciate the intricate, almost inseparable relationship between the concepts of home and the family in these writers' works.

Writing across the Chinese diaspora

For the purpose of this book, I am interested in the close reading of poetry by contemporary diasporic Chinese poets writing across the different geographical regions of the Chinese diaspora, and to offer the contextual backgrounds in which their writing took place. Despite their affinity in ethnicity and cultural roots, these poets differ in their literary voices and thematic preoccupations, and often offer their different ways of understanding home and identity. As Shu-mei Shih argues, the term 'Chinese' has many hidden assumptions, tensions or complications:

> The term 'Chinese' functions as a category of ethnicity, language, and culture only to the extent that it designates the Han, excluding all the other ethnicities, languages, and cultures. The term 'ethnic Chinese' is therefore a serious

misnomer, since the 'Chinese' nationality should designate not one but fifty-six ethnicities, if not more. In short, there is no such group called 'ethnic Chinese', only groups that can be specifically designated as Han Chinese, Tibetan Chinese, Uyghur Chinese, or Hmong (Miao) Chinese. The reduction of Chineseness to Han ethnicity in places outside China is the inverse of the hegemonic claims on Chineseness by the Han majority within China. Historically, various ethnic peoples have contributed significantly to what 'China' has become today.[27]

One of the key factors that we need to be informed about contemporary Chinese writers (especially those who are Anglophone writers) is the one that straddles and inhabits multiple places and languages. To a certain extent, they write for both the East and the West. An Asian-American scholar who has taught and researched in both Anglophone Chinese-American literature and Sinophone Chinese-American literature since the 1980s, Sau-ling C. Wong, has pointed out in 'Global Vision and Locatedness: World Literature in Chinese/by Chinese (Shijie huawen/huaren wenxue 世界華文/华人文學) from a Chinese-Americanist Perspective' the similarity and difference between *huawen wenxue* (world literature in Chinese) and *shijie huaren wenxue* (world literature by Chinese).[28]

In this book, I have chosen a range of poets of Chinese ethnicity born and grew up in different locations, whose poetry has interpreted concepts of home and identity in exciting new ways. What I wanted to show is that these poets – with their cultural inheritance, personal journeys, racial positioning and assumed poetics – have interrogated and penetrated the meanings of home and diasporic identities in different ways. Through these close readings, I will also contextualize their work in terms of the idea of a 'home-land' rather than 'nation', 'country' or 'nation-states', and to analyse how they express their culturally specific identities in the originality of their poetics.

As we appreciate that these poets writing across different places are unique in their own poetics and their ethnic backgrounds, ultimately their work needs to be in the foreground of our discussion. But to analyse and compare their works and their representation or mapping of 'home' within a broader, transnational context is fundamental. In my discussion, Ramazani's transnational framework guides these readings through 'circuits of poetic connection and dialogue across political and geographical borders and even hemispheres' and highlights the cross-cultural 'confluences in poetry'. Specifically, I investigate the poetics of homeland among these poets by situating their poetic language within their socio-political and linguistic environments, and analyse their common grounds and stylistic differences. Based on Steven Vertovec's definition, diaspora emerges as a form of consciousness layered and malleable with its 'multiplicity of histories, communities and selves'. Diaspora also reflects an 'adaptive strength' that arises from the 'fractured memories' of the diasporic people. These critical definitions will add context for our understanding of how these diasporic poets – to varying extent – identify themselves and their works in terms of not just where they reside but where they 'belong'.

In my study, I will look at how the diasporic poets use their poetic language(s). Ha Jin, prominent Chinese-American immigrant known for his prize-winning novel *Waiting* (1999), talked about his dilemma on language: 'I have been asked why I write in English. I often reply, "For Survival." [....] In a writer who migrates to another language, necessity, ambition, and estrangement usually come to bear at the same time.'[29] This reveals the dilemma of Chinese diasporic writers find in articulating themselves. At the same time, despite his struggle to become a skilled and professional Anglophone writer in a foreign land, Ha Jin admitted in his interview with *The New Yorker*, to enjoying the freedom of using the foreign language to write:

> I had written a few poems in Chinese, but I wasn't happy with them. The Chinese language is very literary and highbrow and detached from the spoken word. It doesn't have the flexibility that English has. So I slowly began to squeeze the Chinese literary mentality out of my mind.[30]

This goes to show that a bilingual Chinese writer's relationship with his or her own language can also be ambivalent or even conflicting.

Ien Ang points out that critical diasporic cultural politics should privilege neither host country nor (real or imaginary) homeland, but keep our focal point to the creative tension between 'where you're from' and 'where you're at', where 'Chineseness becomes an open signifier, which acquires its peculiar form and content in dialectical junction with the diverse local conditions in which ethnic Chinese people, wherever they are, construct new, hybrid identities and communities'.[31]

Where or what is the Chinese diaspora?

For centuries, there has been a constant migration movement of the Chinese population across the globe. The scattering of and literary production by writers of Chinese descent is of great significance to the study of the multiple meanings of home and diaspora. While substantial scholarship has been done in studying the Chinese diaspora in terms of history, geography and sociology, there is still considerable room for understanding of the literary output by writers from the Chinese diaspora in a more holistic way, particularly in exploring the connections and overlapping themes between these writers.

In the past few decades, much scholarship on contemporary Anglophone Asian literature has focused on that from the Asian- or Chinese-American diaspora, while Asian-American literature is clearly defined in a number of encyclopaedias such as *The Oxford Encyclopedia of Asian American Literature and Culture*. There are also the genre-specific, influential criticisms such as Steven Yao's *Foreign Accents: American Verse from Exclusion to Postethnicity* and Dorothy Wang's *Thinking Its Presence: Form, Race, and Subjectivity in Contemporary Asian American Poetry* which examined Asian-American experimental writing and shed light on the questions of race.

As Tan Chee Beng points out in his seminal work, *The Routledge Handbook of Chinese Diaspora*, the existing labels can be confusing and insufficient to locate the exact meaning or field of Chinese diaspora writing.[32] Tan argues that the Chinese diaspora can be understood in terms of the family ties and cultural practices of the overseas Chinese population.[33] In *Interpreting the Chinese Diaspora: Identity, Socialisation and Resilience,* Guanglun Mu and Bonnie Pang acknowledge the resilience of family ties and socialization in Chinese diaspora as crucial to appreciating the literary merit of writers from the Chinese diaspora.[34] A pre-eminent scholar on the Chinese diaspora, David Der-wei Wang talks about the concept of 'Sinophone literature', which redefines 'Chinese literature' as a field determined by language rather than purely by geography, although there are also issues in differentiating literature purely on the basis of language. After all, some of the poets writing across the diaspora are actually bilingual (if not multilingual) and are increasingly able and willing to explore multiple languages in their work, or these writers may choose to write in different languages at different points in time.[35]

David Wang favoured the term 'overseas Chinese' when referring to people of Chinese ethnicity living outside China, objecting to the older term *huaqiao,* which risks the political use and implication that overseas Chinese are subjects of China, and which has been used as a way to label 'a single body of overseas Chinese'.[36] In my view, despite the limitations of the term and the difficulty to arrive at a ready consensus on its scope, the reference to 'Chinese diaspora' is still very helpful in appreciating a broader *imagined* community that crosses nation-states. In other words, the Chinese diaspora encompasses the people who choose to live in places outside Mainland China.

To better appreciate the development of contemporary Anglophone Chinese diaspora poetry, the migration history of the Chinese population will need to be accounted for. Back in the Qing Dynasty, the Chinese government decided to send their first, handpicked cohort of students to America.[37] Their main aim was for the Chinese cohorts to learn from the West, to bring back useful innovation and improved practices which would strengthen China as a country. Subsequently, most of the early Chinese immigrants worked as coolies, as traders, as labour corps in the First World War. Later, Chinese migrants who went abroad were mainly labourers who helped achieve industrial expansion in the late nineteenth century.[38] For example, in 'The coming of the Chinese' in *Asian American: Chinese and Japanese in the United States since 1850,* Roger Daniels charts out the history of labour agitation against the Chinese and the lack of prestige and authority faced by the Chinese merchants in Western countries.[39]

The Chinese communities in North America and in Europe and Australia share a similar history of Oriental labour needed to relieve labour shortages during the industrial expansion of the nineteenth century, to be 'marred by an emergent ideology of anti-Orientialism', when the Chinese race was seen

Figure 1 Chinese students, 1872, Albumen print, 22 cm × 29 cm. Courtesy of Loewentheil Photography of China Collection. Attributed Milton Miller.

as 'culturally undesirable and racially inferior'.[40] Edited by Erika Lee and Judy Yung, *Angel Island: Immigrant Gateway to America* traces the history of racial inequality for the early Chinese immigrants in the United States – the setting up of Angel Island as an immigration station and the main point of entry for Asian immigrants but which also 'plays a key role in removing and deporting', coupled with the reverberating impact of the Chinese Exclusion Act of 1882 and the subsequent Immigration Act of 1924.[41]

According to Stearns, the diaspora grew from a movement of around 150,000 Chinese individuals who left China each year to more than 500,000 a year by the 1920s, with nearly half of Chinese emigration consisting of Cantonese speakers to the gold fields of North America and Australia and of indentured labourers to sugar plantations in places like Cuba and Peru from 1820 to the 1850s. In addition to the movement of over 20 million Chinese migrants who relocated to Southeast Asia from 1840 to 1940 after 1880, a more 'distinct Chinese diaspora built on cultural and economic bases' emerged from transnational connections and effects of globalization.[42]

In the period after the Second World War, the 'entrenchment of civil rights and a growing social acceptance of values of equality and multiculturalism' in these

Figure 2 Detention Barracks 1, 2021. Courtesy of Angel Island Immigration Station Foundation.

countries, coupled with the abolition of immigration restrictions, has led to an increase in Chinese immigrants, while immigrants arriving in these countries came from a more diverse educational and occupational background.[43] Combining images with interviews, *Oriental Silk* (2020), Xiaowen Zhu follows the story of a Chinese-American immigrant, Kenneth Wong, who set up his family business, an Oriental Silk shop in Los Angeles, while his father fought her the US in the Second World War.

While the concept of a unifying 'homeland-nation' is problematic, Shelley Chan's concept of understanding history in terms of 'distinct moments'[44] is very useful in appreciating a diasporic experience of time, addressing the impact of significant moments like the Chinese civil war and the Cultural Revolution and their impact on Chinese literature, especially the representation of intergenerational histories, whether it is Sinophone or Anglophone literature. In *China Unlimited*, Gregory Lee retraced the roots of anti-Chinese racism to the 19th century imagining of China.[45]

As Peter Stearns pointed out, one needs to acknowledge a 'new Chinese diaspora that emerged along with globalization after the 1970s', which consisted of a new generation of Chinese immigrants, with some affluent Chinese families who became 'cosmopolitan, investing in a diverse portfolio of multiple passports; multiple homes; children educated in business, law, and engineering in different nations; and family members managing branches of family businesses around

Figure 3 Oriental Silk shop in Los Angeles. Courtesy of Kenneth Wong from *Oriental Silk* (Hatje Cantz, 2020) by Xiaowen Zhu.

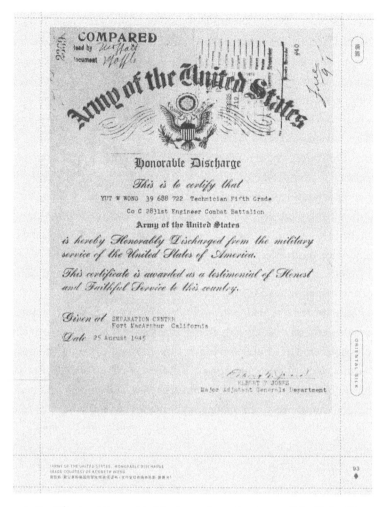

Figure 4 Certificate – Honorable Discharge from the Army of the United States belonging to the father of Kenneth Wong. Courtesy of Kenneth Wong from *Oriental Silk* (Hatje Cantz, 2020) by Xiaowen Zhu.

the world'.[46] Interestingly, Stearns also indicated the diasporic population's shifting sense of home, where 'many overseas Chinese prefer to claim a cultural affinity with other Chinese rather than a political tie to China – although not all people of Chinese descent identify with this diaspora'.[47]

In my discussion, I examine a transnational spectrum of leading contemporary poets from the Chinese diaspora across communities, whose works articulate the unsettling experience of otherness. Ramazani's transnational framework guides these readings through 'circuits of poetic connection and dialogue across political

Figure 5 Kenneth Wong, owner of Oriental Silk shop in Los Angeles, 2014. Photograph, inkjet print on paper. Courtesy of Kenneth Wong from *Oriental Silk* (Hatje Cantz, 2020) by Xiaowen Zhu.

and geographical borders and even hemispheres' and highlights the cross-cultural 'confluences in poetry'.[48] Specifically, I investigate the poetics of homeland among these poets by situating their poetic language within their socio-political and linguistic environments, and analyse their common grounds and stylistic differences. Based on Steven Vertovec's definition, diaspora emerges as a form of consciousness layered and malleable with its 'multiplicity of histories, communities and selves'. Diaspora also reflects the diasporic people's 'adaptive strength' that arises from the 'fractured memories'.[49] As such, writers who have lived outside China for a long time and writing about their lived experience of cultural journeying should be considered. Given the length of this book, I will focus my discussion based on the selected 'Chinese' poets in the UK and the United States and Hong Kong, since the poetry by Anglophone poets living in Southeast Asia, e.g. Singapore, involves a much more elaborate discussion that will hinge on how one defines and understands the poetry arising from poets from the region. One needs to bear in mind that there are many poets who resist or have ambivalent feelings about being connected with the 'Chinese' diaspora as such. With 75 per cent of its population being ethnically Chinese, Clammer argued that Singaporeans are characterized by citizenship and not national identity.[50] With a wide range of ethnicity(ies) of the population, Singapore has long been an independent nation-state since 1965 with its own policies, governance and linguistic environment, where Mandarin rather than Cantonese is predominantly spoken.[51]

In fact, Robbie Goh points out that Anglophone poetry has played a central role not only in the development of a national literature in Singapore in the first few decades after independence, but in the articulation of a kind of national consciousness.

Also, the use of English is much more common than in Chinese-speaking societies in Hong Kong, for example. There is a flourishing literary scene with very diverse voices.[52] Altogether, it has its very distinct ecosystem and concepts of home and identity. Chee Kiong Tong's _Identity and Ethnic Relations in Southeast Asia: Racialising Chineseness_ has provided some very fascinating observations about the identity of Singaporeans.[53]

Timothy Yu's latest _Diaspora Poetics_ discusses the concept of an Asian diaspora as a framework to understand Anglophone Asian writing beyond America, across geographically distinct regions such as Canada and Australia, taking into account the acceleration of globalisation and political solidarities, and the phenomenon of an evolving 'decentering' of Asian American poetics.[54]

It is important to acknowledge the complex and multiple belongings of poets writing across the diaspora. For example, most recently launching his first collection _Imperium_ with Carcanet, Jay Gao is a Chinese Scottish poet who has moved to the US in 2019. Through linguistically and formally adept poetics, Gao's poetry poses challenging questions to the reader on the unknowability or multiplicity of the weary traveler 'speaker', situated within the context of an intimate, original reimagined narrative of Homer's _Odyssey_. In his interview with _The London Magazine_, Gao questions the problematic 'dichotomy between "East" and "West"':

> On one hand, being born in the UK meant that Greek and Roman antiquity – with its standards of beauty and art – easily becomes a period of fascination and desire. Yet being in the UK means that I am also a part of an imperialist and colonialist legacy that trafficked in Orientalism, Chinoiserie, exoticism. _Imperium_, in small ways, is an attempt at reframing these biases, or trying to reconcile them. How might I lean so heavily on a pillar of the European canon whilst also engaging with art, culture, and perspectives from different parts of the world that come with their own aesthetic signatures?[55]

In this volume, I have chosen to include poets whose parents are both Chinese and those who have only one Chinese or a half-Chinese parent, precisely because the relevance or connectedness of their fractured memories and consciousness is not necessarily proportionate to their racial identity. I include Hannah Lowe – born in England to a Jamaican-Chinese father and a British mother – because her work *Chick* (and to some extent *Chan*) deals directly with the re-imagining of home culture and the diasporic identity via the fractured memories and migration narrative of her family.

In addition to the above authors, I broaden the question of cultural identity to reflect on the work of the pre-eminent Chinese poet, Bei Dao (Zhao Zhenkai 趙 振开), a Beijing-born diasporic poet who experienced the Cultural Revolution. I include Bei Dao to shed light on the significance of his identity as a Chinese exile poet, having lived and taught abroad for decades. Writing in Chinese, he is often perceived as a forerunner of Chinese 'misty poetry', a genre of literary and social significance in the post-Mao era. Bei Dao went into exile in 1989 because of his alleged involvement in the Tiananmen student protests in China. With his specific background as a dissident poet in exile and since a wide range of his works have been translated into English, he has achieved considerable recognition or influence in both China and the West. He has been repeatedly nominated for the Nobel Laureate in Literature.

Contextualizing Orientalism and double consciousness

I adopt an inter-disciplinary, transnational-focused approach that incorporates cultural, sociological translational and postcolonical theory on identity and the problem of representation; interrogate diaspora and home as transnational spaces; and explore cultural hybridity and double consciousness through close readings of the texts. Criticisms of place and ethnicity in contemporary African-American and Asian-American literature tend to perceive race primarily as a struggle of the minority against colonial oppression. W. E. B. Du Bois, whom Marilyn Chin cites as a crucial influence on her work, emphasizes the conflicting ideals that exist within an ethnic minority's consciousness:[56]

> It is a peculiar sensation, a double consciousness, this sense of always looking at one's self through the eyes of others, of measuring one's soul by the tape of the world that looks on in amused contempt and pity. One feels his twoness – an American, a Negro; two souls, two thoughts, two unreconciled strivings, two warring ideals in one body[.][57]

While Du Bois' concept of 'double consciousness' has specific relevance to the history of African-American experience, it offers a way to understand the question of identity by engaging with the liminality of transnational space as opposed to locating identity within the fixed boundaries of nation-states. The concept also sheds light on the complexity of belonging and kinship, in which an individual experiences conflicts or doubt within himself as to where he belongs or with whom he identifies with, in relation to as well as beyond his place of origin.

An important issue on the subject of diasporic poetry is the question of exoticism, which affects the perspectives of both writers and readers.[58] In his seminal work *Orientalism*, Edward Said discussed the concept of the Other as the exoticized and culturally hybrid subject. Nevertheless, Said's theory about the Other is broadly based on the Middle East diaspora, and offers a rather polemical, fixed East-West power relation where the East is constantly being threatened by the West and vice versa, a perspective that needs to be updated to understand contemporary diasporic poetics. According to Homi Bhabha, the demographics of the present 'internationalism' refers to 'the history of postcolonial migration, the narratives of cultural and political diaspora, the major social displacements of peasants and aboriginal communities, the poetics of exile, the grim prose of political and economic refugees'.[59] While postcolonial perspectives are useful in understanding the relationship between diasporic space and the perception of otherness, I am wary of over-simplifying self-identity as a site of oppression against the colonial aggressor. Edward Said has defined 'Orientalism' in terms of 'the journey, the history, the fable, the stereotype, the polemical confrontation'; and above all has drawn the reader's attention to 'the lenses through which the Orient is experienced'. In parallel, one should be alert to the danger of over-generalizing this 'polemic confrontation' when analysing East-West poetics.[60]

Diaspora encompasses the possibility or necessity of constructing a home away from home, to envisage different layers of home and senses of belonging. It is possible to feel at home in multiple places, or to feel belonging in a foreign place. For those who have experienced diaspora, their identities are best articulated through a creative, hybrid use of language. By mapping out how hybrid language and an exilic poetic imagination are related to socio-historical contexts, I highlight how a poet's identity is modified by interaction with their environments. According to Steven Yao, Marilyn Chin's poetics demonstrate how an ethnic minority poet can challenge the assumptions of linguistic transparency and the adequacy of English language as a medium for asserting one's ethnic subjectivity.[61] Yao's discussion offers a constructive and accessible paradigm for appreciating the different linguistic and formal experiments of Chinese-American poets, but his work has focused primarily on the formal techniques and the performance of identity, rather than the relationship between textual performance and the writer's sense of home.

Locating ethnicity and ethnic minority poetics

Instead of building on a postcolonial-only framework typically adopted for reading contemporary Asian or Chinese-American poetry, I would like to apply the significance of Stuart Hall's notion on location and representation, which offers a bridging framework 'between culture and politics, between the symbolic and the social', specifically the dialectic between culture and power.[62] According to Hall, we are all 'ethnically located', and otherness is largely socially constructed:

> We all speak from a particular place and time, from a history and a culture which is specific. What we say is always 'in context', *positioned*.[63]

His discussion acknowledges individual difference among people of the same ethnicity, emphasizing the many aspects of 'specificity' of the 'identity-stories' while interpreting identity as a dynamic product of cultural and historical contexts.[64] Building on his argument, my project examines how a poet of cultural hybridity cannot escape nor embrace his or her own culture and history entirely, as one cannot locate a utopian, 'pure' sense of belongingness within diasporic narratives.[65]

In situating ethnic minority poetics, Dorothy Wang's *Thinking Its Presence: Form, Subjectivity, and Race in Asian American Poetry* provides a refreshing reading of Chinese-American poetry as minority literature.[66] Wang argues that the act of reading and interpreting ethnic minority literature is complicated by the Western reader's inclination to appreciate or 'pigeon-hole' writers of a minority race, instead of evaluating the poetry in terms of literary merit:

> In the US academy and society at large, the words 'identity', 'identitarian', and 'identity politics' are often automatically conflated. Used synonymously, all three function as a reductive shorthand to refer to an essentializing and unthinking 'identity politics' – almost always regarded, explicitly or not, as the provenance of minorities with grievances.[67]

This critique draws our attention to the relationship between the diasporic poet and the reader, and sheds light on the phenomenon that the narratives by ethnic minority writers are often read as autobiographical or semi-autobiographical accounts of grievances or racial injustices, as some readers of these narratives are eager to locate the 'identity politics', and are only capable of appreciating such literature as 'an ethnographic window into another "subculture"'.[68] The relationship between the diasporic poet and the reader can also be read in conjunction with Wenbo Sun's argument that Anglophone Chinese diasporic poets over-represent their 'Chinese-ness' vis-à-vis Chinese writers in China as a way to differentiate themselves and justify their existence to Western readers. According to Sun, diasporic poets feel the compulsion to exert their 'Chinese-ness', since the poets who have not left their motherland can experience the immediacy of Chinese history without relying on 'Chinese-ness' to explain their cultural identity.[69] In effect, the diasporic poets confront their 'marginality' as a new cultural experience and identity, while faced with certain expectations from the 'foreign' readership.

The arguments by Wang and Sun have pointed out the bidirectional relationship between the poet and the reader in terms of interpreting ethnicity and identity. For the diasporic or culturally hybrid poet, how does he or she articulate or find the right vocabulary to express a diasporic imagination? How is it possible to amalgamate poetics from the East and the West without losing the authenticity of the poetic voice? Shu-mei Shih, a pre-eminent scholar of Sinophone comparative literature, has identified the danger of an 'over-Westernized' diasporic literature and the 'culturalization' of ethnicity in an increasingly globalized landscape.[70] I argue that it is related to the inevitable reflection on authenticity in a culturally hybrid person's identity.

Ramazani's advocacy for the 'citizenship of a poem' offers a relevant context for understanding the transnational imagination and the impact of literary influences on a poetic mind.[71] As Janet Neigh points out, Ramazani's contribution of a global vocabulary is key for appreciating the cross-cultural production of poetics.[72] In 'Communitarianism, How to Build East Asian Theory', Hillenbrand points out the necessity of a new cartography of knowledge that encompasses knowledge from across the Sinophone and Anglophone cultures and histories, one that does not give undue preference to Western thought and theories.[73] Altogether, the poetic imagination is best appreciated through the specificity and collectivity of diasporic experiences in the context of racial identity politics, cultural history, linguistic landscapes.

Notes

1   Edward Said, *Reflections on Exile and Other Literary and Cultural Essays* (London: Granta Books, 2001), 173.

2   Philip Gleason, 'Identifying Identity: A Semantic History', *The Journal of American History*, 69.4 (1983), 911.

3   Erik H. Erikson, *Identity: Youth and Crisis* (New York: W. W. Norton, 1968), 22. See also Gleason, 'Identifying Identity', 911, 914.

4   Erikson, *Identity*, 22–3.

5   Ien Ang, *On Not Speaking Chinese Diasporic Identifications and Postmodern Ethnicity* (London and New York: Routledge, 2001), viii.

6   *Oxford English Dictionary*, <http://www.oed.com.oxfordbrookes.idm.oclc.org/view/Entry/64786#eid5295519> [Accessed 1 June 2018].

7   Werner Sollors, *Beyond Ethnicity* (New York and London: Oxford University Press, 1988), 28.

8   Sigrid Weigel's 'Families, Phantoms and the Discourse of "Generations" as a Politics of the Past: Problems of Provenance – Rejecting and Longing for Origins', in *Narrating the Nation: Representations in History, Media and the Arts*, edited by Stefan Berger, Linas Eriksonas and Andrew Mycock (New York and Oxford: Berghahn Books, 2008), 142.

9   Gleason, 'Identifying Identity', 929. See also Joseph and Gary Hentzi, *The Columbia Dictionary of Literary and Cultural Criticisms* (New York: Columbia University Press, 1995).

10 James Clifford, *Routes: Travel and Translation in the Late Twentieth Century* (Cambridge, MA: Harvard University Press, 1997), 257.

11 C. Wright Mills, *Sociological Imagination* (London: Penguin, 1970), 3.

12 Khachig Tölöyan, 'The Nation-State and Its Others: In Lieu of a Preface', *Diaspora*, 1.1 (1991), 5.

13 Steven Vertovec, 'Migrant Transnationalism and Modes of Transformation', *International Migration Review*, 38.3 (2004), 977. See also Arjun Appardurai, *Modernity at Large: Cultural Dimensions of Globalization* (Minneapolis: University of Minnesota Press, 1997), 189.

14 Vertovec, 'Migrant Transnationalism and Modes of Transformation', 977.

15 David Morley, *Home Territories: Media, Mobility, and Identity* (London: Routledge, 2000), 3.

16 *Oxford English Dictionary*, 3rd edition (Oxford: Oxford University Press, 2014). <http://www.oed.com.oxfordbrookes.idm.oclc.org/view/Entry/52085> [Accessed 1 June 2018].

17 Stéphane Dufoix, *Dispersion: A History of the Word Diaspora* (Leiden: Brill, 2016), 28.

18 *Oxford English Dictionary* <http://www.oed.com.oxfordbrookes.idm.oclc.org> [Accessed 1 March 2018]. The definitions of home include: 'a person's own country or native land'; 'the country of one's ancestors'; 'the place where one lives or was brought up, with reference to the feelings of belonging, comfort, etc. associated with it', to 'the family or social unit occupying a house'.

19 Erikson, *Identity*, 22.

20 Avtah Brah, *Cartographies of Diaspora* (London: Routledge, 1996), 192.

21 Ibid., 183.

22 David Damrosch, *What Is World Literature?* (Princeton and Oxford: Princeton University Press, 2003), 6.

23   Brah, *Cartographies*, 208–10.

24   Agnes Heller, *Aesthetics and Modernity: Essays* (Lanham, MD: Lexington Books, 2011), 208.

25   Agnes Heller, *Everyday Life* (London: Routledge and Kegan Paul, 1981), 239.

26   *Kangxi Dictionary*, Chinese Text Project <https://ctext.org/dictionary. pl?if=gb&char=%E5%AE%B6> [Accessed on 7 May 2017]. See also Zhang Zailin, 'Theories of Family in Ancient Chinese Philosophy', *Frontiers of Philosophy in China,* 4(2009), 343–59.

27   Shu-mei Shih, 'The Sinophone as Places of Cultural Production', in *Global Chinese Literature: Critical Essays,* edited by Jing Tsu and David Der-wei Wang (Leiden: Brill, 2010), 30–1.

28   Cynthia Sau-ling Wong, 'Global Vision and Locatedness: World Literature in Chinese/by Chinese (Shijie huawen/huaren wenxue 世界華文/举人文學) from a Chinese-Americanist Perspective', in *Global Chinese Literature: Critical Essays,* edited by Jing Tsu and David Der-wei Wang (Leiden: Brill, 2010), 30, 68.

29   Ha Jin, *The Writer as Migrant* (London: University of Chicago Press, 2009), 32, 78, 79. See also Kenny K. K. Ng, 'The Migrant Voice: The Politics of Writing Home between the Sinophone and Anglophone Worlds', *Journal of Modern Literature in Chinese*, 1.14 (2017), 139. See also Alexa Olesen, 'A Conversation with Ha Jin', Virtual China, <http://www.virtualchina.org/lei sure/features/1119-hajinfinal. html> [Accessed 5 November 2022].

30   Dwight Garner, 'Ha Jin's Cultural Revolution', *The New York Times Magazine*, 6 February 2000, <https://www.nytimes.com/2000/02/06/magazine/ha-jin-s-cultural-revolution.html?pagewanted=1> [Accessed 10 December 2021].

31   Ang, *On Not Speaking Chinese,* 35.

32   Chee Beng Tan, *The Routledge Handbook of the Chinese Diaspora* (London and New York: Routledge, 2013), 17.

33   Ibid., 2–4 and 17–21.

34   Guanglun Mu and Bonnie Pang, *Interpreting the Chinese Diaspora: Identity, Socialisation and Resilience according to Pierre Bourdieu* (London and New York: Routledge, 2019), 44.

35   David Der Wei Wang, *A New Literary History of Modern China* (Cambridge, MA and London: Harvard University Press, 2017), 24.

36   Jing Tsu and David Der Wei Wang, *Global Chinese Literature: Critical Essays* (Leiden: Brill, 2010), 30.

37   Tan, *The Routledge Handbook*, 22.

38   Ibid., 22.

39   Roger Daniels, 'The Coming of the Chinese', in *Asian American: Chinese and Japanese in the United States since 1850* (Seattle and London: University of Washington Press, 1988), 42.

40   Tan, *The Routledge Handbook*, 24.

41 Erika Lee and Judy Yung, *Angel Island: Immigrant Gateway to America* (Oxford and New York: Oxford University Press, 2010), 9.

42 Peter N. Stearns, 'Chinese Overseas', in *The Oxford Encyclopedia of the Modern World* (Oxford and New York: Oxford University Press, 2008), 143–4.

43 Tan, *The Routledge Handbook*, 25.

44 Shelley Chan, *Diaspora's Homeland: Modern China in the Age of Global Migration* (Durham, NC: Duke University Press, 2018), 9–10.

45 See the following: Shelley Chan, *Diaspora's Homeland: Modern China in the Age of Global Migration* (Durham: Duke University Press, 2018). Gregory B. Lee, *Chinas Unlimited: Making the Imaginaries of China and Chineseness* (Oxford and New York: Routledge, 2021). For background on Anglophone Singaporean poetry, see anthologies: Angelia Poon, Philip Holden, Shirley Lim (ed.), *An Historical Anthology of Singapore* (Singapore: NUS Press, 2009); Lee, Aaron and Alvin Pang (ed.), *No Other City: The Ethos Anthology of Urban Poetry* (Singapore: Ethos Books, 2000) and *Tumasik: Contemporary Writing from Singapore* (Iowa: Autumn Hill Books, 2009).

46 Peter N. Stearns, 'Chinese Overseas', in *The Oxford Encyclopedia of the Modern World* (New York: Oxford University Press, 2008), 143–5.

47 Ibid., 144.

48 Jahan Ramazani, *A Transnational Poetics* (Chicago and London: University of Chicago, 2009), x–xi.

49 Stephen Vertovec, 'Three Meanings of Diaspora, Exemplified among South Asian Religions', *Diaspora*, 7.2 (1998), <http://www.transcomm.ox.ac.uk/working%20papers/diaspora.pdf> [Accessed 7 May 2017].

50 John Clammer, *Singapore Ideology, Society, Culture* (Singapore: Chopmen, 1985), 25, 27.

51 Ibid.

52 They include poets like Alvin Pang, Daren Shiau, Felix Cheong, Pooja Nansi, Grace Chia, Edwin Thumboo, Toh Hsien Min, Yeow Kai Chai, Wang Gungwu, Wong Phui Nam, Wong May, Ng Yi-Sheng, Lee Tzu Pheng, Leong Liew Geok, Danjl Lim, Joshua Ip, Marilyn Jan and more.

53 Chee Kiong Tong, *Identity and Ethnic Relations in Southeast Asia: Racialising Chineseness* (London: Springer, 2010).

54 Timothy Yu, *Diaspora Poetics* (London and New York: Oxford University Press, 2021), 1, 18, 29.

55 Jay Gao, 'An interview on Imperium', *The London Magazine*, 2022, <https://www.thelondonmagazine.org/interview-jay-gao-on-imperium/> [Accessed 23 September 2022].

56 Appendix, 'An interview with Marilyn Chin', 172.

57 W. E. B. Du Bois, *The Souls of Black Folk: Essays and Sketches* (London: Archibald & Constable Co., 1905), 3.

58 In tracing the beginnings of Orientalism, Said points out, 'Schwab's notion is that "Oriental" identifies an amateur or professional enthusiasm for everything Asiatic, which was wonderfully synonymous with the exotic, the mysterious, the profound, the seminal.' In other words, 'Oriental' interest, prompted by curiosity, is built on demarcating difference. Edward Said, *Orientalism* (London: Penguin Books, 2003), 51.

59 Homi Bhabba, *The Location of Culture* (Oxford and New York: Routledge, 1994), 7.

60 Said, *Orientalism,* 58.

61 Steven Yao, *Foreign Accents: Chinese American Verse from Exclusion to Postethnicity* (Oxford: Oxford University Press, 2010), 268–9.

62 David Morley and Kuan-Hsing Chen, *Stuart Hall: Critical Dialogues in Cultural Studies* (London and New York: Routledge, 1996), 396.

63 Stuart Hall, 'Cultural Identity and Diaspora', in *Identity, Community, Culture, Difference*, edited by Jonathan Rutherford (London: Lawrence & Wishart, 1990), 222.

64 Ibid., 502.

65 See also Chapter 4.

66 In understanding the term 'minority', I refer to its numerical and political aspects, usually defined by disadvantage or under-privilege, which has increasingly been identified in terms of one's racial or ethnic group. In particular, it is important to note that immigrants or other diasporic individuals only become members of minority after they travel to or reside in another location away from home. Ellis Cashmore, et al., *Race and Ethnic Relations*, 4th edition (London: Routledge, 1996), 242–4.

67 Dorothy J. Wang, *Thinking Its Presence: Form, Race, and Subjectivity in Contemporary Asian American Poetry* (Stanford: Stanford University Press, 2013), 12–13.

68 Ibid., 20.

69 Wenbo Sun, *Writing in Relativity* (Beijing: Peking University Press, 2010), 4–6.

70 Shu-mei Shih, 'Global Literature and the Technologies of Recognition', *PMLA*, 119.1 (2004), 22.

71 Jahan Ramazani, *A Transnational Poetics*, 25.

72 Janet Neigh, 'Ramazani's Global Vocabulary for Poetry', *Journal of Modern Literature*, 34.3 (2011), 200.

73 Margaret Hillenbrand, 'Communitarianism, or, How to Build East Asian Theory', *Postcolonial Studies*, 13.4 (2010), 320–1.

1

Bei Dao: A Sinophone diasporic poet and the poetic language of exile

Exiled from China since 1989 and writing in the Chinese language, Bei Dao's work examines the distance between self and society, and depicts the mind as a distant, utopian place of conscience and resistance.

Born in Beijing in 1949 to a middle-class family from Shanghai, Bei Dao (Zhao Zhenkai) studied at one of the top schools in Beijing. As a student, he joined the Red Guards but was later disappointed by the movement's inability to improve the livelihood of the population. In 1969, at the start of the Cultural Revolution, he was sent away to be 're-educated' as a construction worker and blacksmith for ten years.[1] In 1978, Bei Dao and Mang Ke co-founded *Jintian* ('今天' meaning 'today'), a journal that has developed into one of China's most influential literary journals distributed widely both inside China and overseas, featuring a diverse range of contemporary local as well as diasporic Chinese poets. From 1989 onwards, he went into forced exile in both Europe and America, and taught at various universities, while his wife and daughter were not allowed to travel abroad to visit him.[2] In 2007, he ended two decades of exile and returned to Asia, taking up a teaching position in Hong Kong. He is the author of *The Rose of Time: New and Selected Poems* (New Directions, 2010); *Unlock* (2000); *At the Sky's Edge: Poems 1991–1996* (1996); *Landscape over Zero* (1995); *Forms of Distance* (1994); *Old Snow* (1991); and *The August Sleepwalker* (1990). Despite winning many international awards and being repeatedly nominated for the Nobel Prize for Literature, his works and public appearances are substantially suppressed in Mainland China even today. While his poetry is written in Chinese, English editions of his books have been translated by Bonnie McDougall and authorized by Bei Dao.[3] As a leading poet of Chinese ethnicity who has spent decades in exile, Bei Dao's poetry has been widely read and influenced many Chinese writers in China and abroad.

Combining an abstract, private poetic language with unfamiliar, obscure metaphors, his poetry is often perceived as a forerunner of Chinese misty poetry, a genre of literary and social significance in the post-Mao era of 1980s to 1990s.[4] By misty poetry, I refer to Li-hua Ying's definition, a genre representing a major literary breakthrough in the post-Mao era, characterized by 'oblique imagery and cryptic syntax'.[5] The enigmatic quality of poems taps into the power of hidden meanings. Distinct from the use of the oblique in English poems, the imagistic, elliptical nature of 'misty poems' expresses 'aspirations for freedom and spirituality', and represents a distinct form of protest literature against 'totalitarianism and ideological tyranny'.[6] Bei Dao's works reflect a new poetics, focusing on the poet's need for survival from feelings of alienation and homelessness in times of exile. His use of refreshing imageries and individualized language articulates his political resistance against manipulated poetic language and government propaganda.

In this chapter, I will discuss the ways in which Bei Dao's metaphorical and surreal language captures the universal through the personal, a poetic language that has influenced my own writing. In his poetry, home is experienced as a matter of time, in which the present brims with memories, while the past holds the key to the future. I am interested in his identity as both an insider and outsider of his own country, which has led him to a self-portrait of double and often contradictory allegiances. Moreover, one is struck by the subtlety with which he assimilates Chinese and European poetics in the use of symbolism.

Bei Dao has published numerous books of poetry, fiction and essays in Chinese, but to give a more distilled overview and analysis, here I base my discussion on *The Rose of Time*, the comprehensive bilingual edition of his collected poems edited by Eliot Weinberger.[7] In addition, I supplement my reading with the original editions in Chinese and the first English editions of collections translated by Bonnie McDougall and David Hinton. In this way, I adopt David Damrosch's approach of 'detached engagement', a reading approach that emphasizes the dialogue with the work from a distance.[8] This approach is based on the notion that we cannot read the work within its original cultural context, but to appreciate how the work 'reaches out and away from its point of origin'.[9] This perspective makes it possible to engage with translated world literature by regarding it as a literature of its own, while taking into account any cultural information that will be relevant.[10] To do so, I read Bei Dao's work in the context of the Chinese literary scene that suffers from the fears of censorship, in which poetic language evolves constantly to escape from surveillance. Quoting Cooppan, in accessing and appreciating world literature, we need to be 'locally inflected and translocally mobile'.[11] I interpret this as the possibility to articulate a locality with a poetic language that incorporates the local and the foreign, such that the place is experienced in a way that transcends the fixity of the place.

Characterized by a timeless, dream-like landscape, Bei Dao's poetry invites the reader into an intimate, personal and morbid sphere of dreams, fears and imagination. In many of his poems, there is the unusual juxtaposition of natural symbols such as the wind, trees, flowers, stones, mountains, valleys, with man-made artifices such as memorials, flags, markets, highways and newspapers. Such juxtapositions of objects from the personal and public realms evoke a space that is surreal, offering a setting where the self can escape from the immediate reality, and to envisage the possibilities of a new and unfamiliar world. Instead of treating natural landscapes as settings, elements from nature in Bei Dao's poems are often imbued with emotions and a sense of agency. For example, in 'Harbor Dreams', we are presented with stars that continuously search for their daylight positions in the compass of the sky.[12] In 'At the Sky's Edge', there is 'love among the mountains' and 'patience of the earth'.[13] In 'Untitled', that begins with 'at the mother tongue', the rose is said to sip water or dawn-light via 'stem-tubing'.[14] In 'The Next Tree', the snowstorm is capable of stirring up a lie in the air, an imagery that I interpret as the invisible quality of anxiety about language in the society.[15] Such animate landscapes are in strong contrast to the melancholic overtone of his poems, so often filled with death, violence, ill omens and disasters. They also reveal Bei Dao's poetics as a platform to show the stark contrast between vision and reality, and the mind's experience of both hope and despair.

In 'The Rose of Time', the rose is a symbol of suffering, seen to constantly 'emerge in disappearance', and 'cry in the conspiracy'. It is also a source of metaphysical power and ephemeral beauty, blooming despite the harsh sounding of gongs from the East. In the last stanza, Bei Dao suggests that the rose can inspire a process of awakening or 'rebirth', the way a poet can create something timeless by registering a moment of poetic beauty:

in the mirror there is always this moment
this moment leads to the door of rebirth
the door opens to the sea
the rose of time[16]

Jacob Edmond interprets it as Bei Dao's elusive language as a strategy to expose the gap between text and reality, and to undermine the fixity of the world he seeks to describe:

> As the contrasting readings of his work illustrate, allegory not only establishes a correspondence between text and world; it also reveals the gap between the world and our words for it. [...] Instead it produces forms of alienation that stress a continuous process of re-presentation and rereading. His work undoes the apparent fixity of its own allegorical relations between text and world.[17]

Building on this theory of allegory, it is of particular interest to note that, in Bei Dao's poems, the lyrical 'I' often has no fixity in his location and implies his sense of alienation as an exile, being as both an observer and implied participant in this surreal world. In 'Along the Way', the refrain of 'I adjust the time/so as to pass through my life' suggests an individual of volition.[18] However, this lyrical self is also portrayed as a passive, helpless observer of apocalyptic scenes surrounding him: the violent attacks against the tourists, the sudden swarm of bees that pursue the wanderers, the sick baby intoxicated by cigarettes in the mother's womb and the mysterious appearance of blood on the map.[19] This highlights the poet's experimentation with a self that attempts to narrate history and meaning, and yet is unable to fully engage with or change his world. This sense of alienation in his poetic language reflects his identity as an exile, burdened by his memory and nostalgia and feeling the distance between himself and his homeland.

Dian Li describes Bei Dao's poetry as 'an exercise in survival, a battle of voices, a performance in resistance'.[20] Li's interpretation of Bei Dao's poetry as a poetics of resistance can be explained in terms of the poet's frequent use of declarative language and a heroic voice. An example is 'Background', one of Bei Dao's best-known poems on identity written in around 1940.[21] The poem articulates the poet's moral dilemma in deliberating his return to his hometown: as he allegedly supported the pro-democracy movement in the Tiananmen Incident in 1989, a 'repentance' or 'confession' from his former political position is necessary for him to be allowed back into the country. In McDougall's translation, the poem begins with a powerful, declarative line:

> the background needs revising
> you can return to your hometown[22]

Referencing the Chinese original, and taking into account Chinese grammar, the couplet should actually read or mean 'one [you] must revise the background / in order to return to the hometown'. Written in a deliberately impersonal tone that makes it unclear who is asking him to revise his background, the Chinese original conveys a sense of threat that preys on the protagonist's mind, while it also ridicules the impossibility of return, since one's background has already been written. In the first half of the poem, the speaker alludes to the small triumphs gained with 'time-shaken words', followed by 'a string of failures' experienced in one's ideological struggle. The speaker is also acutely aware of his sense of place being obliterated by 'heavy snow' and the scarcity of time ('pressing toward the huge clock of old age'). In the second part of the poem, he portrays the exile's partner, an anonymous female figure in a family gathering, a figure symbolic of personal, emotional attachments:

> the woman closest to you
> always wears the worried look of history
> gazes into snowdrifts, double space to
>
> darkness in which voles believe absolutely[23]

Punctuated by a line of spacing, the anxiety of the passive woman who worries about her husband's exilic life is in sharp contrast with the movement of the hopeful voles. At the end of the poem, the darkness has ambiguous meanings. On the one hand, it is a deprivation of light and hope, as people can hardly see through the thick snow, a metaphor for the context of a troubled historical past. At the same time, the voles are used to represent one's instinctive search for light and clarity in a dark place, and the striving against deprivation. This juxtaposition of the self in relation to society corresponds with Vincent Geoghegan's theory on the power of group and individual memories in constructing alternative realities:

> These memories provide much of the raw material for the vital utopian dimension of their politics. […] It thus opens the door for a utopianism, which is grounded in the historically evolving memories of groups of individuals. The future, in this conception, is not a return to the past but draws sustenance from this past. Memory is the means in the present to ground the future in the past.[24]

In analysing Bei Dao's work, one should not overlook the complexity of the self's responsibility and complicity. When asked about his views towards his controversial poem 'The Answer', which was adopted by student protestors during the Tiananmen Incident of 1989, he remarked:

> My feelings about it are complicated because I wasn't there. I wasn't at the Square and students were facing death with my poetry. I even feel guilt that my poems tried to encourage students to die. They sacrificed themselves with my poetry.[25]

For Bei Dao, the journey of the self is far more complex and difficult than a purposeful, linear movement. A poem written for his then five-year-old daughter, Tiantian, 'A Picture', captures the poet's love and hope for his daughter, whom he was unable to see for a long time during his exile.[26] Moreover, it is a poem that parodies the distance between a poet and his words. In this poem, Bei Dao imagines his daughter drawing a picture on a warm, beautiful morning, while he is a 'hedgehog in exile/taking with him a few unintelligible characters' who 'has left your painting'.[27] The refrain 'how vast is a five-year-old sky' expresses the poet's longing for the innocence of a child's mind, and the reference to the pictorial image of his daughter's name 田田, a Chinese character consisting of the pictograms of two windows. He imagines that one opening of the window points towards 'a sun with no clockhands' and the other 'toward your father'.

This suggests an individual's sense of place or vision as being split between the past and the future, the family and the nation (with the sun being used as a metaphor for the mother country where she remains). Comparing himself to a hedgehog in exile, he associates his exilic journey with darkness, while at the same time the poet is seen as someone who leaves his native place for a noble cause, bringing with him 'a bright red apple' on his journey, a symbol of hope and goodness. In other words, the poem captures the poet's pride as an idealist and dreamer uncompromised in his beliefs, as well as his guilt as a father.[28]

Beyond the camouflage of surreal landscapes and detachment, Bei Dao's poetry aims to expose hidden truths and the power imbalance between the self and the society. Dian Li refers to this as the poet's 'strategy of mapping out the vanishing self against all alienating forces in contemporary societies, real or imagined'.[29] In particular, Li remarks on the 'ideological ambiguity and contradiction' present in Bei Dao's work.[30] In his later poem, 'Black Map', written around the time of his first return to China in 2001, the poet reveals an increasingly ambiguous attitude towards one's position in society, and in particular, questions the ideal or feasibility of a real homecoming. Bei Dao remarked in his interview with *Southern Metropolis Weekly* that the poem is self-contradictory, in the sense that while the titular 'map' is a tool to plot the location, 'black' suggests concealment:

in the end, cold crows piece together
the night: a black map
I've come home – the way back
longer than the wrong road
long as a life[31]

The poet reflects on his efforts to return 'home', be it a location or an untroubled past, a journey in darkness. In subsequent stanzas, the poet expresses his sadness to see his ailing father whose life is now 'small as a pea', and is daunted by a realization that the long years of absence from the family makes him no more than a distant 'echo'. He has also lost his lover, who now 'hides in a wind/swirling with letters', which refers to the fact that an exile can only experience love from the letters he receives from home. The irrevocable loss of his family ties and anchorage culminates in the sense of rejection expressed in the scene where the protagonist stands in a queue at the customs, where there is an unsympathetic small window:

> I wait in line until the small window
> shuts: O the bright moon
> I go home – reunions
> are one less
> fewer than goodbyes[32]

In this condensed, unusual run-on sentence, the poet reflects on how rarely he has been allowed to go home and visit his family, and how he is dreading the prospect of death of his ailing father, a 'goodbye' that is final and filled with regret. Here, the poet seeks solace from the bright moon, evoking the Chinese poetic tradition where the moon is often regarded as a muse, and acknowledges that what remains in his mind is a different version of home now. In other words, the return to one's country can also be a journey of getting lost again, since what used to be there has all disappeared and cannot be re-constructed.[33] In his essay, 'Under a Foreign Sky', Bei Dao talks about his views on the relationship between place and identity:

> To an individual, a city is his centre, irrespective of its size nor its geographical importance. In the same way, the world map published in each country inevitably evolves around itself, but luckily the earth is round, so nobody needs to be too upset about it […] After all, having been away for so long, the concept of home has become blurred. Sometimes, when I was driving under a foreign sky, I would be overcome by a sense of uncertainty: where am I? Is this my home? […] My home is in between different signposts.[34]

'Black Map' also reflects Maghiel van Crevel's claim that, other than physical exile, Bei Dao has, like his Chinese contemporaries, undergone a period of 'inner exile' or 'exilic retreat into the mind', and corresponds with Bei Dao's own claim that the poet is never at home anywhere.[35]

Geoghegan remarks that the future draws sustenance from the past.[36] For Bei Dao, the utopian longing for a true home where the past and the future can co-exist is also evident in his philosophy behind *Jintian*. In an interview with LaPiana, Bei Dao explains that *Jintian* reflects his belief in the writer's power to traverse or transcend places and cultures, and to create an imaginative place free of ideological bounds:

> We [*Jintian* writers] are a kind of intermediate territory between China and the outside. There is a dialogue, an interaction with Western culture. Also, we are not Hong Kong, not Taiwan, not the mainland. We transcend all these boundaries. We are also trying to be free of the forces of ideology, which dominated China for so long, and of commercialism, which dominates it now. We have a special place. Also, our journal is cross-cultural. This is a change from Chinese literary journals in the past.[37]

Exposing the poet's distrust of language, many of Bei Dao's early poems have been termed as examples of 'misty poetry', and have been compared with works by other misty poets such as Gu Cheng and Shu Ting.[38] These poems are characterized by unusual syntax, run-on lines and inaccessible meanings. 'A Local Accent', for example, articulates one's paradoxical relationship with or distrust of language.[39] Written in around 1989 or 1990, at the beginning of the poet's exile, the first-person voice describes the process of practising his mother tongue, Chinese, in front of the mirror, amidst every day, calming rituals such as making coffee and putting on the music. He jolts and arouses the reader's attention by bringing flies into this scene:

> I speak Chinese to the mirror
> a park has its own winter
> I put on music
> winter is free of flies
> I make coffee unhurriedly
> flies don't understand what's meant by native land
> I add a little sugar
> a native land is a kind of local accent[40]

In understanding this poem, it is necessary to appreciate Bei Dao's comparison of his own poetics to film techniques: 'I try to introduce in my poetry the technique of film montage, and by creating juxtaposed images and changes in speed, I want to arouse people's imagination to fill in the substantial gaps between the words.'[41] He relies on this poetic technique to stir the reader's imagination so that 'the gaps between the words can be filled'. Here, the strange syntax reminds one of the fixed verse form in a sestina, where the last words of certain lines (e.g. 'winter', 'flies', 'native land') are repeated at the beginning of other lines, a form of poetic echoing that prompts the reader to reflect on the meaning hidden in each word. The juxtaposition of images also suggests the presence of two places that the poet inhabits at once: the immediate land where he is, where he makes coffee and speaks to himself out of loneliness, a new place with 'its own winter' and is 'free of flies', as well as the place he has left behind or is absent from, a distant land with warmer climate.

In describing the imagined insects, Bei Dao offers the curious observation that 'flies don't understand what's meant by a native land'. The poet imagines that, having only lived in one habitat, it is natural that the flies would have no idea what a native land is, unlike the poet himself. On the other hand, the poem's ending moves from the poet's assertion that 'native land is a kind of local accent', and coming to the shocking conclusion that 'I hear my fright /on the other end of the phone line'.[42] The closing couplet appears completely out of context, detached from the sestina-structure, and upsets the reader's expectations, since the poem begins with the poet's self-speech in front of the mirror. However, it is also a powerful evocation of personal memories and hallucinatory fears of language associated with that distant, native land, triggered by a seemingly innocent phone call, which mirrors the poet's interior monologue at the start of the poem.

In Bei Dao's work, poetic language is used as an instrument of testimony as well as self-mockery or irony. It provides access to new vision and understanding, but at the same time it cannot be fully trusted. In his dialogue with Steven Ratiner, the poet admitted that 'the most important struggle in China has been who has control over the language'.[43] As such, the difficult semantics and obscure meanings inherent in Bei Dao's poetry reflect his search 'for a new language of expression'.[44] The poem also suggests a difference between Chinese and Western contemporary poetry in this period, where different cultural environments have led to different perspective about the meaning of poetry. In 'The Meaning of Poetry and Chinese Contemporary Poetry', Wenbo Sun discusses how poets living under an absolutist regime are likely to focus on the logic of living, as opposed to poets living in a democratic society who are more engaged with the meaning of life itself.[45] In this sense, the fact that Chinese contemporary poetry is often preoccupied with social reality demonstrates how the language of misty poetry is not so much a choice but an enactment of the social-historical condition of censorship in China, made necessary to evade government surveillance.

While Bei Dao has acknowledged his indebtedness to Chinese poetic tradition and the possibility to respond to the past,[46] his literary influences include a range of early-to-mid-twentieth-century poets in Europe, such as Paul Célan, Federico García Lorca, Trakl, Tomas Tranströmer and Dylan Thomas. In particular, he feels a strong sense of affinity with Célan, in the way Célan 'combines the sense of pain with language experiments'.[47] Writing in Chinese, Bei Dao's poetry fuses the use of Chinese misty poetry and declarative language with his appreciation for European poetry such as Celan's and Tranströmer's epiphanic, cryptic lyricism.

From natural landscapes to human isolation or misunderstanding, Tranströmer's poetry engages in a distilled, imagist description of life's paradoxes and mysteries and conveys a fervent sense of hope – a craft which Tom Sleigh describes as the ability to 'imagine the spaces that the deep then inhabits, like ground water gushing up into a newly dug well'.[48] Similarly, by juxtaposing images of natural and urban landscapes, Bei Dao's imagist poetry questions the value of human existence by evoking hope and alienation.[49] Technically, Bei Dao characteristically attaches stylistic adjectival or adverbial modifiers to the images which effect a Misty character or 'twist', disqualifying them from full adherence to Chinese origins and questioning the reader's first impressions. As Gustafsson pointed out, Tranströmer's poetry expresses through metaphors a 'utopia of the moment', which rests on the premises of 'a paradise lost' and at the same time unwavering faith towards a reality beyond oppression.[50] Captured in more violent and apocalyptic images suggestive of oppression, hunger and punishment when compared to Tranströmer's language, Bei Dao's poetry reveals a utopian ideal that is out of immediate reach but utterly plausible.

In his interview with Ratiner, it is also evident that time is a central theme that underlies his poetry and his worldview as a poet. He claims that democracy is not a sudden revolution. It is 'inevitable' and a slow process, or 'a question of time'. He felt that the people in the West have viewed China in 'oversimplified terms' and have ignored the fact that poetry is more like a 'silent revolution' that enters the consciousness of people.[51] With this in mind, one can appreciate his later poem, 'The Rose of Time', as a form of fable and lyrical testimony, since poetry is 'a way of keeping secrets'.[52] Eleanor Goodman, a leading translator of contemporary Chinese poetry as well as a poet who has lived in Beijing, indicated the distrust towards language that is unique to Chinese-language poets in China:

> From my experience as a translator and from my personal observation in Beijing, I think there is a difference [to Chinese poetic language.] Chinese poets today are acutely aware of their language as having been and still being used to political purpose, and that sense of language as being manipulated or "unclean" (*bu gan jing*) produces a sense of self-awareness and an awareness of the implications of that language, which American poets may not have. [I]n China poets are more suspicious of their own language, especially among the older generation of poets, who are aware their language has been manipulated or abused for various purposes.

Set in a timeless landscape where 'bird roads define the sky', the poem is packed with metaphors such as 'a pen draws the horizon' and 'the door opens to the sea'.[53] The recurring motif, 'the rose of time', refers to a priceless thing the poet embraces even as he grows old, an object of conviction and beauty that is constantly appearing and disappearing from his horizon. Considering that this poem was written in the 1990s, when the poet was abroad, it is symbolic of the poet's experience of losing hold of his homeland but gaining new vision in a non-native land. Even without mentioning the poet or placing the poem in any specific political or social context, Bei Dao articulates the power of poetry to transcend time and physical barriers, unlocking the suffering individual from the captivity of exile and the ideology of time.

Conclusion

By employing a distilled, obtuse and lyrical language that is deliberately hard to access, and crafting surreal, timeless and symbolic landscapes that are geographically unrecognizable, Bei Dao has created his own purposeful and experimental poetics by assimilating traditional Chinese poetics and Western literary influences. In his poems, he portrays an individual necessity to confront and resist an alienating environment dictated by social and political forces, and expresses the individual's distance from home and society in terms of temporal, ideological and physical boundaries. He also raises questions about the responsibility and idealism of personal choices and journeys. While the self is often positioned as a witness to history and estrangement, it is also an active, humanist self in search of utopian truth and visions for the future. Such poetics capture the difficulty of elucidating meanings or sharing one's emotions under an oppressive regime, where words are opaque constructs and language is either distrusted or feared. What is gained in the process, on the other hand, is a way to keep and pass on secrets within an introspective, self-preserving language where paradoxical metaphors operate to reveal the complex, contradictory nature of life.

Notes

1   Please see Chee Lay Tan, *Constructing a System of Irregularities: The Poetry of Bei Dao, Yang Lian and Duoduo* (Newcastle upon Tyne: Cambridge Scholars Publishing, 2016), 64. Also, see Lucienne Loh and Malcolm Sen (ed.), *Postcolonial Literature and Challenges for the New Millennium* (London: Routledge, 2017).

2   Maghiel van Crevel, *In Times of Mayhem and Money*, 150.

3   Also, note David Damrosch on differentiating reading the poetry of Bei Dao in Chinese and in English in *What Is World Literature?* (Princeton University Press, 2018), 22–3.

4 Zicheng Hong, 'The Early Poems of Bei Dao', *Journal of Hainan Normal University*, 1.1 (2005), 4–10.

5 Li-hua Ying, *Historical Dictionary of Modern Chinese Literature* (London: Rowman & Littlefield, 2022), 22.

6 Ying, ibid, 140.

7 Bei Dao, *The Rose of Time: New and Selected Poems*, edited by Eliot Weinberger, translated by Yanbing Chen, David Hinton, Chen Maiping, Iona Man-cheong, Bonnie McDougall and Eliot Weinberger (New York: New Directions, 2009).

8 David Damrosch, 'World Literature, National Contexts', *Modern Philology*, 100.4 (2003), 527–9.

9 Ibid.

10 Ibid., 529.

11 Vilashini Cooppan, 'World Literature and Global Theory: Comparative Literature for the New Millennium', *Symploke*, 9 (2001), 33.

12 Bei Dao, *Rose*, 29.

13 Ibid., 115.

14 Ibid., 125.

15 Ibid., 163.

16 Ibid., 281.

17 Jacob Edmond, *A Common Strangeness*, 96.

18 Bei Dao, *Rose*, 65.

19 Ibid.

20 Dian Li, *The Chinese Poetry of Bei Dao 1978–2000* (New York: Edwin Mellen Press, 2006), 2.

21 For context, see the interview with Bei Dao, *Southern Metropolis Weekly* (2010), <http://blog.renren.com/share/113186301/5240090640> [Accessed 20 April 2017].

22 Bei Dao, *Rose*, 137.

23 Ibid.

24 Vincent Geoghegan, 'Remembering the Future', *Journal of the Society for Utopian Studies*, 1.2 (1990), 67.

25 Li, *Chinese Poetry*, 5.

26 His wife and daughter were not allowed to visit him in the United States while he was in exile, and their family reunion happened only after his marriage ended. [See Steven Ratiner (ed.), *Giving Their Word: Conversations with Contemporary Poets* (Amherst and Boston: University of Massachusetts Press, 2002), 235]. In his essay 'Daughter', Bei Dao refers to his daughter as 'anchor': 我跟田田分开了六年,从她四岁到十岁。我满世界漂流事,暗自琢磨,恐怕只有田田这个锚,才能让我停下来。My translation: 'I was separated from Tian-tian for six years, since she was four, and we remained apart until she was ten. When I was in exile, sharpening my

skills and knowledge, it is only Tian-tian, my anchor, who could bring me to a halt.' [Bei Dao, *Selected Works of Bei Dao* (Wuhan: Changjiang Literature and Art Press, 2012), 206.]

27   Bei Dao, *Rose*, 85.

28   'Though she doesn't show up in my writing often, my daughter Tiantian plays an important role. She is the anchor for my drifting boat and the latent reader that pushes me to write. […] But I believe that someday she truly will understand. I want to tell her my life stories, including the tears on history's mask, the shattered myths and enemies; and we will travel beyond all this, reaching a way beyond countries; I am there, she is there, along with countless others.' [See also Bei Dao, 'Drifting', translated by Jody Beenk, in *Chinese Writers on Writing*, edited by Arthur Sze (Texas: Trinity University Press, 2010), 141–2.]

29   Li, *Chinese Poetry*, 5.

30   Dian Li, 'Ideology and Conflicts', *Modern Chinese Literature,* 9.2 (1996), 372.

31   Bei Dao, *Rose,* 253.

32   Bei Dao, *Rose,* 137.

33   Bei Dao, *Southern Metropolis Weekly.*

34   Original text reads: 一个城市对于一个人,往往就是中心,不在乎其大小、地理位置重要与否。这就好比每个国家出版的世界地图都把自己置于中心,好在地球是圆的,永不着为这打架[……]说实话离开故乡久了,家的概念变得混乱。有时我在他乡的天空下开车,会突然感到纳闷:我在哪儿?这就是我家吗?我家,在不同的路标之间。[Bei Dao, 'A Foreign Sky' (他乡的天空), *The Selected Works of Bei Dao,* 278–9.]

35   Maghiel van Crevel, *Chinese Poetry in Times of Mind, Mayhem and Money* (Leiden: Brill, 2008), 177–8.

36   See Note 20.

37   Siobahn LaPiana, 'An Interview with Visiting Artist Bei Dao: Poet in Exile', *The Journal of the International Institute*, 2.1 (1994) [Accessed 28 November 2016].

38   Gu Cheng and Shu Ting are leading Chinese misty poets. For their works translated into English, see *New Selected Poems,* translated by Joseph R. Allen (New York City: New Directions 1993); and Eva Hung (ed.), *Shu Ting: Selected Poems* (Hong Kong: Renditions, 1994).

39   Bei Dao, *Rose*, 80.

40   Ibid.

41   Bei Dao, 'About Poetry', in *Notes from the City of the Sun: Poems by Bei Dao* (New York: Cornell East Asia Papers, 1983), 79.

42   Bei Dao, *Rose*, 80.

43   Ratiner, *Giving Their Word*, 223.

44   Ibid., 229.

45 '社会刺激人的思考。所以,说中国当代诗的生产是社会存在刺激的产物, 其
    根据是确切的:没有上一个世纪80年代社会生活的变动,解除思想束缚后大
    规模的解放运动带来的向外看, 和与外部世界的比较, 就不会有先锋诗的产
    生。朦胧诗之争,"口语化"与"非口语化"之争,从表面上看属于语言形式、
    审美观念的争论,但内里反映的则是不同的文化观念之争。' My translation is:
    'What happens in a society prompts us into thinking. Therefore, it is safe to assume
    that contemporary Chinese poetry is a product stimulated by the society: without
    the social changes in 1980s, the outward-looking perspectives that arise from the
    unfettered thoughts of the collective liberation movement, and the accompanying
    comparisons with the outside world, forward-looking poetry will not be borne.
    The competition in the field of misty poetry, the conflict between formalism and
    colloquialism in poetry, seem to be a controversy regarding forms of language and
    aesthetics, but in fact they suggest the internal conflicts of cultural perspectives.'
    [Wenbo Sun, 'The Meaning of Poetry and Chinese Contemporary Poetry', in
    Writing in Relativity (Beijing: Peking University Press, 2010), 90.]

46 Bei Dao remarked: 'The emphasis traditional Chinese poetry lays on imagery
    and poetic space is in the end our own wealth ... When I do readings abroad,
    I sometimes feel that Li Bai, Du Fu and Li Yu are standing right behind me ...
    That's what tradition means. If we have the capability, we can enter into this
    tradition and enrich it; otherwise we're just failures.' [Bei Dao, 'Interview with
    Xiaodu Tang', *World Literature Today*, 82.6 (2008), 20–36.]

47 Gabi Gleichmann, 'An interview with Bei Dao', *Modern Chinese Literature*, 9
    (1996), 390. 'Of all the poets mentioned earlier, I like Célan best because I think
    there is a deep affinity between him and myself in the way he combines pain with
    language experiments. He transforms his experience in concentration camps into a
    language of pain.'

48 Tom Sleigh, *Interview with a Ghost: Essays* (Minnesota: Graywolf Press, 2006), 215.

49 'Bei Dao's imagism [...] has a new life of its own. Although it coincides with the
    imagist manifesto of absolute freedom in choice of subjects, expression in free
    verse, and the use of commonplace vocabulary and strong imagery, Bei Dao
    further challenges the clarity of the poetic pictograms by blurring the images
    and altering the conventional portrayal of hard and strong images advocated by
    imagists to form a new image, which I term the "Image Phrase". [Chee Lay Tan,
    *Constructing a System of Irregularities: The Poetry of Bei Dao, Yang Lian, and
    Duoduo* (Newcastle Upon Tyne: Cambridge Scholars Publishing, 2016), 81.]

50 Lars Gustafsson, '"The Utopia of the Moment": The Poetry of Tomas Tranströmer',
    World Literature Today, 64.4 (1990), 596–7.

51 Ratiner, *Giving Their Word*, 231.

52 Maghiel van Crevel, *Mind, Mayhem and Money*, 180.

53 Bei Dao, *Rose*, 281.

2

Li-Young Lee: Exile, nostalgia and Oriental spirituality

Introduction

Lyrical and deeply introspective, Li-Young Lee's poetry explores the impact of exile, memory and Oriental values on the diasporic individual's self-identity. Taking on a lyric, universal 'I', Lee's poetry articulates the irrevocable sadness and loss in exile, as well as his longing for spirituality that transcends racial and cultural divides. While his poetry reflects on his experience of exile with his family from Indonesia to the United States, it also emphasizes the healing power of memory, and a transcendental, utopian vision that assimilates Taoism and Confucianism through a receptive self.

As a young boy, Lee and his family moved from one country to another, before settling in America. Lee's particular family past and his father's political exile in Indonesia have contributed to the complexity of Lee's sense of self-belonging. In his work, the self is constantly questioning and returning to the family past. I will analyse the reworking of the family past in Lee's poetic language and imagery, as well as the sense of healing brought about by a higher poetic order, as the self undergoes a continued, transformative process of introspection and self-translation.

Looking into the 'Invisible'

Born in Jakarta, Indonesia, in 1957 to Chinese parents with powerful blood ties and political connections, Lee's mother was the granddaughter of Yuan Shi-kai, China's first republican president. His father was a physician who once worked as Mao Zedong's private secretary and was imprisoned for political reasons in Indonesia amidst anti-Chinese sentiments. After his release, the Lee family fled through Hong Kong, Macau and Japan, arriving in the United States in 1964.[1]

Lee was introduced to Christian doctrines, classical Chinese literature and Taoist beliefs through his father, a background that underlies the philosophical enquiry in his work.

Based in Chicago, Li-Young Lee is one of the most prominent Asian-American first-generation immigrant writers whose works have been recognized within the mainstream American poetry canon.[2] He is the author of *Rose* (BOA Editions, 1986), which won the Delmore Schwartz Memorial Poetry Award; *The City in Which I Love You* (BOA Editions, 1990) which won the 1990 Lamont Poetry Selection; *Behind My Eyes* (W. W. Norton, 2008); *Book of My Nights* (BOA Editions, 2001); *From Blossoms* (Bloodaxe Books, 2007); the pamphlet *The Word from His Song* (BOA Editions, 2016) and *The Undressing* (W. W. Norton, 2018). He received a Lannan Literary Award for Poetry in 1995. His memoir, *The Winged Seed: A Remembrance* (1995), received an American Book Award. Lee's honours include fellowships from the National Endowment for the Arts, The Lannan Foundation and the John Simon Guggenheim Memorial Foundation, as well as other writing grants.

Nevertheless, it is striking that Lee's poetry is marked by a deliberate absence of direct references to political figures or events. This is a bold distinct direction to resist the code of the Asian-American ethnic writing community. After all, Joseph Bruchac, editor of *Breaking Silence: An Anthology of Asian American Poets* (Greenfield Review Press, 1983), highlighted the need to celebrate the diverse Asian-American voices as a way to resist the rampant racial stereotypes and 'xenophobic animosity' in America.[3] Instead, his poems are lyrical, spiritual narratives of the family and the self, where identity is accessed via nostalgia and visions. In his interview with Tod Marshall, he admitted that his role as a poet is to 'deal with the invisible, not the visible'.[4] Moreover, he claimed to harbour little or no interest in offering 'a dialogue with cultural existence': 'Culture made that up – Asian-American, African-American, whatever. I have no interest in that. I have an interest in spiritual lineage connected to poetry'.[5] Geographically speaking, America is Lee's homeland, where he has spent most of his life. Nevertheless, the presence of Asia or China is deeply embedded in his exploration of family history, rituals and memory.[6]

A Confucian self and father-son relationship

Lee's poetic self is delineated in terms of his relationship to the family and fragmentary recollections of the family past, which reflects an ongoing preoccupation with the father figure. While acts of love, nurturing and care are repeatedly associated with the father figure (such as mending the son's clothing), the figure also represents absence. For example, in the poem 'Arise, Go Down', Lee suggests that he grows 'more fatherless each day' ever since his father has left him, and he, by necessity, has to embrace life 'without my father's help'.[7] The self harbours ambivalent feelings towards the father: admiration, guilt, awe, fear and love. The description is visceral and spiritual: 'The rose announces on earth the kingdom/of gravity. A bird cancels it. / My eyelids cancel the bird'.[8] What is surprising is that the portrait of the father is both intimate and distant at the same time, alluding to the 'absolutely binding' and yet nourishing or cultivating father-son relationship in the Chinese doctrine of filial piety.[9]

In his poem, the father figure is a haunting body on which the poet projects his unresolved feelings towards his family past. The poet describes his epiphany that the world he inherits is from his father, even though he imagines his father speaking: '*I didn't make the world I leave you with,* /he said, and then, being poor, he left me /only this world'.[10] In other words, the poet is aware that his knowledge and freedom are both derived from his father, and that the father figure – strongly connected with the biblical father – is for him the crucial connection between the past and the present. The poet's selfhood gravitates, at the same time, to both the presence (the here and now) and absence (the distant or re-imagined past). While Lee's use of the father motif highlights his Confucian thinking as a filial, obeying son, the romantic nostalgia imbued in the narrative represents an affective mode of expression that is more Western than Chinese, On the one hand, it demonstrates Lee's conviction that poetry is a medium for encouraging synthesis and erasing ethnic or cultural allegiances. On the other, it echoes Yao's argument that Lee's distinctive poetics embrace 'a strictly idiosyncratic knowledge of his heritage tradition that informs the deployment of Chinese cultural reference' and his incomplete knowledge of Chinese.[11]

This location of the missing place, a gravitational anchor, is elucidated in 'With Ruins', marked by 'a place where things /were said and done', and an architectural space that connects the reader (i.e. 'you') and the poet ('I'). It is an unreal and paradoxical space, with its 'roofless floor' and 'columns/supporting nothing', and is characterized by absences, being 'a three-/dimensional grid negotiating /absences'.[12] The poet describes the organic space of total freedom created by self-choice:

> You think
> of a woman, a favorite
> dress, your old father's breasts

the last time you saw him, his breath
brief, the leaf

you've torn from a vine and which you hold now
to your cheek like a train ticket
or a piece of cloth, a little hand or a blade –
it all depends
on the course of your memory.

This remembered space represents an invisible, subjective territory where one can only enter through imagination, and changes each time he visits. It is also a place where the poet and the reader converge in 'you(r)' consciousness.

From memory to spirituality

The creative tension between past and present, memory and imagination, is of utmost significance in Lee's poetry. Contrary to other Asian-American writers of his time whose work engages more directly with their immigration experience, Lee's poetic language is imbued with nostalgia, impersonality and spirituality, exemplifying a mode of 'lyric testimony' that Steve Yao describes as characteristic of early Asian-American poetry. In his interview with Tod Marshall, Lee explains his interest in quest poetry. What fascinates him is 'a dialogue with his truest self', and has a keen interest in 'spiritual lineage connected to poetry-through Eliot, Donne, Lorca, Tu Fu, Neruda, David the Psalmist', even though he acknowledges that is part of the hybrid culture and traditions he inherits'.[13]

Lee's rose motif in *Rose* and *The City in Which I Love You* (1990) best illustrates the spiritual essence of his poetry. From *Breaking the Alabaster Jar: Conversations with Li-Young Lee*, we are told that Lee's father loved growing roses, and used to teach his son that life is like a great big flower, opening perpetually. Moreover, Lee's mother sometimes would add roses to her home-cooking.[14] By choosing the rose to embody purity and beauty, Lee incorporates a spiritual essence into his poetry. It is a more accessible symbol for the Western reader than the lotus, the latter used as the traditional symbol of goodness and righteousness in Chinese literature. Instead of taking this symbolism for granted, in 'Always a Rose', he claims it and transforms it into his own tantalizing image, a flower-body that is 'odorous', 'tender' and 'bitter', representing both love and death. The poet adores the fragile and beautiful body of the rose. The poem moves from contemplation to the ingestion and incorporation of the rose into his own body, fusing it with his father's dead body: 'I eat you to put my faith in grief. /[...] /I eat you /down to your secret.'[15]

In Lee's poetry, selfhood originates from feelings of love and the longing for home; yet, the home represented in his poetry is more abstract and spiritual than autobiographical. It is an open architecture of the mind, rooted in both the past and the present, and is consummately articulated in *The City in Which I Love You*. It is a lyrical narrative or lament that traces the close-knit relationship between father and the son, and their reconstructed dialogue throughout the years of exile from Indonesia to America. By traversing time in a subjective, non-linear manner, the rekindled family past gives rise to new meanings and questionings of the self.

As Xiaojing Zhou points out, the poem re-articulates erotic love with the intensity and sensuality similar to *The Song of Songs,* and echoes Walt Whitman's *Leaves of Grass.*[16] On the one hand, Lee's use of sensuous language seems to suggest Lee's ability to articulate his longings in a poetic idiom that is more accessible to readers of American literature. On the other, in 'Furious Versions', claiming that 'memory revises me', the narrating voice shifts between the perspectives of the father and the son, and these overlapping voices recount the departure from the family's home in Indonesia to a new country where the diasporic self preserves the memory of the distant land:

America, where, in Chicago, Little Chinatown,
who should I see
on the corner of Argyle and Broadway
but Li Bai and Du Fu, those two
poets of the wanderer's heart.[17]

Throughout the lyrical narrative, the poet registers the impossibility of fleeing from the past, as memories of home and the familiar keep returning, just as the poet encounters the apparitions of Chinese poets when he experiences America. Zhou argues that Lee's diffuse lyric persona as a 'guest' allows him to relate to the others without losing the individuality of his self or reducing the alterity of the other.[18]

While in this poem the father urges his son not to forget what has happened, in the following poem, 'The Interrogation', the poet brings together the voice of the deceased father and the son's questions about the family past: '*Who rowed the boat when our father tired?*' The father is portrayed as exhausted from the trial of persecution, and repeats 'I'm through /with memory'.[19] Remembering the teaching of the afflicted father, the son keeps his promise not to forget.

Between the personal and the impersonal

Often, Lee's protagonists are faceless silhouettes or family members engaged in their rituals, against a dreamy, sweeping and timeless backdrop. His chosen poetics seem to be unusual, considering that anthology editors, critics and poets alike focus predominantly on poetry that is 'essentially Asian', i.e those with explicit ethnic markers. Timothy Yu remarks that Lee's refusal to thematize the categories of 'Asian' and 'American' is a deliberate act that makes his work more universal and effective.[20] I see Lee's use of a diffuse, universal self as being influenced by the Confucian view of selfhood as the site of creative tension, where the self is motivated to adjust his differences with the world and to reconcile conflicts, in order to achieve a moral and cosmic order of harmony.[21]

Shifting between personal memories and the longing for a more cosmic order of harmony, the poetic voice becomes both personal and impersonal.[22] In his interview with Matthew Fluharty on the relationship between his poetry and identity, Lee also draws on the multiple selves that contribute to the essence of poetic-ness: 'There are many selves in me. As I am speaking to you now, I am speaking out of one self, the self that is in conversation. But there is a self that was dreaming last night. [...] Poetry accounts for the many-ness of who we are.'[23] Likewise, in the long poem 'The Cleaving', the speaker tries to see affinity with the butcher ('He could be my brother'): Such a sorrowful Chinese face, / nomad, Gobi, Northern [...] warlike forehead' and 'He could be my brother[.]'[24] Throughout the poem, the idea of eating up what he can see seems a way to process grief, even if the butcher figure reminds him of the traumatic past of war, of death, of injustices that could have happened to any race: his 'warlike forehead' and 'the death- /in-a-strange-land, these Chinatown / deaths, these American deaths'.

At the end of the poem, the poet leave us with:

> this Jew, this Asian, this one
> with the Cambodian face, Vietnamese face, this Chinese
> I daily face,
> this immigrant,
> this man with my own face.[25]

Lee confronts his own face, his face of an immigrant, as he reflects on his affinity with the marginalized, other people from other places.

Lee's title poem, 'In the City Where I Love You', captures such convergence of the personal and the impersonal. Time and again, the protagonist – an immigrant who searches for meaning of self in a nameless city – comes across people who resemble him, only to discover that none of them is himself. At the end, the protagonist finds his way to re-enter the city 'without retreat or help from history', offering a route to appropriate his self-identity by looking inward.[26] The poet is haunted by the painful memories of anti-Chinese persecution his family experienced in Indonesia; yet, at the same time he denies these memories:

[T]hat man was not me;
his wound was his, his death not mine.
And the soldier
who fired the shot, then lit a cigarette:
he was not me.[27]

The poetics of negation reflects the poet's sense of alienation and indignation against social injustices. In my interview with Lee, he said: 'Globally speaking, all I see is the sign of the scapegoat. There are scapegoats everywhere on this planet. [...] What can "home" mean to anyone these days except crisis? Our earth-home itself is suffering massive crisis.'[28] In essence, the search for meaning in this poem sequence reflects the poet's quest for 'a logic of peace and a science of life' that transcends nation-state, class, racial, gender and other divides. According to Lee, his allegiance is inclined towards 'a logic of peace' and 'a science of life' that is more important [...] than any other allegiance including home, country, family, race, class, gender, sexual preference, poetic school, you name it'.[29] In other words, for Lee, home is never free from trauma, and he looks for a sense of belonging that is not just rooted in a physical location or even identification with a race, culture or a tribe. Instead, he is longing for peace with himself and with history.

A receptive, cosmic order where self resides

Lee's poetry is characterized by an open-ended response towards names and meanings, corresponding to the open-handedness in Chinese philosophy and cultural values that is often expressed in delicate, lyrical or opaque language to communicate a transcendental view of the world. 'For a New Citizen of These United States' begins with a poignant image of a moth trapped in the damask, and yet the speaker reassures the reader, saying there is no need for alarm or sadness.[30] In Taoist philosophy, the soul of the deceased can metamorphose into a moth, and in this way the deceased revisits their loved ones in bodily form.

In the poem, 'father-shadow' is described as part of the natural elements in his line of vision, side by side with 'cloud-shadow' and 'wing-shadow'.[31] This image of the moth crystallizes what can be seen and what remains unseen, capturing a reality where both the past and the present co-exist, and where the self dwells in both *here* and *there*.

Despite his assertion that the rain brings nothing, claiming that he will not speak of the past because he assumes the reader ('you') has already forgotten about it, images of his previous home, relatives and familiar home scenes, are scattered throughout the poem:

> But you don't remember, I know,
> So I won't mention that house where Chung hid,
> Lin wizened, you languished, and Ming –
> Ming hush-hushed us with small song.[32]

The passage of time in *these* United States is, in fact, observed and measured by family habits and memories, such as the way he can tell the arrival of each spring by the scent of his mother's favourite flower, lilac. In Lee's poetry, naming, or more often the refusal to name, becomes a powerful means of narrating racial trauma. There is a deliberate blocking out of memory or fears by replacing the unnamed with the symbol of flowers, houses, touch and other sensations. It is as if the poet finds it unbearable to remember or articulate a history that goes outside the realm of personal history.

Although the poem starts with a reminder of personal history – the death of his father and hence the return of the moth and the 'father-shadow' – the poem zooms out to situate this event within the broader context of his social reality, where his family history is merely 'years in a book of years'.[33] There is the mention of 'other families on a crowded/railroad platform'.[34] Hence in conveying the sensations and emotions associated with the family past, the poet identifies historical events and social history that lie outside his immediate experience but nonetheless belong to the same temporal space, articulating his affinity with families like theirs, whose lives and homes are irrevocably changed as a result of moving to a new country.

Opaque poetic language and Taoist outlook

In 'Of Nonlimited Locality/Identity: Chinese Diaspora Poetry in America', Benzi Zhang points out that central to the experience of diaspora is a 'dramatic change in the politics of place, which starts to redefine place beyond the historical opposition of *here* versus *there*, since, to a certain extent, *there* has both emerged and been merged in the very characterisation of *here*.[35] Diaspora, according to him, is a process of mutual translation and interaction.[36] Within this poem, Lee explores the self and unfulfilled desires in an urban but surreal landscape, where the city is at once the object of desire and yet perpetually out of reach. The feeling of emptiness is embodied in the elusive body of the city, or the lover 'you': 'Morning comes to this city vacant of you. /Pages and windows flare, and you are not there.'[37] The tone of this poem corresponds with the Taoist pathos, which Wai-lim Yip described in *Diffusion of Distances* as a deverbalized world ('*wu-yen*').[38] In the Taoist world, 'conscious efforts to generalise, formulate, classify, and order' will result in 'restriction, reduction, or even distortion'.[39] Lee's opaque poetic language echoes the Taoist belief in open-mindedness where, quoting Zhuang Zhi, 'the vital force is an emptiness ready to receive all things.'[40] Such spirituality is commonly adopted by classical Chinese poets such as Wang Wei, where one does not make a judgement on things but simply receive the world and the relations of objects as they appear.[41]

The poetics of elsewhere

In *Imaginary Homelands*, Salman Rushdie speaks of the past as 'a country from which we have all emigrated, that its loss is part of our common humanity'.[42] Assuming universality in the experience of loss, Rushdie argues that the writer who is 'out-of-country' or 'out-of-language' is inevitably preoccupied with such discontinuity and the sense of being 'elsewhere'.[43] Homi Bhabha refers to such discomfort arising from the gap between the self and its place as an 'unhomely moment', a moment that occurs when the borders between home and the world become confused, and how moments like these relate to the 'ambivalences of a personal, psychic history to the wider disjunctions of political existence'.[44] For Lee, the poetic self is restless and filled with unknowing because of this unhomely predicament. While it seeks to flee from the past, it also keeps returning to the past, especially family history, for affirmation.

In his latest collection, *The Undressing* (2018), Lee's poetic voice becomes even more elusive and introspective, creating a sense of cosmic, spiritual order beyond ethnic experiences and allegiances, and exploring the potency of the unspoken and the invisible. In my interview with him, Lee said: 'I think, in order for us to be more fully human, and in order for us to answer to today's challenges, the best of East and West are going to have to be fully synthesized. I don't perceive any natural conflict between East and West.'[45] In 'Folding a Five-cornered Star so the Corners Meet', Lee returns to his birthplace and marks the locale with the imagery of a rice-cake vendor.

> I was born in the City of Victory,
> on a street called Jalan Industri, where
> each morning the man selling rice cakes went by
> pushing his cart.[46]

In the above poem, the birthplace marks the beginning of one's consciousness. At the same time it is a place of self-doubt and melancholy. Instead of showing us a glimpse of childhood, the poet conveys a deep sense of loneliness and sadness and suggests that 'maybe it's my father's'.[47] The couplet 'Five in a bed, and none of us can sleep./ Five in one body, begotten, not made' evokes the image of a family in exile, haunted by fear and insecurity.[48] Alluding to the stars on the Chinese and American flags, we are reminded of the poet's dual identity as an ethnic Chinese as well as an American citizen. Looking up at the 'insomniac' stars, he calls himself the earthbound descendant of stars. Lee's elusive poetic language suggests that his identity is, to a certain extent, inexplicable and forever out of reach.

When asked about his definition of home, Lee admits the impact of violence and silencing on his writing:

> I was born to scapegoats. My mother and father and the families they came from were violently scapegoated in China, where my parents were born. After escaping China, my parents started a family from scratch in Jakarta, Indonesia, where I was born, and where my parents found themselves to be the open targets of violent scapegoating yet again, this time with their own children at hazard. After escaping Indonesia and finally arriving as refugees in the United States, a country at war at that time with an Asian country, we were scapegoated here. [...] So, what might 'home' mean in such circumstances? Everything, except safety. Everything, except security. Everything, except membership that confers privileges or protection. Everything, except a place one may return to for rest or sanctuary.[49]

This is, of course, a startling definition of home, but Lee's negotiation of such wounds or racial trauma is achieved through a nuanced use of the lyric.

Conclusion

Lee's articulation of an intimate yet universal selfhood reflects his ability to embed Chinese philosophical and spiritual beliefs in lyric poetry. Fusing philosophy, metaphorical language and the invention of new poetic forms, his poetry moves beyond confessional, lyrical poetry to articulate a self that belongs to both the present and the past, the home and out-of-home terrain. Approaching selfhood from a more detached, philosophical and transcendental perspective that recalls Taoism and Confucianism, the subtlety of his language and deliberate silences represent a creative tension between suffering and healing, between belonging and alienation, as the poet looks for meaning within a process of remembering, omissions and self-knowledge.

Notes

1   Tod Marshall and Li-Young Lee, 'Interview with Li-Young Lee'. 'To Witness the Invisible: A Talk with Li-Young Lee', *Kenyon Review*, 22.1 (2000), 129.

2   His poems are widely anthologized, and have featured in mainstream American literary anthologies such as *The Norton Anthology of American Literature, The Norton Anthology of Modern and Contemporary Poetry*, as well as Asian-American anthologies such as *The Open Boat: Poems from Asian America* by Garrett Hongo.

3   Joseph Bruchac, *Breaking Silence: An Anthology of Contemporary Asian American Poets* (New York: Greenfield University Press, 1983), viii.

4   Marshall and Lee, 'Interview with Li-Young Lee', 132.

5   Ibid.

6   Ingersoll writes in his Foreword to *Breaking the Alabaster Jar*, 'if compelled to confront questions of his ethnicity, he [Li-Young Lee] stresses very forcefully that although he was born in Indonesia he rejects any effort to label him Indonesian [...] As he strongly emphasises... his parents were ethnic Chinese, who felt forced to emigrate from China [...]' [Earl Ingersoll, *Breaking the Alabaster Jar: Conversations with Li-Young Lee* (New York: BOA Editions, 2006), 1.]

7   Li-Young Lee, *In The City in Which I Love You* (New York: BOA Editions, 1990), 37.

8   Ibid., 38.

9   'The father-son tie is a constraint, a limitation, and a bondage; yet through its constraining, limiting, and binding power, it provides a necessary means for self-cultivation for the father as well as the son'. [Wei-ming Tu, *Confucian Thought: Selfhood as Creative Transformation* (Albany: State University of New York, 1985), 118–21.]

10   Li-Young Lee, *City*, 38.

11   Steven Yao, *Foreign Accents: Chinese American Verse from Exclusion to Postethnicity* (Oxford and New York: Oxford University Press, 2010), 161.

12   Li-Young Lee, *City*, 43, 44.

13   Yao remarks: 'lyric testimony' since the 1970s refers to 'as a narrative of 'personalised history that exemplify racial/ethnic identity as a traumatic condition of either

problematic difference from mainstream society or debilitating cultural loss that necessitates an act of recuperation'. [Yao, *Foreign Accents: Chinese American Verse from Exclusion to Postethnicity*, 14.]. See also, Marshall and Lee, 'Interview with Li-Young Lee', 132.

14 Ingersoll, *Alabaster Jar*, 22.

15 Li-Young Lee, *From Blossoms: Selected Poems* (Tarset: Bloodaxe Books, 1986), 52.

16 Xiaojing Zhou, *The Ethics and Poetics of Alterity in Asian American Poetry* (Iowa: Iowa University Press, 2006), 46, 48.

17 Li-Young Lee, *City*, 23.

18 Zhou, *Ethics and Poetics of Alterity*, 47.

19 Lee, *City*, 34.

20 Timothy Yu, 'Form and Identity in Language Poetry and Asian American Poetry', *Contemporary Literature*, 41 (2000), 144, 440.

21 Li identifies five key features of Confucian notion of harmony, in which 'tension follows naturally when it leads to coordination and, further, to cooperation'. According to Li, Confucian harmony is understood as 'a cosmic order and a moral value. […]' [Chen-yang Li, *The Confucian Philosophy of Harmony* (London and New York: Routledge, 2014), 9.]

22 His writing voice sheds light on what T. S. Eliot calls a 'surrender' of the poet 'as he is at the moment to something which is more valuable', 'a continual extinction of personality'. However, since Lee's lyrical 'I' expresses his personal emotions, I find it more akin to the Chinese vision of the self than T. S. Eliot's theory of an extinguished self. See T. S. Eliot, 'Tradition and the Individual Talent' (1919), Poetry Foundation, <https://www.poetryfoundation.org/resources/learning/essays/detail/69400> [Accessed 10 May 2017].

23 Matthew Fluharty, 'An Interview with Li-Young Lee', *Missouri Review*, 23.1 (2000), 81–100.

24 'The Cleaving', in *In the City in Which I Love You*, edited by Li-Young Lee (New York: BOA Editions, 1990), 37.

25 Ibid.

26 Lee, *City*, 57.

27 Ibid., 54.

28 Jennifer Wong, 'An interview with Li-Young Lee', Appendix, 168.

29 See Appendix, 172.

30 Lee, *City*, 41.

31 Ibid.

32 Ibid., 81.

33 Ibid.

34 Ibid.

35 Benzi Zhang, *Asian Diaspora Poetry in North America* (New York and London: Routledge, 2011), 5.

36   Zhang, *Asian Diaspora Poetry*, 56.

37   Li-Young Lee, *City*, 56.

38   Yip Wai-lim, *Diffusion of Distances: Dialogues between Chinese and Western Poetics* (Berkeley and California: University of California Press, 1993), 66.

39   Ibid.

40   Ibid., 73.

41   Ibid., 72. Original text from *Chuang-tzu-chi-shih* (Taipei: Ho Le, 1974).

42   Salman Rushdie, *Imaginary Homelands: Essays and Criticisms 1981–1991* (London: Granta Books, 1991), 12.

43   Ibid., 12.

44   Homi Bhabha, *The Location of Culture* (Oxford and New York: Routledge, 1994), 13–15.

45   Jennifer Wong, 'Redeeming Desire: A Conversation with Li-Young Lee', *World Literature Today*, 92.1 (2018), <https://www.worldliteraturetoday.org/2018/january/redeeming-desire-conversation-li-young-lee-jennifer-wong> [Accessed 20 April 2018].

46   Li-Young Lee, *The Undressing* (London and New York: W. W. Norton, 2018), 48.

47   Ibid.

48   For a more detailed discussion of Lee's use of the lyric and the relationship between the spiritual and the healing self, in *The Undressing*, see my book review in *Poetry Review*, 108.2 (2018), 117–20.

49   Wong, 'An interview with Li-Young Lee', Appendix, 167.

3

Marilyn Chin's feminist poetics of protest

Fuelled by the Civil Rights Movement and African-American activism in the United States in the 1960s, the emergence of Asian-American literature in the 1970 to 1980s was a collective response against ethnocentrism and racial stereotypes. This gives rise to a culturally hybrid voice within the larger American identity. In the 1970s, Asian-American literary anthologies, such as *Aiiieeeee! An Anthology of Asian-American Writers* edited by Frank Chin and *Roots: An Asian-American Reader* (1971) edited by Amy Tachiki, have promoted interest in an inter-ethnic imagination, recognizing new poetics on selfhood, cultural otherness and informed protest against homogenized culture, as Asian-American writers redefined their identity and allegiance to America via a literature of dissent. It is within this larger socio-historical context that the deeply activist, feminist and formally dexterous poetry of Marilyn Chin assumes its significance.

Born in Hong Kong in 1955 to Chinese parents, Marilyn Chin moved with her family to Portland, Oregon, in the United States when she was seven years old. She received a BA from the University of Massachusetts, Amherst, in Chinese literature and an MFA from the University of Iowa. She is the author of *Dwarf Bamboo* (Greenfield Review Press, 1987); *The Phoenix Gone, The Terrace Empty* (Milkweed Editions, 1994); *Rhapsody in Plain Yellow* (W. W. Norton, 2002); *Revenge of the Mooncake Vixen* (W. W. Norton, 2009); *Hard Love Province* (W. W. Norton, 2014), which won the 2015 Anisfield-Wolf Book Award; and *A Portrait of the Self as Nation: New and Selected Poems* (W. W. Norton, 2018). She co-directed the MFA programme at the University of San Diego. She is Professor Emerita at San Diego State University and serves as a Chancellor at the Academy of American Poets. Her awards include the United Artist Foundation Fellowship, the Radcliffe Institute Fellowship at Harvard, the Rockefeller Foundation Fellowship at Bellagio, the Anisfield-Wolf Book Award, two NEAs, the Stegner Fellowship and a Fulbright Fellowship to Taiwan. In 2017, she was honoured by the Asian Pacific Islander Caucus and the California Assembly for her activism and excellence in education. In 2020, she received the Poetry Foundation's 2020 Ruth Lilly Poetry Prize in recognition of Chin's outstanding lifetime achievement. In addition, her works have featured in anthologies including *The Norton Anthology of Literature by Women* and *The Norton Anthology of Modern and Contemporary Poetry*, *The Penguin Anthology of 20th Century Poetry*. She has translated poetry by Asian writers, notably Ai Qing and Ho Xuan Huong.

Through her collection *Rhapsody for Plain Yellow* (2002), we catch a glimpse of her 'fusionist', feminist poetic language and imagery that amalgamate Chinese and Western poetics. This bold experimentation of poetic language and voice captures the position of the Asian-American female whom Shirley Lim calls 'an overlapping of categories that will enable the conventional and stereotypical hostility between ethnic cultures, traditionally organised for patriarchal ends, and emerging women's identities, expressed in socially transforming concerns for the rights of women, to be defused, synthesized, or merged into a new sensibility'.[1] Published in 2014, *Hard Love Province* is anchored in elegies of love and grief and reflects her racial imaginary as a woman writer of colour. The book won the Anisfield-Wolf award in recognition for its the book's contribution towards the understanding of racism and diversity. Anchored in elegies of love, *Hard Love Province* reflects her racial imaginary as a woman writer of colour. In this chapter, I will explore the way Chin fuses the personal with the political to forge a new poetics of protest.

A Chinese-American writer who has lived in both Asia and America, Chin possesses multiple cultural roots. Her poetry often parodies the stereotypes of the Asian diasporic individual. By 'diaspora', I refer to the subjective consciousness layered and malleable with its 'multiplicity of histories, communities and selves' and the 'fractured memories' of the diasporic people.[2] It is precisely this sense of multiplicity and destabilized poetic voice that differentiates Chin's work. In Chin's poetry, we see how the diasporic poet has a need to respond creatively to her state of longing and unbelonging, to locate oneself across different histories, cultures and homelands.

Humour as a language of self-defence

In *Rhapsody for Plain Yellow*, humour is adopted as an effective language to counter male aggression and to defend one's position in a racist, patriarchal society. For example, in 'Chinese Quatrains (The Woman in Tomb 44)', the grown-up daughter reveals the secret of unhappiness of her Chinese mother who was unable to conceive a male child. The rhyming pattern of the quatrain, juxtaposed with an unusual choice of metaphors for a poem on childbirth (e.g. worm, fat corpses), conveys a sense of macabre and foreboding. The use of quatrains echoes the penta-syllabic quatrains of *jue-ju* within Chinese poetics, which is in itself a parody of the paradoxical situation: the seemingly simple poem on stereotypes boasts a form that has a history dating back to the Tang dynasty. The tragicomic poem dwells on the frustration against patriarchal rule, governed by the traditional Chinese family belief that favours boys over girls:

> Baby, she's a girl
> Pinkly propped as a doll
> Baby, she's a pearl
> An ulcer in the oyster of God.[3]

The word 'Baby' is a double entendre, revealing the poet's ownership of two languages: while 'Baby' is a typical, everyday endearing term in American culture, here it only expresses the husband's shock and disappointment over the birth of the baby girl. The subtitle for the poem has complementary meanings derived from English and Chinese languages. In English, the word 'Tomb' refers to the woman's 'womb', while the number 44 is the unluckiest number in Chinese, making it a circulatory pun on the unfortunate mother and daughter who feel unloved in a patriarchal community. Yet instead of simply seeing her own birth as a misfortune, she questions the benevolence of human nature. The poet offers unusual and grotesque imagery in describing her parents:

> The worm has entered the ear
> And out the nose of my father
> Cleaned the pelvis of my mother
> And ringed around her fingerbone[4]

The poem draws on the philosophy of Hsün Tzu, who believes that human nature is evil, motivated by gain, and that strife and rapacity will follow if man follows his own tendency (*hsing*).[5] It is as if the daughter has lost faith in her parents as her protectors, and the poem concludes with an emotionally deprived, barter-like relationship between her parents:

> She married him for a green card
> He abandoned her for a blonde.[6]

The barter is practical, necessary and at the same time disillusioning. At the end of the poem, the reader is presented with an abstract image of a female corpse in the tomb, adorned with jewels and gemstones on her face, robbed 'again and again' (ibid.). As such, her poems are rebellious and revolutionary in subverting the stereotypes of a traditional Chinese family and in speaking out against injustices. This is in stark contrast with Li-Young Lee's work which positions the family as an emotional anchor, and home as a transcendental state of mind where suffering and love meet.

In an interview with Ken Weisner, Chin concedes that the passionate, tragicomic poetic voice is a product of her unsettling family situation: '[W]e had to laugh deep from our guts to keep from crying. Our situation at home was unbearable. I had a gambler bigamist father, an overbearing grandmother, a grandfather who didn't recognize girls, and a deeply depressed and oppressed mother all under the same roof.'[7] Chin's psychoanalysis and self-justification unearth an important area of identity of Chinese-American women writers: their close relationship with and ambivalence towards the Chinese family, and the effect the family has on their writing.

Redefining the Asian woman

In *Rhapsody of Plain Yellow*, Chin portrays the female body as a visible and political site, where she encounters the conflicted meanings of her ethnicity and gender.

The prose poem 'The True Story of Mr. and Mrs. Wong' exposes the disgrace of a Chinese wife who cannot bear a son. Unsatisfied that there is no male heir to inherit his restaurant business, the husband divorces her and marries a foreigner, who bears him three sons:

> He now loves his new wife, whose name is Mrs Fuller-Wong. At first she couldn't conceive. Then, the Good Lord performed a miracle and removed three large polyps from her womb. She bore Mr Wong three healthy sons and they all became corporate tax accountants.[8]

The married name of the second wife, Fuller-Wong, is ironic, as if Wong – the husband – depends on the woman to give him 'fullness' or completeness in life. The poet compares childbirth to the 'removal of three large polyps', alluding to the abnormality and whimsicality of the second family: not only are the births of three boys unnatural, they all choose to be corporate tax accountants, a profession that signals upward social mobility compared to the father's profession as a restaurant owner. Through the use of stark humour, Chin exposes the female body as a site where racial and cultural stereotypes are challenged.

At the same time, the poem parodies the inferiority complex of female Chinese immigrants, particularly their struggle to transcend the typical role of a potential wife or lover of men – American men or Chinese men – and their desire to survive and become self-sufficient. The daughters in the poem become the source of embarrassment for the father and are married off to men with steady jobs, except for one daughter who decides to run away to Hollywood and become a successful sound specialist. By imagining avenues of fulfilment for Chinese immigrant women other than marriage, the poet asserts the power of self-reinvention and the courage for women to rebel against family influence as a way of survival.

Chin's strident writing serves to counter that filial obedience expected of Chinese daughters, and is a way to talk back to the patriarchy and oppressive racist structures. I also see her rebellious voice as a way of responding to the image of early Chinese immigrant women who were interrogated severely at and beyond Angel Island, often perceived as dependents of male immigrants and often suspected for immoral behavior.[9] In 'Summer Sonatina', the speaker rejects her family's warnings and subterfuge:

> Don't tell them, says mother, they will deport you.
> Don't tell them, says father, I was a paperson.
> Don't tell them, says brother, our misery is our own.[10]

To a certain extent, the speaker idealizes the foreigner: 'He is so fair you could see the Thames pulsing in his temples.'[11] She is wary of the rift between herself and the other race, and frustrated by his ignorance about Taoism and the Haiku:

> He said, *The Tao is untranslatable and the Haiku is dead.*
> I thought, *pink and swollen, something sad about his body.*[12]

The poem ends with the speaker's disillusionment about the adopted country: 'Fake paradise, imported palmettos.'[13] Liberated from family teachings as well as her fantasy about the white male, the speaker asserts her sage-like aloofness: '[S]he stands lonely on that hillock observing the pastures./The world scoffs back with bog and terror.'[14]

In 'Horse Horse Hyphen Hyphen (Border Ghazals)', a similar tension can be felt as the speaker negotiates her bicultural inheritance and her allegiances to her family:

> I hate, I love, I don't know how
> I'm biracial, I'm torn in two [...]

In a slow hovercraft of dreams
I saw Nanking from a bilge

Some ashes fell on his lap
I'm afraid it's my mother

The protocol is never to mention her
While we are fucking.[15]

According to Shirley Lim, the ethnic woman uses transgressive language to assert her identity away from the site of her own ethnicity, displacing and reinventing herself within the Western ideological context. Chin subtitles this poem as 'Border Ghazals', even though these are not conventional ghazals, and reinforces the homelessness of a split identity. The poem evokes a longing to be loved and the fear to be disappointed. The speaker denies the father ('Your father is not a car, not a compass and not God'). But no matter how much she would like to separate herself from the family, both the mother ('the protocol is not to mention her/while we are fucking') and the father ('He kept crawling back to us, back to us/Each time with a fresh foot mangled') return to haunt her.[16]

The speaker adopts a transgressive, fragmentary language to depict a love-hate relationship with the present, as her mind drifts to traumatic moments in history such as the Rape of Nanking ('I saw Nanking from a bilge') and her fear as a writer ('the bad conceit police will arrest you'). Such fragmentary form captures the 'multiplicity of histories' in the diasporic mind, where the personal and the collective overlap, and where the surreal past and present collide.

Breaking down stereotypes

Chin's poetry is also marked by a bold use of poetic language and symbolism. She is unafraid to expose the artificiality of stereotypes by creating new words and meanings based on those stereotypes. The title of the collection – *Rhapsody in Plain* Yellow – recalls the sense of hybridity in Gershwin's *Rhapsody in Blue*, which fuses classical music with jazz. However, Chin deepens the irony in the title of the collection by calling her work a rhapsody in 'plain yellow', signalling her self-awareness as a woman of colour.[17]

'Blues on Yellow' – the first poem in the collection – in part a lament of the traumatic past of early Chinese immigrants. Chin evokes the stereotypes: the

Chinese gold miner who dies en route to digging up a fortune, and the wife whose American dream is lost. There is the repetition of the word 'yellow' to highlight protest, a symbolic colour and a somewhat archaic, racist term to stand for Chinese ethnicity. The cooking in Chin's kitchen focuses on the cracking of an egg, where the yellow 'oozes into the white', a metaphor for the influx of the Chinese immigrants that disrupts the American society. At the same time, by calling it 'Blues on Yellow' and italicizing the text, Chin beckons our attention to the form while she acknowledges the influence of the blues in African-American culture on her work, an aesthetic which Amiri Baraka describes as an 'expression of sorrow' and 'a reference to [our] sad African slave lives'.[18]

In my interview with Chin, she acknowledges how she has been influenced by African-American women writers, e.g. the early writers like Angela Davis: 'I was also influenced by Bessie Smith, the blues singer when I wrote Rhapsody in Bright Yellow … My African American friends loved it and can hear the blues in it … My aesthetics reflects hybridity and creates a diaspora. I try to merge traditions.'[19]

The poem suggests the urgency of a power conflict, though the cause is not identified. The focus is rather on how to resist against the aggressor:

If you cut my yellow wrists, I'll teach my yellow toes to write.
If you cut my yellow fists, I'll teach my yellow feet to fight.[20]

By creating new names and meanings based on stereotypes, Chin offers a hyphenated, counter-language that captures a hybrid imagination. The voice of dissent also reminds one of the protest poems the early Chinese immigrants carved onto the walls on Angel Island Immigration station a long time ago. The poet first imagines violence and amputation, and then revenge. The colour becomes loaded with political meanings, recalling the yellow peril against the nation's body politic, and the stereotype of the Chinese immigrant figure illustrates Steven Yao's argument on Chin's potent and semi-transparent language of dissent:

Chin's verse points consistently to the irreducible specificity of the ethnic (Chinese) cultural heritage that she seeks to represent. In this way, she repeatedly challenges the assumptions about linguistic transparency and the adequacy of English as a medium for the representation of individual ethnic subjectivity in particular that underwrite the hegemonic mode of lyric testimony.[21]

By portraying an adamant Chinese female fighter who fights back the aggression against her 'yellow' body, the poet situates her work within the racial imaginary

Figure 6 Writing on Walls, 2019. Courtesy of Angel Island Immigration Station Foundation.

of Chinese-American literature such as Maxine Hong Kingston's *The Woman Warrior*, a classic studied in Asian-American studies. In her interview with Maxine Hong Kingston, published by *MELUS* in 2002, Chin admits that *The Woman Warrior* was a very important book in her life, having discovered it in 1977 in the Jeffrey Amherst Book Store in Amherst, Massachusetts, when she was an undergraduate.[22] In fact, Chin confesses how she identifies Brave Orchid in *The Woman Warrior* as her grandmother and Moon Orchid as her sad mother. In other words, the female fighter figure is for her a way to engage with both her personal and the collective history of her community.

Figure 7 Chinese Poetry in Barracks – Poem 69 – 'detained in this wooden house'. Courtesy of Angel Island Immigration Station Foundation.

The subversive part of the poem lies in the daughter's rebelliousness and her wilful desertion of the mother, while reassuring the mother not to be afraid 'to perish', because the Buddha will be compassionate to her. Instead of wishing her mother were safe, the daughter believes that '*your babies will reach the promised land*'.[23] Although the situation that causes the separation is uncertain, the imagery of a departing boat may refer to the journey of the immigrant family. It is as if the only way to survive and retain an independent identity is to break free from the family.

This is illustrated in 'The Colonial Language is English', which articulates a Chinese-American daughter's attitude towards both her native Chinese language and her acquired English, the latter referred to as 'the colonial language'.[24] Drawing on Taoist texts, she creates her own dialect to represent as well as deny her otherness. Juxtaposing her inherited culture with the disillusionment of the first Chinese-American immigrants who arrived at Sutter's Mill for the Gold Rush, she asserts her creative freedom based on poetic citizenship:

The Tao of which we speak is not the eternal Tao
The name that we utter is not the eternal name

My mother is me, my father is thee
As we drown in the seepage of Sutter Mill.[25]

While assuming that immigrants can, in theory, transform and integrate themselves into this ideologically bound sense of nationhood, Chin's poetry highlights the intersectionality between race and class, reflecting the economic and socio-cultural hurdles that immigrants often encounter in this assimilation process. In my interview with Chin, she points out how her class struggle begins from her ancestors, and how her feels connected with the early immigrants:

> Unlike Li-Young Lee, I am from working class. My family came from Toisan, that whole generation that needed to get out of Guangdong to go to the US to work. They were the coolies, the working class, who sent money back to China. I am part of the Cantonese American experience. The Cantonese, the rebels! I feel connection with the early immigrants.

Here in 'The Colonial Language is English', she portrays immigration as a collective experience of trauma. The activist nature of her poetry recalls the Chinese poetry of dissent inscribed on the walls of the Angel Island detention centre against the racial hostility arising from Chinese Exclusion Acts in America.[26]

In her ars poetica poem, 'So, You Fucked John Donne', Chin questions her conflicted identity as a poet, especially as a woman poet of colour.

> So, you fucked John Donne.
> Wasn't very nice of you.
> He was betrothed to God, you know,
> a diet of worms for you![27]

The metaphor of making love to John Donne and John Keats ('*Poor thang*, you h-d no self worth then/you fucked them all for a song') alludes to the poet's attempt to appropriate white power or the Western canon in her language.[28] On one level, such uninhibited display of female desire contradicts the Confucian teaching of preserving and concealing the body. On the other, by comparing Western or Romantic poetry to a decadent, ill-disposed body, Chin asserts her role as a colonizer rather than the colonized. Moreover, she, a woman poet of colour, can also appropriate the Romantic or Western tradition just like any other white poet, and in the process reinvent a language of her own.

Stylistically, Chin's ability to interpret her immigrant experience by using hybrid forms, neologism and bold experimentation with language and voice, serves to assert the poet's belief in the possibility to embrace and merge disparate worlds.

In *Rhapsody of Plain Yellow*, Chin portrays the female body as a site where she encounters the conflicted meanings of her ethnicity and gender. Having studied Chinese literature at university, Chin is well-versed in Classical Chinese texts, and she contrasts the metaphors of the body in Chinese and American literature. In *Xiao Jing*, the classic Confucian text on filial piety, the Confucian Master said: 'The crimes that are addressed by the Five Punishments number some three thousand, and none of them is graver than to be wanting in family reverence' (五刑之屬三千,而罪莫大於不孝). It also teaches that 'your physical person with its hair and skin are received from your parents. Vigilance in not allowing anything to do injury to your person is where family reverence begins' (身體髮膚 授諸父母).[29]

Figure 8 Childhood photo of poet Marilyn Chin (girl on the right). Courtesy of Marilyn Chin.

Bearing in mind the poet's knowledge, it is surprising to note how the female body in *Rhapsody for Plain Yellow* becomes a recurrent motif that is highly visible and political. For example, in 'The Colonial Language is English', the daughter is torn between her need to be accepted and loved in the family, and the mother's preferential treatment for the brother:

> My mother loved me, I am certain
> She molded my happiness in her womb
> My mother loves my brother, certainly
> His death was not an enigma
> Yes, it too, had its mystery
>
> I had willed it in my heart
> I had condemned him in his crib
> When I touched his round, Buddha face[30]

The poet subverts the mother figure by blaming the mother for favouring the son, while expressing her vengeance against her brother, willing him to disappear.

Chin's activist verse is empowered by the use of an expressive, humorous female self, fetishized, gazed upon, and yet also a curious onlooker who subverts Western society and culture. In her interview with Weisner, she remarks on her position as a poet:

> I believe that as a minority writer in this country, I must be an oppositional force. This is expected of me, no? To shake things up? [...] So, while I have the page, I must rattle some cages.[31]

In other words, Chin sees a necessary relationship between poetry and activism or politics for the minority writer.

Hard Love Province: Writing as a political act

Following from *Rhapsody in Plain Yellow* (2002), *Hard Love Province* charts the shift of Chin's poetics from the personal and familial realms to bold, universal questions on self-identity and race. The title suggests the individual's return to his or her origin. The word 'province' has a political overtone in that the province belongs to a nation-state, while at the same time 'Hard Love' also indicates that it could be just an imaginary place. In the form of love poems and elegies, the book explores what it is like to come from a foreign country, a feeling of alienation common to migrants. At the heart of the collection is the question of race, and Chin's awareness of her multicultural lineage as a writer and the necessity to rebel against the stereotype of a minority writer. Instead of a focus on the immigrant narrative, here we see a multicultural racial imaginary that amalgamates influences, questioning the notion of citizenship and the marginality of the diasporic individual as both the insider and outsider.

Chin's activist verse is empowered by the use of an expressive, humorous female self, fetishized, gazed upon, and yet also a curious onlooker who subverts Western society and culture. In my interview with her, she explains how teaching in higher education and other feminist writers have influenced her work:

> Early on, I was informed by theorists such as Cixous, Said, Spivak, Gates and mostly postcolonial and feminist theorists. I learned a lot from the black arts movement. I loved reading black feminist thinkers on my own (outside of academia) – Audre Lorde, Barbara Smith, Angela Davis, June Jordan, bell hooks, etc. Tough women poets/thinkers like Gloria Anzaldua and Tri Min Ha. And of course, Adrienne Rich.[32]

Assimilating these influences into her poetics, the poet claims her right to embrace what Jahan Ramazani calls a 'poetic transnationalism', which generates poems formed by both 'unwilled imaginative inheritances and elective identifications across national borders'.[33]

In 'From a Notebook of an Ex-Revolutionary', Chin contrasts consumerism in America with the burden of history endured by immigrants who have left so much behind. The first few sections of the fragmentary narrative suggest the poet's memories of trivial banter and conflicts in one's social circle ('I dreamt that I was naked save a pair of designer stilettos and was ruthlessly networking at a benefit soiree').[34] In his California home, the Chinese immigrant (ex-revolutionary) confesses to his wife his haunting guilt of having sent his own mother to death, alluding to the hostile persecution en masse during the Cultural Revolution when children would accuse parents of 'political crimes' to the authorities ('*History made me do it! History made me do it!*').[35] Recalling Eliot's *The Waste Land*, Chin evokes the ex-revolutionary's ineradicable memories of a war driven by unjustified hatred and racism:

> The ash fell all day today
> Fell all day yesterday
> Will fall all day tomorrow
> From Dachau to Buchenwald[36]

By evoking a bleak, surreal landscape tinged with traumatic memories of war and oppression, Chin depicts those in society who shift between place and displacement, personal and collective history.

In 'Kalifornia (A portrait of the poet wearing a girdle of severed heads)', Chin offers an ironic self-portrait on the privilege of experiencing diaspora. Addressing herself as 'you', she congratulates herself as a Goddess with sexual freedom ('You have your fresh lovers') and 'a castle /With a vestibule'), and that anything she pens will be understood as a moment of diaspora, an exotic dialect:

> Your poems will write themselves on parchment
> Your manuscripts will illuminate
> Any moment now
> The diasporas will form a new dialect[37]

As Dorothy Wang argues, Chin's strategy of using irony often disguises her political accusations of racial prejudices in America, particularly since her ironies require careful decoding, and her voices entail some level of complicity, instead of merely pitting a Chinese-American female against the oppressor. In 'Kalifornia', her address to 'you' in a half-congratulatory, half-mocking tone creates discomfort in the reader. The poet celebrates her achievement in being recognized by the others for her writing, even though she acknowledges the oppressor's power over the ethnic minority poet. She also mocks the superficiality of racist judgements: 'They will paint you black /They will paint you white.'[38] By doing so, she successfully merges the personal with the political, to speak about as well as against stereotypes.

In 'Black President', a poem inspired by the former President Barack Obama before the Trump era, the speaker ridicules the logic of racist attitudes and racial discrimination:

> If a black man could be president
> Could a white man be his slave?
> [...]
> If the terminator is my governor
> Could a cowboy be my king?[39]

By reversing the racial stereotypes, the poet re-imagines or longs for an America where racial equality is possible. While the subject matter is essentially contemporary, Chin uses the Chinese poetic form *dui dui zi*, characterized by strict rhymes, syllabic symmetry and rhetorical questions.

Wielding a poetic language that fuses American culture, a re-imagined Far East and the surreal, Chin's confessional verse reveals the inner conflicts of a diasporic individual who is at once the insider and an outsider – informed by a double consciousness socially, linguistically and politically – and challenges the social inequalities that exist in modern day America.[40] The poem ends with the following image:

> Blood on the altar   Blood on the lamb
> Blood in the chalice not symbolic but fresh[41]

This imagery of sacrificial blood is politically charged and suggests the history of violence in American history, and to call it 'not symbolic but fresh' is a bold statement against its history of racism and violence.

In *Cartographies of Diaspora*, Brah said that diasporic space is inhabited by both migrants and the indigenous, and that peoples of different ethnicities in the same location influence each other. Because the indigenous is also continuously influenced by other incoming cultures from migrants, no one is truly 'native' because 'the native is as much as a diasporian as the diasporian is the native'.[42] In this sense, Chin's poetry represents a deliberate, politicized poetic language.

Conclusion

Chin's poetics of dissent reveal a subjective and unstable ground where the divided female immigrant self is constantly displaced, shifting between racial and gender stereotypes, her allegiance to the family and her desire for self-definition and independence. Stylistically, Chin's ability to interpret her immigrant experience by using hybrid forms, neologism and bold experimentation with language and voice, serves to assert the poet's straddling of disparate worlds. Questioning Confucian values while paying homage to her feminist influences, Chin empowers her narrative with a culturally hyphenated hybrid language. Her poetry is tinged with ambivalence towards the family and the self's resistance against a society denominated in patriarchal values and filial piety. The poet reveals her allegiances to becoming a global citizen and a hybrid, political language that will capture her diasporic imagination. Reworking and mocking racial and gender stereotypes, Chin asserts her poetic citizenship and power to dissent as a Chinese female, writer and immigrant.

Notes

1 Joyce W. Warren and Margaret Dicki (ed.), *Challenging Boundaries: Gender and Periodization* (Athens, Georgia: University of Georgia Press, 2000), 116.

2 Stephen Vertovec, 'Three Meanings of Diaspora, Exemplified among South Asian Religions', *Diaspora*, 6.3 (1997), 282.

3 Marilyn Chin, *Rhapsody in Plain Yellow* (New York and London: W. W. Norton, 2002), 24.

4 Ibid., 25.

5 Antonio Cua, *Encyclopedia of Chinese Philosophy* (New York and London: Routledge, 2003), 376.

6 Chin, *Rhapsody*, 26.

7 Ken Weisner, 'Interview with Marilyn Chin', *MELUS*, 37.3 (2012), 225.

8 Chin, *Rhapsody*, 55.

9 Erika Lee and Judy Yung, *Angel Island: Immigrant Gateway to America* (Oxford and New York: Oxford University Press, 2010), 79–80.

10 Chin, *Rhapsody*, 89.

11 Ibid.

12 Ibid., 90.

13 Ibid.

14 Ibid., 91.

15 Lim, Geok-lin, Shirley, 'Feminist and Ethnic Literary Theories in Asian American Literature', *Feminist Studies*, 19.3 (1993), 590.

16 Chin, *Rhapsody*, 69–70.

17 Amiri Baraka, *Digging: The African-American Soul of American Classical Music* (Berkeley and Los Angeles, CA: University of California Press, 2009), 23 and 26.

18 Baraka, *Digging*, 23, 26.

19 Wong, 'An interview with Marilyn Chin', Appendix, 172.

20 Chin, *Rhapsody*, 13. Lee and Yung, *Angel Island*, 102–3. See also Figures 6–7: 58–9.

21 Steven Yao, *Foreign Accents: Chinese American Verse from Exclusion to Postethnicity* (Oxford and New York: Oxford University Press, 2010), 190.

22 Marilyn Chin, 'An Interview with Maxine Hong Kingston', *MELUS*, 16.4 (2002), 62.

23 Chin, *Rhapsody*, 13.

24 Ibid., 20.

25 Ibid., 21.

26 Lee and Yung, *Angel Island*, 102–3. See also Figures 6–7: 58, 59.

27 Chin, *Rhapsody*, 82.

28 Ibid.

29 Henry Rosemont and Roger T. Ames (eds), *The Chinese Classic of Family Reverence: A Philosophical Translation of the Xiaojing* (Hawaii: University of Hawaii Press, 2009), 112.

30   Chin, *Rhapsody,* 20.

31   Weisner, 'Interview with Marilyn Chin', 225.

32   Wong and Chin, 'Marilyn Chin Talks to Jennifer Wong', *Asian Review of Books,* 28 August 2020, <https://asianreviewofbooks.com/content/marilyn-chin-talks-to-jennifer-wong/> [Accessed 6 August 2016].

33   Jahan Ramazani, *A Transnational Poetics* (Chicago and London: University of Chicago, 2009), 21.

34   Marilyn Chin, *Hard Love Province* (New York and London: W. W. Norton, 2014), 44.

35   Ibid., 45.

36   Ibid., 46.

37   Ibid., 57.

38   Ibid.

39   Ibid., 48.

40   Jennifer Wong, 'Walking to Jupiter: The Place of the Personal for Chinese Women', *Poetry London*, 84 (2016), 53–5.

41   Chin, *Province,* 48.

42   Ibid.

4

Hannah Lowe: Hybridity, multicultural heritage and class

Introduction

According to Deirdre Osborne, the problem of synthesizing Black and Asian into a single category when discussing the value of postwar British literature has blurred nuanced understanding of race, while only those who can be aligned to the 'white-majority culture and its traditions' stand a higher chance of being recognized.[1] Exploring the relationship between place, culture and identity through celebrating the personal and the re-imagined, the poetry of Hannah Lowe and Sarah Howe has gained considerable attention in the contemporary literary scene, accompanied by a growing readership for immigrant narratives and multicultural voices. Their works have been recognised early in their careers: Hannah Lowe has been named as one of the Next Generation Poets in 2014 by the Poetry Book Society, while Sarah Howe has won the T. S. Eliot Prize in 2015 for her debut collection, *Loop of Jade*. In 2022, Hannah Lowe won the Costa Book of the Year with her poetry collection, *The Kids* (Bloodaxe Books).[2] Their poetry has raised important questions of identity arising from their multicultural family backgrounds. Their writings have opened up new ways of interpreting family history and mixed-race identity, highlighting the difference between poetry and life writing: an influence that cannot be neglected in catalysing a new generation of British Asian poets. Despite their partially Chinese heritage, the two writers are seldom included in Asian-themed poetry anthologies, except for the fact that Sarah Howe's poetry was included in *Eight Hong Kong Poets* (2015) edited by David McKirdy and Peter Gordon.[3] In the case of Sarah Howe, interviews on her Chinese (or half-Chinese) identity and cultural hybridity did not appear until after she won the T. S. Eliot Prize, an accolade that highlights her 'Anglo-Chinese heritage'.[4]

Conscious of their partial Chinese ancestry, these poets articulate their experience of cultural hybridity, and how that perception has affected their own mixed race. Because of their multicultural heritage and upbringing, their poetry reflects what it means or feels to self-perceive or be taken as 'the other', even though Sarah Howe describes herself more often as a half-Chinese poet compared to Hannah Lowe. Hannah Lowe's collections, *Chick* and *Chan,* as well as Sarah Howe's *Loop of Jade,* have brought new perspectives towards the representation of otherness and cultural inheritance. In their writing, family becomes the foreground for revisiting and re-imagining one's cultural past. It is a place of constant departure, return and ambivalence, from which identity evolves.

Drawing on memories of her Chinese-Jamaican father who emigrated to England in the 1940s, and her own childhood growing up in a multicultural area in Essex, Hannah Lowe's first collection, *Chick,* is a narrative of family love and regrets. The book focuses on a culturally hybrid protagonist's unresolved feelings for her family, particularly her disavowal of her father on the grounds of his racial difference. In the narrative, Lowe explores the significance of family attachment and the need to exorcise the past to achieve self-autonomy.

Exploring her childhood years in Hong Kong and her fascination with her Chinese mother's life before relocating to England, Sarah Howe's *Loop of Jade* is a finely crafted and experimental collection that articulates the poet's mixed heritage. Born in Hong Kong to a Chinese mother and an English father, Howe spent her childhood years in Hong Kong before relocating to England at the age of seven. Inspired by her fascination with cultural hybridity and her Chinese heritage, Howe's poetry conjures an intimate and complex narrative of cultural crossings, where questions of personal identity, language and history are intertwined.

According to Stuart Hall, ethnicity is the pivotal point where an individual's cultural identity and specificity of his or her own history begins:

[W]e all speak from a particular place, out of a particular history, out of a particular experience, a particular culture, without being contained by that position as 'ethnic artists' or film-makers. We are all, in that sense, *ethnically* located.[5]

Both Hannah Lowe and Sarah Howe explore in their poetry the specificity of their positions within personal and social history, given the different ways with which they are connected to their birthplace and the homelands of their parents. At the same time, thinking of the importance of cultural positionality and specificity, their identities are not bound by their particular ethnic locations. Their poetry enhances our understanding on the convergence of self-identification, political positioning and self-representation.

Hannah Lowe: Confronting otherness in a multicultural self

Born in Essex to an English mother and a Chinese-Jamaican father, Hannah Lowe's poetry explores the inner conflicts of the mixed-race self, blending fiction with family history and social reality. Experimental in her play of hybrid poetic forms, imagery and language, Lowe articulates the richness and complexity of multicultural heritage and identity.

The power of Lowe's poetry lies in her use of an accessible and lyrical voice to convey the complexity of identity politics. Katy Evans-Bush's review of *Chick* – Lowe's first collection that draws from memories of her Chinese-Jamaican father – observes Lowe's 'deliberately informal style' and the visual quality of her poetry.[6] In my interview with the author, Lowe points out her emphasis on an accessible poetic language, and that form has always served as a 'great scaffolding' for her work. 'Dance Class', for example, conveys the unresolved feelings of the protagonist as she confronts her own otherness. Dressed in her ballet costume, the daughter aspires to be part of the clique, 'the best girls', who are gracefully poised as 'poodles at a show'. She is uneasy about her own figure and identity, and calls herself 'a big-footed /giant in lycra'.[7] The dramatic self-portrait or self-parody echoes Judith Butler's argument on the political performativity of gender:

> As the effects of a subtle and politically enforced performativity, gender is an 'act', as it were, that is open to splittings, self-parody, self-criticism, and those other hyperbolic exhibitions of 'the natural' that, in their very exaggeration, reveal its fundamentally phantasmatic status.[8]

An unusual sonnet, the poem adopts a circular structure, connecting the past and the present, the daughter's hybrid self and the father's black identity. The daughter finds it unbearable to see her father – a Black man – standing in the foyer, waiting for her to come out from the dance class. Here the class not only serves as a site to contest her identity, but triggers the knowledge of her otherness, as she perceives the difference between her and her peers, as well as between her and her own father.[9] The last line, '*he's the cab my mother sends for me*', exposes her guilt and her wish to renounce her non-white father.[10] According to Susan Stanford Friedman, women's writings from the 1990s onwards reflect a third

Figure 9 Ralph Lowe and friend in London, *c.* 1950s. Courtesy of Hannah Lowe.

wave feminism which moves beyond gender to the 'geopolitics of identity' that accounts for multicultural configurations of race and gender.[11] Here the image of the female body also moves from a gender-only focus to the dialectics of race and gender.

Food rituals and exoticism

In *Chick*, Lowe uses the food motif to articulate the coherence of a shared culture. Lowe often creates tension through the contrast of perspectives and the manipulation of settings and the poetic voice. In 'Sausages', the experience of otherness and emotional ambivalence is told through an aloof, detached voice.[12] The husband is not visible in the scene, but his presence is obvious from the concoction of exotic spices, as he cooks Chinese preserved sausages at home. The poet observes the physical closeness of her parents, yet notices the difference between the parents' cultural upbringing. To her, her father's Chinese cooking is a signifier of his different origin as well as *their* difference from other families in England. Despite the visible signifier, China and Jamaica remain distant places to her because she did not grow up in either of these countries. Understanding that difference, or otherness, of her father and themselves as a multicultural family, and its implication on her own identity, becomes a core narrative in the book. Lowe's use of the eating motif here to articulate racial and cultural difference can be compared with the family meals represented in Li-Young Lee's 'Eating Together'. In Lee's poem, eating with the family reinforces his self-identity as a Chinese person and an insider to his inherited culture. In Lowe's poems, the dining ritual causes her to reflect her identity as both an insider to that minority culture (Chinese culture) and an outsider to it (as she perceives the Chinese food as exotic).[13] In my interview with Lowe, she explains the importance of re-constructing her place of origin and family history in order to understand herself: '[E]ven though I did not know where Jamaica or China were, or why my dad was from Jamaica or why his dad had come from China, they were always anchors in my understanding of myself.'[14]

In the poem Lowe re-imagines the mother's longing to while connecting this curiosity or desire for the foreign with the idea of physical hunger and food consumption: 'Her mother told her /not to marry a foreigner. *You always wanted /to be different* she hissed. *Now this*.'[15] There is a curious ambivalence of feelings towards the mother, seeing her both in light of the grandmother's disapproval, and in light of the mother's self-contentment towards her own marriage: '[H]e is like good food to her.'[16] By comparing her father to food, the poet directs her gaze at the father as if he were an exotic, edible object. This act is symbolic of her subconscious attempt to fetishize the father. Homi Bhabha argues in *The Location of Culture* that the colonial subject is often trapped in a site of 'fixity and fantasy':

> The construction of colonial discourse is then a complex articulation of the tropes of fetishism – metaphor and metonymy – and the forms of narcissistic and aggressive identification available to the Imaginary [...] The taking up of any one position, within a specific discursive form, in a particular historical juncture, is thus always problematic – the site of both fixity and fantasy.[17]

In the concluding part of the poem, the father assumes a more submissive position in the relationship, while the mother takes on a dominant position of agency: 'Tonight they will eat sausages together /and she will lick the oil and spice /from his hands.'[18] The imagery suggests the mother's fantasy or fixity at the narcissistic and aggressive drives is at play in a colonial discourse, enhanced by the processes of fantasy and stereotyping.

Such a representation of the 'exotic' mixed-race Chinese is necessarily rooted in stereotypes. As explained in Witchard's essay for the Migration Museum's, 'China Limehouse and "Mr Ma and Son"', during the 1910s, the politicians began to 'exploit the dramatic potential of Chinese Limehouse in London as a locus of drug-trafficking, gambling and the sexual ensnarement of young white women'. It was later believed that 'the sinister "Chinamen" lured innocent white women into their opium dens'. These various stereotypes have perpetuated a sense that the Chinese are a source of threat to the British society.[19]

In 'A Man Can Cook', the reader is introduced to a symbolic set of perspectives that complicate the relationship between the colonizer and the colonized. Lowe recalls her father's inherited food culture as a 'colonial mixture'.[20] The protagonist is curious about his exotic cooking, yet keen to distance herself from her father and his world:

> You at the stove, the air spiced up with ginger,
> nutmeg, clove. I know you won't turn round
> but I can stand here can't I, watch the fire [111]
> [...] You can't turn around,
> too busy with your strange colonial mixtures.[21]

The word 'strange colonial mixtures' refers to the father's way of cooking red snapper with Asian spices, which seems to suggest a mixture of Chinese and Jamaican food ingredients. The speaker's decision to stand and gaze at her father from a distance, watching his work, suggests an act of 'surveillance'. The line 'I know you won't turn around/but I can stand here can't I, watch the fire' suggests that she sees herself as the agent of power and knowledge, while the father is rooted in his own world and culture, allowing himself to be watched and exoticised.[22] In effect, she aligns herself with the white race that defines and gazes at her own father. The speaker's alludes to the uncomfortable curiosity and exoticism associated with perceiving the foreign race, imposing a feeling of complicity onto the reader, who shares the poet's subjective gaze of the father.

Between nostalgia and topographia

Lowe's use of places transforms physical locations into recreated spaces coloured with emotions and re-imagination. In 'Three Treasures', the poet suggests the amalgamation of cultures as if it were a Chinese dish or restaurant.[23] She shifts between different objects and experiences that relate to her Chinese, Jamaican and English heritage:

> China in the won-ton skin,
> gold songbird on the brittle porcelain,

pink pagoda silk settee
[…]
England for the English in graffiti
on the roundabouts and bus shelters,
Please Sir! on TV

By naming and bringing together animals and objects from different origins and cultures, Lowe blurs the boundary between them, highlighting her connection with those objects and their exotic qualities. It also encapsulates the 'elsewheres' brought by London's immigrants from different places of origin, representing an 'intercultural space' that contains similarities and differences between cultures.[24]

Figure 10 Chinese art hangings from Hannah Lowe's childhood home in Essex. Courtesy of Hannah Lowe.

By evoking the foreign through recognizable objects, the poet adopts a tourist's perspective and mocks the attempt to over-simplify culture and race.

The poem ends with her father's refusal to speak his own dialect: 'China in the Cantonese he knew /but wouldn't speak[.]'[25] This suggests that the diasporic individual's alienation is suffered at multiple levels. On the one hand, her father's native tongue is an important, defining part of himself and his identity; at the same time it suggests alienation and otherness. Despite his ability to understand the language, he deliberately refuses to speak it in England, resisting to be defined and assimilated linguistically, in order to erase his difference from the others. Lowe elaborates on the context for this denial in her interview and the importance of Chinese food (rather than the language) as a cultural signifier:

> The thing about my Chinese side in the family is my grandfather, who is a migrant in Jamaica. My dad [...] is not on good terms with his own father. There is a denial of that [Chinese] culture. [...] My dad has learned how to make Chinese food from him, particularly Hakka cuisine, a food I grew up eating. It was a big part of our family life.[26]

In the final stanza of the poem, the imagery of a flying origami bird ('China in an origami butterfly, that flew') alludes to the diaspora: those originally from China have left China for 'greener pastures' on the other side of the world.[27] The word 'origami' indicates the impossible directions in diaspora. Just as an origami bird cannot fly, those who leave their own country can never leave their culture behind entirely.

Lowe presents the two cultural worlds she inherits in parallel and constantly draws the reader's attention to the similarity and difference between these two worlds. In 'Poem with a Plantain in It', the poet describes with humour the qualities of plantains – a popular Caribbean food – their resemblance to, as well as subtle differences, from bananas:

> Unpeeled, those bright supermarket bananas
> have pale and yielding throats,
> so different from the plantains
> I buy in Brixton market
> with their mucky skins
> that snag like stuck zips,
> their tough and pungent flesh.[28]

Lowe conveys the impossibility to find authentic plantains in London. Their unattractive and sexualized features found in Brixton market ('mucky skins', 'tough and pungent flesh') seem to suggest a racial stereotype. Their resemblance to and differences from bananas, in terms of colour and texture, allude to the poet's identity as a person of mixed heritage, who almost passes as a British woman but she is not. As Robert Young describes, hybridity is the site where the meaning of sameness and difference become disrupted or exaggerated:

> Hybridity thus makes difference into sameness, sameness into difference, but in a way that makes the same no longer the same, the different no longer simply different. In that sense, it operates according to the form of logic that Derrida isolates the term 'brisure', a breaking and a joining at the same time, in the same place: difference and sameness in an apparently impossible simultaneity.[29]

The poet's contrast plantains in London (her 'local place') with that in Jamaica (the 'real' home of plantains). Taking into account Young's argument, the poem articulates the culturally hybrid person's obsession with the meaning of adequacy and authenticity, despite the impossibility to experience absolute sameness or difference.

Interrogating citizenship and class

In her second collection, *Chan*, Lowe retells the migration story of the early Jamaican immigrants, focusing on the feelings of hope, disillusionments and alienation experienced by those in diaspora through merging fiction with life history.[30] Using first-person narratives, these poems are re-imagined accounts of Jamaicans who boarded the transatlantic passenger ship, *Ormonde*, in 1947 to travel to England. Despite their inferior status as early immigrants of limited means and employment opportunities and who constantly struggle against stereotypes, these Jamaican characters on board *Ormonde* actually speak in iambic verse. Lowe admits: '[I]n my writing I am deliberately and consciously political.'[31] By adopting this stylistic measure of gentrifying the immigrant' voice, Lowe mocks at the many unnatural changes and inequality the immigrants are prepared to confront in order to survive and assimilate in a new country.

In 'Dressmaker', Lowe highlights the immigrant's dreams and aspirations for a better home and hints at the unrealistic nature of this imagined future. The superficial change of dress code as the passenger travels from Jamaica to England highlights her ignorance of the destination country, a place where she does not belong and has never lived. She imagines that there she will live a life of affluence: '[n]o more /my threadbare skirt or patched-up pinafore'.[32] Instead, she will wear 'long sleeves, a gathered waist, /one tier of voile, one poplin, double-skinned /for England's winter-time, and the cold sea-wind'.[33] While this highlights an immigrant's eagerness to re-invent her identity and to become local in her new, acquired place, it also reveals the dressmaker's expertise of self-fashioning. The speaker sympathizes with the protagonist's unilateral hope or naive thought to adopt a new country or culture by dressing in a certain way:

> I dreamt myself – on a red bus passing Whitehall,
> or walking on the Strand. There was a tea-room
> where I wiled away my idle afternoons
> and in every scene I wore my dress, bright red
> for pillar box and rose [...][34]

The word 'dreamt' refers to both the immigrant's naive dreams and hopes, as well as the unrealistic nature of assimilation. It also articulates the immigrant's longing to identify herself with a new 'colour'.

In Lowe's poetry, homecoming is an almost unattainable state, as the diasporic confront their losses and gains. Aptly titled to highlight the complexity of place and belongingness, the poem 'In' offers a powerful narrative on the disillusioned immigrants:

> In *England*, you're in England
> In the shop, a rock of last week's bread you carry home
> in snow, your slipping soles and god knows how the world went white like this[35]

England is italicized to emphasize the location as a somewhat distant and unreal place for the immigrant, a country that promises a better future. In reality, what one experiences is the harshness of poverty and deprivation, indicated by the stale bread and the slippery shoes in the snow.

Lowe's use of 'in' to commence each line satirize the whole situation, that no matter how hard one tries, the immigrants will never feel truly belonged: 'In the labour queue, ten men ahead the same as you – you're /in, no no, some other fellow's in, new worry rising like the wind.'[36] The poem ends with humiliation, culminating in a scene where the protagonist is beaten up by a fellow immigrant in a pub, in the presence of spectators, signalling the unfair treatment in the immigrant's encounters in a new country: 'the arms you are sinking like a puppet /in.'[37] The word 'puppet' suggests his helplessness.

Lowe said: 'When you are diasporic, you have an imagination of those places, which may not have been in any way rooted to reality.'[38] By exploring the fluidity of distance and proximity within her own history, and re-inventing the narrative of Jamaican immigrants as they leave behind their native land for England, Lowe articulates the drifting nature of a diasporic imagination, as it travels from one place to another, and transforms elements of different cultures into a close-knit fabric. Moreover, by problematizing memory, self-representation and immigrant narratives, Lowe demonstrates Chambers' theory of writing as 'a constant journeying across the threshold between event and narration'.[39]

In the last section of *Chan*, the prose poems reveal the poet's reflection on her hyphenated multicultural identity. Written as a contemplation of her child's ancestry, 'Yellow River, Milk River', the poet offers a vivid, striking image of her grandfather: '**If you ask me about ancestors I'll tell you** He weighed codfish down with salt.'[40] The reader has the choice of reading the first half of each line in bold, for a narrative on their Chinese ancestors (the collective Hakka community), or the non-bold text on the right-hand side of each line, the latter a migration story of the poet's grandfather who runs a grocery store in Jamaica. The 'Borderliner' form captures the convergence of history, as memories, culture and meanings are passed down from one generation to another.

Figure 11 London Chinatown, 2022, by Jennifer Wong.

In her 'If You Believe' poems ('If You Believe: Ribs', 'If You Believe: Old Paradise Street', 'If You Believe: One Pale Eye' and 'If You Believe: In the Smoke and the Light'), the poet depicts a fictionalized encounter with Joe Harriott, the British Jamaican saxophonist who emigrated to the UK in the 1950s, and also her father's cousin, as she journeys in time. The poet meets Joe in a gig in Gerrard Street, where London's Chinatown is located, and sometimes she plays Joe Harriott's music and weeps for: '[T]hose decades in history/when men like Joe and my father were shadows/on English streets.'[41] In the poem, one was reminded of the thin divide between fiction and history: 'Richard says be careful what you do in poems/to real people (*known* people), but surely this poem/ shows its seams enough.'[42] By fusing reality with imagined events, Lowe reduces the difference and distance between the reader and the immigrants, a strategy that creates sympathy for the colonized.

Notes

1   Deirdre Osborne (ed.), *The Cambridge Companion to British Black and Asian Literature 1945–2010* (Cambridge: Cambridge University Press, 2016), 14–15.

2   Alison Flood, "Uplifting" book of sonnets by Hannah Lowe wins Costa book of the year', *The Guardian*, 1 February 2022, <https://www.theguardian.com/books/2022/feb/01/uplifting-book-of-sonnets-by-hannah-lowe-wins-costa-book-of-the-year> [Accessed 3 March 2022].

3   David McKirdy and Peter Gordon (ed.), *Hong Kong Eight Poets* (Hong Kong: Chameleon Press, 2015).

4   Petit, Pascale, 'Chair of Judges 2015 T. S. Eliot Prize-giving Speech', *Poetry Book Society*, <http://www.poetrybooks.co.uk/projects/47> [Accessed 6 August 2016]. Petit remarked on the 'exciting and ambitious' achievement of *Loop of Jade* as a debut collection, and the poet's accomplishment in bringing 'new possibilities to British poetry, with her scholarly but intimate explorations of her Anglo-Chinese heritage'.

5   David Morley and Kuan-Hsing Chen, *Stuart Hall: Critical Dialogues in Cultural Studies* (London and New York: Routledge, 1996), 447.

6   Katy Evans-Bush, 'Witnessing the Flow: On Hannah Lowe, Matreyabandu, Marianne Burton and Rebecca Goss, New Poets Immersed in the Stuff of Life', *Poetry Review*, 104.4 (2014), 77.

7   Hannah Lowe, 'Dance Class', in *Chick* (Tarset: Bloodaxe Books, 2013), 20.

8   Judith Butler, *Gender Trouble: Feminism and the Subversion of Identity* (London: Routledge, 2007), 200.

9   See also, Figure 9, 72.

10   Lowe, *Chick*, 20.

11   Jane Dowson, Introduction to *The Cambridge Companion to Twentieth Century British and Irish Women's Poetry* (Cambridge: Cambridge University Press, 2011), 2, 119; Friedman, Susan Stanford, *Mappings: Feminisms and the Cultural Geographies of Encounter* (Princeton: Princeton University Press, 1997), 3–4.

12   Lowe, *Chick*, 16.

13   Li-Young Lee, 'Eating Together', in *From Blossoms* (Tarset: Bloodaxe Books, 2007), 57.

14   Wong, Jennifer. 'On Home, Belongingness and Multicultural Britain', *Wasafiri*, 92.2 (2018), <https://www.worldliteraturetoday.org/2018/march/home-belongingness-and-multicultural-britain-conversation-hannah-lowe-jennifer-wong> [Accessed 2 January 2022].

15   Lowe, *Chick*, 16.

16   Ibid.

17   Homi Bhabha, *The Location of Culture* (London and New York: Routledge, 2004), 110.

18   Lowe, *Chick*, 26.

19   Anne Witchard, 'China Limehouse and "Mr Ma and Son"', <https://www.ourmigrationstory.org.uk/oms/chinese-limehouse-and-mr-ma-and-son> [Accessed 20 January 2021].

20   Lowe, *Chick*, 68.

21   Ibid.

22   Ibid.

23   Ibid., 46.

24   Lee Jenkins, 'Interculturalism: Imtiaz Dharker, Patience Agbabi, Jackie Kay and Other Irish Poets', in *The Cambridge Companion to Twentieth Century British and Irish Women's Poetry,* edited by Jane Dowson (Cambridge: Cambridge University Press, 2011), 119. In Jenkins's article, interculturalism is defined as the 'reifying difference between cultures, while eliding difference within cultures'. Further, it denotes 'a discursive space which accommodates differences and commonalities, allowing us to expand the paradigms through which we read women's poetry'. See also Figure 10, 75, on Lowe's objects in her childhood home that remind her of Chinese culture.

25   Lowe, *Chick*, 47.

26   Jennifer Wong, 'On Home, Belongingness, and Multicultural Britain: A Conversation with Hannah Lowe', *World Literature Today*, 92.2 (2018), <https://www.worldliteraturetoday.org/2018/march/home-belongingness-and-multicultural-britainconversation-hannah-lowe-jennifer-wong> [Accessed 20 April 2018]

27   Lowe, *Chick*, 47.

28   Ibid., 49.

29   Young, Robert C., *Colonial Desire: Hybridity in Theory, Culture and Race* (London: Routledge, 1994), 25.

30   This sequence of poems, entitled *Ormonde*, was published as a pamphlet by Hercules Editions.

31   'Family history' panel of the Poetics of Home Chinese Diaspora Poetry Festival, featuring Hannah Lowe, Kit Fan, Jennifer Lee Tsai and Shirley Lim, moderated by Susheila Nasta (1 October 2021).

32   Hannah Lowe, *Chan* (Tarset: Bloodaxe Books, 2016), 36.

33   Ibid.

34   Ibid.

35   Ibid., 42.

36   Ibid.

37   Ibid.

38   Jennifer Wong, 'An interview with Hannah Lowe', Appendix, 178.

39   Chambers, Iain, *Migrancy, Culture and Identity* (London and New York: Routledge 1994), 11.

40   Lowe, *Chan*, 62.

41   Ibid., 11. See also Figure 11, 79, on London Chinatown nowadays.

42   Ibid.

5

Sarah Howe: Pilgrimage, *Chinoiserie* and translated identities

While Hannah Lowe's poetry centres on the re-imagined life of her father as a professional gambler and a multi-ethnic immigrant, Sarah Howe's *Loop of Jade* (2015) evokes her mother's birthplace, her own pilgrimage to China and the grappling with, and translation of, her own cultural identity. *Loop of Jade* has the distinct focus of an intimate and imaginative journey as the daughter revisits China, her orphaned mother's native homeland and reflects on her own identity as half-Chinese. Altogether, the book makes use of poetic narratives, fragments, prose poems and epiphanies to articulate the overlapping territory of personal and collective history, resembling a form of 'border-crossing'.

Sarah Howe

Born in Hong Kong in 1983 to an English father and Chinese mother, Howe moved to the UK at the age of seven. She studied at Christ's College, Cambridge, completing an undergraduate degree in English followed by a PhD in Renaissance literature. Howe first published the pamphlet *A Certain Chinese Encyclopedia* (tall-lighthouse) in 2009, winning the Eric Gregory Award. Howe's first book, *Loop of Jade* (Chatto & Windus, 2015), won the T. S. Eliot Prize in 2016. She is the founding editor of *Prac Crit*, an online journal of poetry and criticism. In June 2018, she was elected Fellow of the Royal Society of Literature. Previous fellowships include a Research Fellowship at Gonville and Caius College, Cambridge, a Hawthornden Fellowship, the Harper-Wood Studentship for English Poetry, a Fellowship at Harvard University's Radcliffe Institute and a Leverhulme Fellowship at University College London. She now works as lecturer in creative writing at King's College London.[1]

In representing family history as constantly re-negotiated and re-imagined territory, these poets suggest new possibilities of narrating and translating home and the feeling of otherness. Lowe's poetry unsettles the reader by challenging racial injustices and class divides across familial and community spaces, while Howe examines the complexity of family lineage through intertextuality and allusions.

The narrative begins with 'Mother's Jewellery Box', a poem about her mother's story:

> the twin lids
> > of the black lacquer box
> > > open away[2]

By opening her mother's jewellery box, the protagonist reveals her curiosity about her mother's past. The poet does not continue to describe the items inside the jewellery box. Instead, she evokes 'a moonlit lake/ghostly lotus leaves/ unfurled in tiers' to suggest the elusive, dream-like landscape of her mind, which serves as an overarching setting throughout the book.[3] This setting corresponds to Daljit Nagra's claim about Howe's writing that it has 'crossed the imaginary line between the personal and the political, between the Occident and the Orient [...] between the real state of arrival and the dream state of pursuit'.[4] While Nagra's comment refers to her pamphlet *A Certain Chinese Encyclopedia*, her oscillation between these spheres is evident in *Loop of Jade,* as the poet tries to locate her mother's story in relation to the eclipsed family past and her identity.

'Crossing from Guangdong' is a cinematic long poem in which the poet describes her visit to Guangdong – a symbolic pilgrimage to China – where her mother was born. The refrain 'Something sets us looking for a place' conveys one's longing to search for or to rediscover a place of significance.[5] The exact reason for her trip to China is never pinned down, and the 'place' is not clearly defined. Howe refers to the journey as a 'strange pilgrimage to home'.[6] It suggests the function of the journey in addressing some spiritual or emotional need, and creates a paradox of distance between the poet and her home or homeland. Howe spoke of her feelings as an 'outsider' when living with her family in Hong Kong: 'I was always something of an outsider in Hong Kong for those first seven years of my life because of being half-English, half-white, and not speaking Cantonese'.[7] The poet portrays the destination of her 'pilgrimage', Hong Kong, as a mythical place: '[t]he island rising /into mist, where silver towers forest /the invisible mountain, across that small /span of cerulean sea.'[8] She connects her mother's childhood ('a screaming /baby') with her own memories of growing up, as though their lives merge in time and space. With its long lines (packed with run-on lines), this heightened poetic form mirrors a person's intimate interior monologue.

For Lowe, her sense of place is anchored in the immediacy of her family history and social reality, Howe's representation of 'place' is ruptured by her etymological approach towards mapping her heritage. In *Loop of Jade*, the poet draws associations between her birthplace, her family and the representation of Chinese culture and history from the perspective of a mixed-race person. In "Journeying is Hard", Mary Jean Chan argues that Howe's poetry is 'difficult' as it challenges the assumption of 'authenticity' and expands it beyond autobiography. The language taps into the complexity of race 'to reveal their historically determined and socially constructed nature as categories'.[9] Howe's narrative articulates the personal in a distant way, which corresponds to the etymological strategy of mapping.[10] In the title poem, 'Loop of Jade', the poet portrays her mother's reminiscences about her life in Asia. Fascinated with her mother's stories, the poet becomes aware of the distance between herself and this place where her mother comes from. By mythologizing or turning 'this place' into a metaphor, she highlights its foreign nature and the impossibility of identifying with it:

I can never know this place. Its scoop of rice in a chink-rimmed bowl, its daily thinning soup.[11]

Despite confessing the difficulty of re-entering her mother's past, the daughter re-imagines what it must be like for her mother to have escaped China. In this long, breathtaking prose poem, historical details are inter-woven with the personal, and it is the unfamiliar music of Cantonese that brings her back to 'the place'. The mother's memoir is constantly interrupted by fragments of the famous Chinese legend of the butterfly lovers (denoted by italicized text), a style adopted to deliberately blur where history ends and storytelling begins. This literary style highlights the poet's performative self-representation.

Compared with Lowe's deliberate use of the colloquial, many of Howe's poems are allusive and intertextual, and resemble a collage of texts and language(s). William Wootten praises Howe's 'considerable stylistic range' and her 'rare ability to write poems that clearly relate to the academic study of literature yet which are not, in the bad sense, academic'.[12] The choice of such a literary style sets up a distance between the reader and the poet, even if part of the poetry is partially autobiographical.

In *Loop of Jade*, intimate storytelling is embedded in the complexity of form and stylistics. On the one hand, the poet provides an intimate account of a mother-and-daughter relationship, not dissimilar from the popular themes in early Anglophone Chinese fiction such as *Wild Swans* by Jung Chang and The *Joy Luck Club* by Amy Tan (with *Wild Swans* named as one of the books that has made a strong impression).[13] On the other, the poet experiments with poetic forms, breaking away from the traditional, chronological model of family reminiscences or narration. Martyn Crucefix emphasizes the poet's 'readiness to experiment', highlighting the spiritual or philosophical inquiry contained in her poetry.[14] The use of 'gaps and elliptical looping' in the book alludes to the complexity of the poet's family origins.[15] At the same time, I would argue that the elliptical narrative structure and language not only serve as autobiographical detail, but suggest the non-linear concept of identity or origin, the impossibility to pin down one's identity in relation to actual places:

> I have this uncanny sense whenever I go to Hong Kong or Guangdong that everyone I pass in the street could potentially be my family – long lost cousins, say. The fact that people from that part of the country do look so much like my mother [...] gives rise in me to this sense of generalized kinship with the place that can't quite be pinned down. [...] I probably do have a host of cousins, aunts, uncles, or other relations still living in that part of China, and yet I can never know who they are. I think this feeling has shaped my poetry's encounters with the place.[16]

Other than the chosen fragmentary form, Howe's poetry articulates a strong sense of cultural hybridity. Several poems are titled as if they were modern-day entries of Borges' *The Celestial Emporium of Benevolent Knowledge*, a book that classifies animals into curious categories. Such an overarching framework for the collection suggests her engagement with the concept of *Chinoiserie* and a curiosity to explore new ways of articulating or countering her biracial identity in terms of 'categories' and 'labels'.[17] Howe explains her own understanding of ethnicity in particular, how she situates herself vis-à-vis a 'Hong Kong identity':

> I don't think I would call myself a "Chinese poet," as that doesn't feel like an identity I can lay claim to; "British-Chinese poet" perhaps, but even that feels like an oversimplification. "Hong Kong poet" is another lens through which I've begun to consider my work more recently. As a label it feels truer to some

extent, if only because Hong Kong's own identity is so cosmopolitan, so bound up with migration, departure and return. I think Western eyes sometimes don't appreciate quite how various a category "Chineseness" is.

By *Chinoiserie*, I refer to David Porter's useful definition:

Any object, whether of Chinese or European origin, that would have been recognised as being in a so-called Chinese style by an observer at the time.[18]

In Howe's poetry, the sense of *Chinoiserie* being evoked has the attribute of being 'at once alluring and repulsive, charming and grotesque, strange and strangely familiar'.[19]

Howe emphasizes the significance of exoticism behind borrowing from Borges' categories to classify her own observations of Chinese culture, saying: 'Being half-Chinese half-English, I always felt Borges's passage of wry *Chinoiserie* was somehow describing me'.[20] In my interview with her, she remarks on the problematic notion of authenticity in capturing diasporic experiences: 'It's very clear to me that *Loop of Jade* isn't some sort of dispatch from an "authentic" China, but the record of a writer trying to forget some sort of tentative relationship with a culture that is very much not a given'.[21] By framing her questions on identity and her curiosity towards Oriental culture within Western philosophical and literary discourses, she has opened up a new 'fantasy space of the *Chinoiserie*' where cultural identity can be translated into an image, or something that can be grasped: 'the Orient as imagined by a European willow-pattern plate or a modernist poet "translating" Li Po' to explore one's specific 'racial and cultural in-betweenness'.[22]

In the collection, personal history is intrinsically linked with the poet's reflection on the relevance of Chinese history to her self-identity. The poem '(j) Innumerable' portrays a young child's recollection of the Tiananmen Incident in 1989, when she witnessed in the protests ('toy-box people chanting and abuzz'), which did not make sense to her at that point in time.[23] The poet surveys her surroundings and realizes her parents have brought her to this 'unusual outing'.[24] Having set the scene, the poet highlights a surreal image on the TV screen:

A few days later there were different pictures on the news. A man with two white shopping bags edging crabwise on a faceless boulevard in another city where twenty-three years later I would struggle for over half an hour to hail a cab.[25]

Evoking the scene where the student protester in China challenges the regime by refusing to leave the demonstration site, despite the threat of a military vehicle, remains to haunt her 'twenty-three years later'. By placing herself in the scene of the action, this powerful line about the protestor's 'crab-wise movement' articulates Howe's dual consciousness. Having grown up in Hong Kong and England, she is an outsider to China physically, and yet, her 'participation' via witnessing history on TV has become an ineradicable piece of childhood memory. Her deliberately long sentences coupled with temporal and geographical conjunctions such as 'in another city' and 'twenty-three years later' allude to the contradictory feelings: she feels part of the Chinese community, and yet sees herself as being distant, at least geographically, an outsider of China. The poem ends with a half-question, half-statement: 'Where they pressed the clumps down, you would never know.'[26]

In her blogpost for *Best American Poetry* on the use of metaphor, Howe reflects on her identity as a British-Chinese writer and the impossibility of achieving authenticity in one's writing when the experience of the homeland is partly autobiographic, and partly mythologized:

> The literary critic part of me suspects this is a naive set of questions to be asking – except that the literary expectations revolving around autobiography and 'authenticity' (I'm thinking now via Graham Huggan's important book, *The Postcolonial Exotic*) seem particularly charged when (female) minority writers are concerned. What I had written in my latter years away from Hong Kong, was it – like the ancestral plains imagined by Denise Riley's homebound Savage – so many 'myths thought up / and dreamed'?[27]

In the article, Howe emphasizes the use of research in her poetry to achieve precision with her imagery and the impossibility of re-imagining homeland without a degree of creative licence. She writes: 'My flurry of Hong Kong fact-checking had, in fact, exposed the clash between a place in the imagination – the backdrop for one's self-mythologizing – and a place where you might sublet a studio flat for five weeks.'[28] In other words, she is suggesting that it is possible to claim a place or culture as one's own even if one is a guest, a diasporic person, to the place.

Howe situates the self – a pilgrim – within the lyrical, dream-like landscape where reality and fiction collide. Her work captures one's curiosity towards the family past, and the impossibility of knowing it entirely. In 'Earthward', the poet is overwhelmed by the evocative power of the past. She recalls a familiar face that haunts her and reflects on the inner state of restlessness linked to the question of authenticity:

more restless still
for being not
the thing itself.[29]

Pascale Petit, chair of the T. S. Eliot Prize panel of that year, remarked on the imagistic[30] quality of Howe's poetry and her adeptness in the use of space in blank verse.[31] In 'Earthward', the adoption of very short, condensed lines, coupled with substantial space on the page, seems to mimic and recall the brevity and imagistic nature of classical Chinese poetry. It also creates a meaningful tension between word and form, and encapsulates the uncertainties arising from the slippery concept of 'authenticity'.

From the poems above, we see that Howe and Lowe differ in the representation of class. Howe's use of intertextuality and the mixture of academic and intellectual registers in her poetic language combine to render a more class-conscious voice in *Loop of Jade*. For example, in '(j) *Innumberable*', the poet alludes to her own privileged background in Hong Kong where her family are members of the Hong Kong Jockey Club, a social club for the elite. Other poems, such as 'A Painting', '(e) *Sirens*', '(g) *Stray dogs*' and 'The Countess of Pembroke's Arcadia', convey a fascination with Renaissance literature, classical myths and the ekphrastic. As for Lowe, many of her poems are set in Essex and the culturally diverse districts of London, such as Brixton, Brick Lane, Hoxton and the Canal. The cultural signifiers used in Lowe's poems, such as pub food ('Now That You Live in Hoxton'), Chinese supermarkets ('Early Morning Swim') and Reggae music ('Reggae Story'), suggest a more working-class culture. This difference in depicting class sets up a distant relationship between the writer and the reader in Howe's poems, as opposed to the more immediate relationship between the writer and the reader in Lowe's work.

Conclusion

Through exploring the power of naming and translating, Howe's poetry offers a new way to understand the possibility of capturing or questioning authenticity through re-imagined narratives. Her poetry is a nuanced and destabilized mapping of the diasporic imagination, through the compelling convergence of reality, imagination, exoticism and myth-making. Above all, by capturing a meaningful tension between storytelling and personal history, Howe's poetry questions the ownership of language and challenges the reader to look beyond a traditionalist notion of 'authenticity'.

Notes

1   Writers Make Worlds, 'Sarah Howe', <https://writersmakeworlds.com/sarah-howe/> [Accessed 7 January 2021].

2   Sarah Howe, 'Mother's Jewellery Box', in *Loop of Jade* (London: Chatto & Windus, 2015), 1.

3   Ibid.

4   Sarah Howe, *A Certain Chinese Encyclopedia* (Luton: Tall-lighthouse, 2009), back-cover.

5   Sarah Howe, *Loop of Jade*, 2.

6   Ibid., 3.

7   Jennifer Wong, 'An interview with Sarah Howe' (2015), Appendix, 185.

8   *Loop of Jade*, 5.

9   Chan, Mary Jean, '"Journeying is Hard": Difficulty, Race and Poetics in Sarah Howe's Loop of Jade'. *Journal of British and Irish Innovative Poetry*, 12(1): 22 (2020), 13.

10   Michael Thurston and Nigel Alderman, *Reading Postwar British and Irish Poetry* (New Jersey: Wiley-Blackwell, 2014), 131.

11   *Loop of Jade*, 14.

12   William Wootten, 'On Jack Underwood and Sarah Howe', *Poetry Review*, 105.3 (2015), 89.

13   Jennifer Wong, 'An interview with Sarah Howe' (2015), Appendix, 194.

14   Martyn Crucefix, 'Forward First Collections Reviewed 5: Sarah Howe', 6 September 2015, <https://martyncrucefix.com/2015/09/06/forward-first-collections-reviewed-5-sarah-howe/> [Accessed 6 June 2021].

15   Wong, 'An interview with Sarah Howe', Appendix, 192.

16   Wong, 'An interview with Sarah Howe', Appendix, 192.

17   Wong, 'An interview with Sarah Howe', Appendix, 184.

18   David Porter, *The Chinese Taste in Eighteenth-Century England* (Cambridge: Cambridge University Press, 2010), 185.

19   Ibid., 10.

20   Sarah Howe, 'Word Play in Borges and Roethke, Fellow-feeling in Pound', *Poetry Society*, <http://poetrysociety.org.uk/publications-section/the-poetry-review/behind-the-poem/sarah-howe-unlocks-wordplay-and-punning-in-borges-and-roethke-and-finds-fellow-feeling-in-pound/> [Accessed 6 June 2016].

21   See Note 197.

22   Jennifer Wong, 'An interview with Sarah Howe', Appendix, 188.

23   *Loop of Jade*, 34.

24   Ibid.

25   For more on exposure and the translation of the relevant image in contemporary culture and the impact of erasure, see Margaret Hillenbrand, *Negative*

Exposures: Knowing What Not to Know in Contemporary China (Durham: Duke University Press, 2020).

26 Ibid.

27 Sarah Howe, 'To China: That Blue Flower on the Map', *The Best American Poetry Blog* (2016), <http://blog.bestamericanpoetry.com/the_best_american_poetry/2016/02/i-to-china-that-blue-flower-on-the-map-by-sarah-howe.html> [Accessed 6 June 2021].

28 Ibid.

29 *Loop of Jade*, 10.

30 Stephen Cushman et al. (eds), *Princeton Encyclopaedia of Poetry and Poetics*, 4th edition (Princeton and Oxford: Princeton University Press, 2012), 674.

31 Mark Brown, 'T S Eliot Prize: Poet Sarah Howe Wins with "Amazing" Debut', *The Guardian*, 11 January 2016, <https://www.theguardian.com/books/2016/jan/11/ts-eliot-prize-poet-sarah-howe-wins-with-amazing-debut> [Accessed 6 June 2021].

6

Race, sexuality and family in the poetry of Mary Jean Chan

Introduction

In the UK, Anglophone poetry by Chinese diaspora poets has become increasingly visible in the last decade, particularly with the T. S. Eliot Prize win by Sarah Howe for her debut collection, *Loop of Jade*, in 2015. Mary Jean Chan's debut collection, *Flèche*, appeared from Faber & Faber in 2019. The first East Asian or Chinese poet published by Faber and Faber their book represented a substantial shift in the contemporary poetry publishing landscape in the UK, was shortlisted for a number of prizes including the Dylan Thomas Prize and Jhalak Prize, and won the Costa Book Award for Poetry 2019.

Born in 1990 to Chinese parents and grew up in Hong Kong, Mary Jean Chan now lives in the UK. Chan obtained an MA and a PhD in Creative Writing from Royal Holloway, University of London, and is now senior lecturer in Creative Writing at Oxford Brookes University.[1]

Mary Jean Chan is the author of *A Hurry of English* (ignitionpress, 2018), a Poetry Book Society Pamphlet Choice, and Chan's debut poetry collection, *Flèche*, was published by Faber & Faber in 2019. Chan was shortlisted in the Forward Prize Best Single Poem category twice and received an Eric Gregory Award in 2019. Winner of the Costa Poetry Award, *Flèche* examines sexuality, desire and postcolonialism through the lens of a queer poet.[2]

In Chan's poetry, the racialized body is the site of conflicting desires and allegiances. Through close readings, I would like to discuss the relationship between racial discourse and poetic language. In *Flèche*, Chan explores the intricate relationships between identity and gender, and the conflicting relationship between mother and daughter in the Chinese family. At the heart of the collection lies a profound redefinition of gender experience and sexuality, where the personal is also deeply political, and the body is experienced as both a racialized space and a site for sexual desires. The title of the book,

Flèche, is a French term meaning 'arrow' and recalls an offensive technique used to surprise an opponent in fencing, a sport that Chan trained in when they attended secondary school in Hong Kong.[3] Divided into three sections, namely 'Riposte', 'Parry' and 'Corps-à-corps', it alludes to the attacks, parries and counter-attacks in a competitive sport that requires the use of a mask and a weapon.[4] Sharing a similar pronunciation to 'flesh' and suggesting the power of naming, it is an apt metaphor for the poet's vulnerability while at the same time a fervent defence of their holistic sense of self and their beliefs against those of their own family and peers. Different types of wounds and trauma permeate the collection, including their own coming out as a queer person, and their mother's traumatic experience in the Cultural Revolution in China.

The book of poems is an intelligent framing of narrative exploring questions of race, sexuality and the articulation of the otherness, particularly the poet's ambivalent identity as a poet of Chinese ethnicity. Chan draws the reader's attention to the dialogue between the poems and the narrative framework. In the preface of the book, the poet sets out a manifesto, the first quote being a political statement as an activist, a worldview with implications about present and the future identities: '[W]e are defined against something, by what we are not and will never be.' The pronoun 'we' is deliberately inclusive and elusive, addressing the reader who may come from any background and who shares the speaker's perspective. The second quote states that '[t]his is a book of love poems', suggesting the constant tension between the inner self and the external world. The collection's epigraph is a quotation from *The Fire Next Time* by James Baldwin, an impassioned non-fiction book on the queer Black writer's struggle against racism in his early life in Harlem in the United States, published in 1963 at the dawn of the civil rights movement: 'Love takes off the masks that we fear we cannot live without and know we cannot live within.' This quote suggests to the reader that, despite the different historical periods and geographical settings, there is a sense of affinity and activism underlying Baldwin's and Chan's work, and their resistance against pre-established notions of allegiances in their worlds.

In her revolutionary memoir *The Second Sex,* Simone de Beauvoir wrote: 'The body is a situation.'[5] Chan's poetry, to a large extent, is also a critique of the body as a situation. Yet what the speaker struggles or battles against in the book is metaphorical and multi-faceted. For example, in 'A Hurry of English', the speaker's situation is filled with carefully hidden desires:

> My desires dressed themselves in a hurry of English to avoid my mother's gaze.
> How I typed 'Shakespeare', then 'homoeroticism + Shakespeare' into Google,
> over and over. My mother did not understand the difference between English

words, so she let me be. A public history seeps into the body, the way tea leaves soak up the scent of a fridge. An odourless room is not necessarily without trauma. We must interrogate the walls. My skin is yellow because it must. Love is kind because it must. Admit it, aloud.'[6]

A prose poem, the interior monologue betrays the speaker's feelings of vulnerability and anxiety, and one's way of searching on the internet for answers or clues to the longing. Similar to the love poems protesting against the oppression suffered by lesbians in Adrienne Rich's *The Dream for a Common Language,* in Chan's collection, the racialized queer body is experienced as a site of trauma and oppression as well as a nourishing source of love. Chan has cited Adrienne Rich on various occasions as an important literary influence. As Linda Barber points out, Adrienne Rich's *The Dream of a Common Language* – published in 1978 – asserts a 'far-reaching impact on lesbian feminism and lesbian theory more generally'.[7] In 'A Hurry of English', the line 'we must interrogate the walls' recalls Rich's 'Origins and History of Consciousness':

No one lives in this room
without confronting the whiteness of the wall
behind the poems, planks of books,
photographs of dead heroines.
Without contemplating last and late
the true nature of poetry. The drive
to connect. The dream of a common language.[8]

Here in Rich's poem, the 'dream of a common language' is pitted against the harsh, white, uncomprehending walls. While Rich's poetics have reflected her vision for social justice and her radical feminism, in 'A Hurry of English' we are confronted with a self-reflexive, politically engaged yet intimate and tender lyrical voice that acknowledges misunderstanding as suffering, as trauma, even if it is silent and invisible. The choice of words 'we must' and 'interrogate' is urgent and politically charged, calling for action and solidarity. In my interview with the poet, Chan asserts the function of poetry and the English language as a way for them to find freedom and locate their identity. They explain: '[A]s a queer poet, I have found freedom and acceptance through poetry in more ways than one, so in a sense, language (the English language in particular) has been my home for the past decade. To me, the English language allows me to be in touch with my most authentic self, even when that self is constantly shifting and morphing into something unknown.'[9]

In an essay for *Modern Poetry in Translation*, Chan points out their perception of the difference in the use of pronoun between Chinese and English, and the process of translating one's sexual identity:

> The pronouns for *he*, *she*, and *it* are phonetically the same in Cantonese (my mother tongue), as well as in Mandarin Chinese. As a bilingual speaker, the notion that I would check someone's use of my pronouns only makes sense within an Anglophone context. I am exploring new words and ways of being: most recently, what it might mean to be *non-binary*. I identify as queer, in all senses of the word in English. In Chinese, there are other names, ones which I seldom use, because those words and their specific connotations do not evoke the ways in which I have become – and am still becoming – queer.

As Chan pointed out, queerness is a defining experience and a process of becoming. For Chan, identity entails the complex intersections of sexuality, language and race. Throughout *Flèche*, the motif of food becomes a powerful metaphor for desire, and the food that each person desires is both culture- and history-specific. 'Flesh' opens with the mother preparing a meal, in what seems to be a poem against eating meat ('Some days I watched shrimp and prawns / suffer: their deaths brutal, yet profoundly ordinary' as their mother would 'season the wounds with garlands of garlic'). By the end, the poem has transformed into a comparison of Chan's own vegetarianism with Mother's three years of vegetarian meals – not out of choice but because of widespread famine during the Cultural Revolution:

> [...] Mother would always have too much
> her rice bowl emptying
>
> so quickly I would never forget the three years
> she became vegetarian: the famine leaving all
>
> the trees bereft of their bark, the villagers
> so grateful for something, anything, to chew on.

In other words, the mother's present appetite brings back memories of hunger and deprivation. At the same time, noting the title of the poem – 'Flesh' – and the notion of 'suffering' shrimps, the reader cannot help but connect the mother's bodily trauma (the mother's experience of the famine) with the shrimps' struggle against their fate to suffer and die. The idea that the villagers might be grateful despite their trauma is deeply ironic. After all, the older generation do not even have the choice to be 'ungrateful'.

In Judith Butler's *Undoing Gender*, the discourse on gender norms and sexual identity is broadened to include 'the performative force of spoken utterance', while the act of confession combines language, the body and psychoanalysis.[10] In the chapter 'Bodily Confessions', Butler remarks on the social construction of gender which includes both what is conceived and the articulated. Butler argues: '[T]o have a confession to make is also to have speech that has been withheld for some time. To have a confession to make means that it is not yet made, that it is there, almost in words, but that the speaking remains in check, and that the speaker has withdrawn from the relationship in some way.'[11] For example, in Chan's 'The Importance of Tea', the speaker mocks their partner's aunt who asks for 'normal tea', bringing in their understanding of what 'tea' means, having grown up in Asia where 'tea' offers a different spectrum of images and meaning:

> When your aunt arrived, she asked for normal tea, which, to my untrained ears, sounded a bit like normality. In Hong Kong, normal tea is green, or white, or red.

The speaker confesses their inability to share the same sense of *normal tea* or *normality* as the partner's aunt: '[n]o matter how many years I've spent in this country, how I interpret normal tea, what is normal to me'. Interestingly, words like 'normality' and 'normal tea' are italicized to call our attention to the foreignness of the terms taken for granted, along with 'Earl Grey' and 'Darjeeling'.

In the closing scene, the couple (addressed by the confessional term of 'we') 'laughed and left the sachets unopened'.[12] In other words, laughter is offered as a response to the aunt's definitive view of the world, with the suggestion that the couple, with their unspoken desires, refuse to be judged or defined by ready categories of normality. By calling into question the slippery meaning of categories and names, Chan captures the complexity and multiplicity of the sexual consciousness of the racialized 'Other'.

Throughout the collection, food and the act of eating become loaded metaphors for longing and the enactment of desires. In '//', which was shortlisted for the Forward Prize for the Best Single Poem, the idea of fluid positionality is captured by the use of '//' as title and a visual metaphor of the same-sex couple with the 'same anatomies':

> To the Chinese,
>
> you & I are chopsticks: lovers with the same anatomies.
> My mother tells you that *chopsticks* in Cantonese sounds
>
> like *the swift arrival of sons*. My mother tongue rejoices
> in its dumbness before you as expletives detonate: *[two*

women] [two men] [disgrace]. Tonight, I forget that I am
bilingual. I lose my voice in your mouth, […]

no apology will be enough.[13]

Despite being 'bilingual', the speaker in the poem refuses to accept or be told
what chopsticks mean in Cantonese. In my interview with Chan, they muse on
their ambivalence towards the native tongue and suggest their fluid positionality
as a writer of colour:

> While I speak Cantonese (my mother tongue), Mandarin Chinese as well
> as Shanghainese, my relationship with these languages remains ambivalent,
> since Cantonese has been the primary language in which I have experienced
> homophobia and verbal abuse. In contrast, English (despite being the coloniser's
> tongue) has been a language of liberation and emancipation for me, especially
> on the progressive notions in gender and sexuality.[14]

In the poem, the act of kissing 'till blood / comes' is more visceral and
authentic than one's grasp of the native tongue. The use of the confessional lyric
voice conjures the intimacy of not just the relationship, but the relationship
with the reader too. Yet, the focus of the poem is on the right to desire,
rather than *ars erotica*, for the memory of intimacy is soon disrupted by the
uncomprehending parents' commentary on youth suicides, which reminds the
lovers of the silent suffering and grief being experienced by the marginalized
community.

In Chan's poetry, oppression can take place in many different forms, including
both the visible and the unseen. Their work also reflects the fundamental tenets
of radical feminism, where 'gender oppression is the most fundamental form of
oppression and precedes the economic structure of patriarchal societies'.[15] For
example, 'The Heart of the Matter' conjures a surreal meeting with the school
headmistress as an 'awakening to a room without walls, by which I mean a room
without eyes'. In a riddle-like, ironic speech, the headmistress confronts the
speaker:

> *There is something you*
>
> *want to tell the world,* she'd say,
>   sipping a sencha tea

On the one hand, the headmistress's provocative suggestion of a hidden 'ache'
prepares the reader for the speaker's compelling urge to 'come out'. On the other,

it also suggests the speaker's need to escape from the oppressive society that surrounds them, into a surreal time and space where thoughts and desires can unravel, where they can embrace the truth'.

One of the remarkable strengths of this collection is the poet's success in crystallizing the complexity of intergenerational trauma, particularly the paradoxical nature of the mother-daughter relationship in a Chinese family, within the larger discourse of gender politics. The daughter is reluctant to accept the mother's story, but feels compelled to understand it. Several sections entitled 母親的故事 are displayed in Chinese characters, meaning 'mother's story', which blur the boundary between the speaker and their mother. Also, in some poems the mother is referred to as 'the poet', including the title for the poem 'what my mother (a poet) might say (I)'. In that poem, the poet has crossed out the lines that reflect on mother's traumatic experiences as well as the lines in which she denies her longings and thoughts:

> ~~that she had scurvy as a child~~
> ~~that I don't understand hunger until I can describe~~
> ~~what a drop of oil tastes like~~
>
> *that Mao wrote beautiful Chinese calligraphy*
>
> ~~that she finds democracy to be the opiate of the masses~~
> ~~that I am a descendant of the Yellow Emperor~~
>
> *that Mao wrote beautiful Chinese calligraphy*

The deliberately crossed-out lines articulate the mother's traumatic experience in the Cultural Revolution in China, as in the previously mentioned 'Flesh':

> her rice bowl emptying so quickly I would never forget the three years
> she became vegetarian: the famine leaving all
> the trees bereft of their bark, the villagers so
> grateful for something, anything, to chew on.

In this poem grief, desire and love are mixed together into something edible that could satiate not only the longing that both mother and daughter regularly feel, but also mend their relationship.

Alluding to the mass shooting in a popular gay nightclub in Orlando in 2016, 'At the Castro' uses a twin-column form to heighten the sense of parallel narratives. The poet shifts from an intense moment of love between dancing couples to a re-imagined moment of terror:

```
what if you had been          stopped
by the bullet          into whose arms
would you have          surrendered

the way skin     is never an apology
but always          an act of faith
```

By situating one's own lived experience within the collective racial and political consciousness, Chan is politicizing the narrative of the personal. They have the ability to capture the provocative, political oppression of radical feminism, 'recogniz[ing] the oppression of women as a fundamental political oppression wherein women are categorized as an inferior class.'[16]

Within gender politics, Chan's poetry also captures one's conflicting feelings when reconciling nationhood and identity, and demands the reader's active engagement with the text. For example, 'Written in a Historically White Space (I)' is a powerful and strikingly original multilingual representation of postcolonial space, and a way of 'talking back' to the white interlocutors:

> The reader stares at my 皮膚 and asks: why don't you write in 中文? I reply: 殖民主義 meant that I was brought up in your image. Let us be honest. Had I not learnt 英文 and come to your shores, you wouldn't be reading this poem at all.

Words related to their identity and political consciousness are transcribed into Chinese characters (皮膚 [skin], 中文 [Chinese], 殖民主義 [postcolonialism]). In this way, the speaker – through maintaining control as a translator – asserts their own linguistic space as a poet of colour, as a way of 'talking back', while representing the paradox of a bilingual, postcolonial upbringing.

In the poem, form becomes part of the language to encapsulate marginality and intersectionality. A prose poem divided into sections of different mental states, 'The Five Stages' explores moments of intimacy as well as sexual awakenings and disillusionments. Instead of line breaks or punctuation marks, double slashes are used to punctuate the poem, blending the narrative with interior monologues:

> // there is a knock // at the door // my heart is a stampede // she slips out of my arms & calls // to our flatmates: *hey,* // *what's up? we were just* // *watching a film* //

Fluent in Cantonese, Mandarin and English, Chan explores the gaps in meaning between these languages, and the power one has in wielding them. In the poem 'speaking in tongues', the mother's Cantonese expressions rhyme with the English words that the daughter muses on. The deliberate misunderstanding or reluctance to understand each other is later referred to in the poem as

I've discovered a secret
that half of my words
have been kept like a key
under a plant

Conclusion

Defiant yet filled with tenderness, Chan's collection redefines the articulation of one's sexuality and identity on multiple levels. With their deft handling of poetic forms and the use of multilingual, multi-layered storytelling, the poet captures the inner life of a queer person and one's struggles to feel accepted, caught between the norms and expectations of the East and the West. Oscillating between the points of view of mother and daughter, Chan delves into the complexity of family relationships and their own conflicted identity growing up in Hong Kong, while at the same time capturing love as a language for survival. Above all, Chan's poetry opens up new directions for discourse on the intersectionality between race and gender. Through experimental forms and the adoption of a confessional lyric, their poetry of testimony captures the instinct for survival and resistance against stereotypes and oppression along the axes of gender and race, calling for the need for love and acceptance.

Notes

1   'Mary Jean Chan', The Adrian Brinkerhoff Poetry Foundation (2021), <https://www.brinkerhoffpoetry.org/poets/mary-jean-chan> [Accessed 3 August 2021].

2   Ibid.

3   Marvin Nelson and Rick Reiff, *Winning Fencing* (Washington: H. Regnery Company, 1975), 42.

4   Berndt Barth, Claus Janka and Emil Beck, *The Complete Guide to Fencing* (Missouri: Meyer and Meyer, 2004), 17.

5   Simone de Beauvoir, *The Second Sex*, translated by H. M. Parshley (New York: Vintage Books, 1989); translation of *Le deuxieme sexe*, 2 vols (Paris: Gaillimard Coll Folio, 1949).

6   Mary Jean Chan, *Flèche* (London: Faber & Faber, 2019), 12.

7   Linda Garber, *Identity Politics: Race, Class, and the Lesbian-Feminist Roots of Queer Theory* (New York: Columbia University Press, 2001).

8   Adrienne Rich, *The Dream of a Common Language* (New York: W. W. Norton, 1973), 30–1.

9   Mary Jean Chan, 'Queerness as Translation: From Linear Time to Play Time', *Modern Poetry in Translation*, <https://modernpoetryintranslation.com/queerness-as-translation-from-linear-time-to-playtime/> [Accessed 1 April 2022].

10 Judith Butler, *Undoing Gender* (London and New York: Routledge 2004), 165.

11 Ibid., 162, 166.

12 Mary Jean Chan, *Flèche*, 67.

13 Ibid., 37. For identity politics and fluid positionality, note the detailed discussion in Linda Garber's *Identity Politics: Race, Class, and the Lesbian-Feminist Roots of Queer Theory* (New York: Columbia University Press, 2001). According to Garber, identity poetics refer to 'the simultaneity of staunchly grounded identity politics and fluid positionality, particularly evident in the work of lesbians of color'.

14 Wong, Jennifer, 'An interview with Mary Jean Chan', mss, (2017).

15 Deborah Madsen, *Feminist Theory and Literary Practice* (London: Pluto Press, 2000).

16 Marsden, *Feminist Theory and Literary Practice*, 152–3.

7

Anglophone-Chinese diaspora poetry in the UK: A new generation

In addition, in the last two decades, catalysed by the call for inclusivity and diversity after the 'Black Lives Matter' movement, the changing publishing landscape in the UK has seen various changes that are responding to the need for – though by no means adequate – a more diverse range of international voices. In 2005 literary activist and writer Bernardine Evaristo urged Arts Council England to investigate the lack of diversity in British poetry. The resulting report, Free Verse, found that only 1% of the poetry published by major UK presses was by Black and Asian poets back then.[1] In response, Bernadine Evaristo and Arts Council England set up The Complete Works (TCW), a national programme, that was directed by Nathalie Teitler selected 10 outstanding Black and Asian poets, and offered them mentoring, seminars, literature retreats and publication in a Bloodaxe anthology.[2] In 2012, Bloodaxe Books published the *Out of Bounds* poetry anthology, edited by Gemma Robinson, James Proctor and Jackie Kay, which reveals 'a newly charted map of Britain as viewed by its Black and Asian poets'. These anthologies showcased the work of contemporary poets from international backgrounds, including poets Shanta Acharya, John Agard, Imtiaz Dharker, Vahni Capildeo, Daljit Nagra, among others.[3] The international anthology series TEN, edited by Bernadine Evaristo in 2010 and by Karen McCarthy Woolf in 2014 and 2017, also featured the work of poets of colour. From the 2000s onwards, the increased use of the term BAME to label poets from Black, Asian and Minority Ethnic backgrounds became more popular even if both labels can also be quite limiting by exaggerating the homogeneity of the group despite the vast range of ethnic and cultural backgrounds. In March 2017, together with Claire Cox and Mary Jean Chan, I co-organised a Poetics of Home – Place and Identity creative writing symposium in the Institute of English Studies, with funding support from Santander Trust and Oxford Brookes Poetry Centre, featuring readings and discussions by poets from international backgrounds and their critics.[4]

In 2016, RAPAPUK – a poetry conference founded by a group of academics from UK and US universities – established a critical-creative dialogue on the subject of race, catalysing a shift in attention from more autobiographical immigration narratives to more politicized narratives centred on the ideology of race. In 2019, the Ledbury Poetry Critics mentorship scheme was founded by Sandeep Parmar (University of Liverpool) and Sarah Howe (King's College London), jointly with the Ledbury Poetry Festival, to encourage diversity in poetry reviewing, cultivating new critical voices.[5] Subsequently, the British Chinese Studies Network, was also set up by Lucienne Loh (University of Liverpool) and Alex Tickell (Open University) to foster outreach planning with community groups across the regions and nations of the UK, and workshops with the Liverpool Chinese British community, including local creative writers.

In October 2021, in collaboration with *Wasafiri*, the Institute of English Studies and writers Jinhao Xie and Laura Jane Lee, I curated a Poetics of Home Chinese Diaspora Poetry Festival in the UK, with publicity partnership from Oxford Brookes Poetry Centre. As it was held during the pandemic period in the UK, the festival was done via Zoom.[6]

In the pandemic, the volunteer-led Besean network also organised a series of activities to 'empower, educate and embrace East and South East Asian (ESEA) communities in the UK', resisting racism and highlighting 'ESEA experiences through platforms and events.'[7]

All these new developments in the literary scene have gradually opened up more opportunities for publishing or showcasing diasporic voices not just from Asia but from other transnational writers as part of the British literary community. In this chapter, we will highlight some of the original voices and their works.

Kit Fan myth-making and bold aesthetics

Born and grew up in Hong Kong, Kit Fan moved to the UK at the age of twenty-one for his studies, where he now lives. He has published two collections, including *Paper Scissors Stone* (Hong Kong University Press, 2011) which won the inaugural HKU International Poetry Prize. His second poetry collection, *As Slow as Possible*, was published by Arc Publications in 2018 and was named a Poetry Books Society Recommendation for Autumn 2018. Crossing geographies and time zones, *As Slow as Possible* captures a migrant's rich racial imagination, from poems inspired by handmade furniture to a dramatic version of ancient Chinese mythology. Winner of a Northern Writers' Award, Fan is also a fiction writer and has published two novels including *Diamond Hill* (2021). His poetry translation of the Chinese Classical poet Tu Fu won one of the Times Stephen Spender Prizes in 2006.

In Antony Huen's review of the collection, he remarks on the ekprastic vision in Kit Fan's work.[8] In my opinion, *As Slow as Possible* demonstrates the distinct lens of a migrant, as the poet explores the intellectual subjectivity of the self and memory through philosophy, myths and visual art. Named after the title of the longest music piece in the world composed by John Cage and performed in Germany, the book is about finding harmony despite contradictions or locating one's identity through art, reinvention and myths. Throughout the book, the poet shifts with ease between Western and Chinese literary traditions, art and language. For example, 'Genesis' is a remarkable, very original long poem that tells the Chinese myths of Pangu and the beginning of the Earth in biblical language:

1. In the beginning there was nothing.
2. And the sky and the land were muddled like an unhatched egg.
3. And Pangu lived in the egg.
4. And in darkness he lived, for eighteen thousand years.
5. And slowly the sky and the land divided.
6. And the place that was cloudless became the land.[9]

Striking in its use of lineation and space, and reassured in voice, Fan's retelling of the Chinese myth resembles a reclaiming of language, a desire to resist a Eurocentric tradition by revisiting the cultural inheritance of the migrant poet.

In 'My Mother in a Velázquez', the speaker imagines himself to be the famous painter, striving to paint his mother in a better light than reality affords: 'You were all blacks and shadows in the kitchen-darkness/where off-whites were still possible on some plates[.]' Later in the poem, the speaker observes and wonders about her 'worrying look in the shadow of your brows/could only have been you, or at least how I or Velázquez/would have painted you'.[10] The speaker assumes the role of a painter or pseudo-painter, trying to set up an aesthetic distance from the mother by seeing her as the object of his art. Yet, the uneasy setting returns to the speaker: 'I remember singing *Joyful, Joyful We Adore Thee* in Cantonese/I'd learned from a School Mass, when the houses were freed/from the hosts[.]'.[11] The word 'freed' exposes the speaker's vulnerability and unease about his social position, and his longing to break free from memory.

In many of Fan's poems, freedom is a key theme, expressed in metaphorical, nuanced ways. In 'Resistance', the poet reveals a sense of moral conscience witnessing the moment a leaf unfurls:

> There comes a time a leaf will furl back to its vein
> with generations of green mouths unbudding
> as a form of protest, a way of branching in.[12]

Throughout the poem, the speaker maintains a language of resistance: '[T]wigs and branches will unfork and loosen/their ties.' Altogether, the movements of the tree are not innocent or coincidental, but necessary for survival. In the ending stanza, it reads: 'It will return to where it once survived and begin / again in the valley of its unmaking.'[13]

Through these subtle yet poignant metaphors from Nature, the reader must ponder at the poet's restlessness and the cause for such resistance. The idea of the tree as geneaology and the motif of 'return' in the poem seem to be politically charged metaphors, alluding to the poet's deliberate relocation or displacement from Hong Kong, the former British colony, back to the UK.

Eloquent and experimental, Fan's work demonstrates the complexity of belonging, and an artist's painterly vision of place and, at other times, displacement. Shifting between the visible and the invisible, between witnessing and introspection, Fan's poetry offers a nuanced reading of the identity of a migrant who resists readymade categories and whose language is hinged on nostalgia and desire.

Theophilus Kwek: Dwelling in history

Born and raised in Singapore, and having studied PPE, history and politics at Oxford, Kwek has published three collections of poetry, including earlier collections *They Speak Only Our Mother Tongue* (2011), *Circle Line* (2013) – which was shortlisted for the Singapore Literature Prize in 2014 – and *Giving Ground* (2016), all of which were published in Singapore; and a pamphlet *The First Five Storms* published by Smith/Doorstop, in the UK in 2017. A former president of the Oxford University Poetry Society, and as co-editor of *Oxford Poetry* and currently editing *The Kindling*, Kwek has also edited several volumes of Singaporean writing. Now living in Singapore, Theophilus Kwek's first UK collection, *Moving House*, was published by Carcanet, a major UK poetry publisher, in 2020: a major breakthrough as a Singaporean poet and UK sojourner of his generation. *Moving House* shifts across time and space: from the story of Mary Magdalene, portrayals of a soldier's training, scenes of Oxford, to the hardships faced by the refugees, the book is a mapping of migration and histories.

What marks Kwek's work from other British Asian diaspora poets is his emphasis on the construction of personal and social history, articulated through the use of more rigorous forms and a deft, elegiac language. Depicting the burial of his grandfather, 'Requiem' exemplifies Kwek's precision with poetic form and rhythm, coupled with the use of a more heroic voice: 'In cupped fingers we scooped the fire-/tempered sand, a cloud of chalk/over the precious hill.' The poem ends with a language of instruction: 'Teach me now to love, at their frayed edges/the left-behind, their washed and ashen fingers.' This ending couplet deepens the sense of grief and examines closely the body that is no longer present ('their washed and ashen fingers'), and the love and longing that remains in the bereaved.[14]

Another interesting observation about Kwek's work is his fascination with history of both the West and the East, and the reworking of symbols. For example, 'Magdalene' is a remarkable portrayal of Mary Magdalene, one of the most loyal apostles of Jesus, reflecting on a pivotal moment in the biblical narrative:

> [...] I watched them leave,
> then stood alone in the tug of wild hyssop
> at the city's sleeve, strong as love or the facts
> of being known: brief night. The lightness of stone.

Instead of depicting her as the first to discover the resurrection of Christ on Easter morning, Kwek crafts an original portrait of Magdalene and her thoughts the night before the resurrection. Here wild hyssop refers to the flowers on the city's edge, at the same time as it evokes Christ's suffering on the cross, while 'the lightness of stone' suggests what is yet to happen – the resurrection, the vindication of her knowledge about Jesus. The unusual choice of first-person voice also offers a refreshing spin to the biblical narrative, letting Mary Magdalene tell her story.

Kwek excels in capturing or re-imagining history by recreating the personal. Made up of two letters Sir Thomas Stamford Raffles – who established a British trading port in Singapore – home to his wife, 'Sophia,' offers a glimpse into the beginnings of Singapore as a colony, seen from the eyes of the colonizer who eyes the island with wonder and excitement:

> that special island
>   so spectral now, yet with its harbour, then
> the pearl of our possessions.[15]

One can approximate their underlying assumptions about the place and their own privileged position: 'How we made/our livings there, rejoicing as we found/ a world so large, and of our own devising, /that you longed to know it, end to end.'

While Kwek's poetry is lyrical and formally dexterous, it is also political in responding to social injustices beyond the immediate personal experience. In 'Strangers Drowning', the reader is led to re-imagine the traumatic experience of refugees as they try to flee from their country, their fate at the mercy of the guard: 'Last one to put your head underwater, still/kicking the wet ledge, you swallow/as the guard kneels to prise your fingers off.'[16]

In exploring the sense of otherness and the meaning of belonging, Kwek looks to history for relevance. For example, in 'The Difference', he explores imperialism and racial difference through an informed reworking of historical texts. Using *Sejarah Melayu* – a significant literary and historical work written in Malay language in the fifteenth century about the Malaccan sultanate – the poem captures the Malaccans' perspective of the foreigners: 'This is how we knew the difference: eyes/like porcelain.' Despite their brief period together, the Malaccans soon realize the motives of the strangers, and this revelation is depicted through an original use of perspective and precision: 'In the end, our children will ask, what was it/that gave them away at the next monsoon? Instead of skin, steel. Instead of matted /curls swept back with laughter, casques.'[17]

Cynthia Miller: A multi-ethnic, diasporic imagination

In her debut collection *Honorifics* – published by Nine Arches Press and shortlisted for the Forward Prize in 2021 – Malaysian-Chinese American poet Cynthia Miller explores with wit and feeling the resilience of family love and one's sense of belonging through imaginative language and experimental forms.

Miller had a very international childhood. Her mother is Malaysian-Chinese and her father an American, she grew up in Nepal, Beijing, India and the United States, before she moved to Edinburgh in adulthood where she now lives. Original and playful, her works explore and question the representation of the multiple, conflicting facets of identity and reflect on her multicultural heritage. In 'Homecoming', a narrative spread across three columns of text, the reader experiences the conflicting emotions of a diasporic individual who revisits his or her own choices in leaving home, or in making a new home in a foreign country. In one column, the voice said: 'In this version you never leave Malaysia,

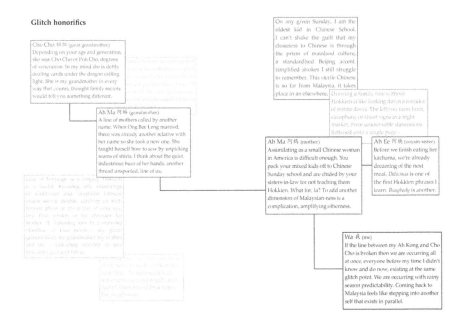

Glitch honorifics

Cho Cho 祖祖 (great-grandmother)
Depending on your age and generation,
she was Cho Cho or Poh Cho, degrees
of veneration. In my mind she is deftly
dealing cards under the dragon ceiling
light. She is my grandmother in every
way that counts, though family secrets
would tell you something different.

Ah Ma 阿嬤 (grandmother)
A line of mothers called by another
name. When Ong Bee Leng married,
there was already another relative with
her name so she took a new one. She
taught herself how to sew by unpicking
seams of shirts. I think about the quiet,
industrious buzz of her hands, another
thread unspooled, line of us.

On any given Sunday, I am the
oldest kid in Chinese School.
I can't shake the guilt that my
closeness to Chinese is through
the prism of mainland culture,
a standardised Beijing accent,
simplified strokes I still struggle
to remember. This sterile Chinese
is so far from Malaysia, it takes
place in an elsewhere. Drawing a family tree without
Hokkien is like looking down a corridor
of mirror doors. The leftover neon hum,
cacophony of street signs in a night
market, three unknowable dimensions
flattened onto a single point.

Ah Ma 阿嬤 (mother)
Assimilating as a small Chinese woman
in America is difficult enough. You
pack your mixed kids off to Chinese
Sunday school and are chided by your
sisters-in-law for not teaching them
Hokkien. What for, la? To add another
dimension of Malaysian-ness is a
complication, amplifying otherness.

Ah Ee 阿姨 (cousin-sister)
Before we finish eating her
kachama, we're already
dreaming of the next
meal. *Delicious* is one of
the first Hokkien phrases I
learn. *Busybody* is another.

Wa 我 (me)
If the line between my Ah Kong and Cho
Cho is broken then we are occurring all
at once, everyone before my time I didn't
know and do now, existing at the same
glitch point. We are occurring with rainy
season predictability. Coming back to
Malaysia feels like stepping into another
self that exists in parallel.

never sell your house to your brother despite your father's boh tua boh suay comments.' In another column, the reader finds out: 'In this version, you leave Malaysia and America opens to you like an animal trap. Everywhere you go children chew their arms off to escape home at 18.'[18]

In 'Glitch Honorifics', Miller captures the complexity of traditional honorifics used within a Chinese family by blocks of multilingual poetic text. Resisting the temptation to 'explain' what these honorifics mean, each enclosed box reveals the personal history, dreams and disillusionments of that family member. For example, the entry for Ah Ma (Mother) reads: 'Assimilating as a small Chinese woman in America is difficult enough. You pack your mixed kids off to Chinese Sunday school and are chided by your sisters-in-law for not teaching them Hokkien.'[19]

In the collection, there are some very surreal and imaginative poems that unravel the poet's roaming imagination and exploration of space. For example, several poems were inspired by NASA's mysterious release of jellyfish polyps into outer space to study how they grow in microgravity. In '[zero gravity]', these jellyfish are given voice, and they confess: '[I]t was just rollercoaster dizziness/ silliness of space mountain + dehydration + mild sunstroke +funnel cake sugar high.' Through the perspective of these transplanted jellyfish, Miller explores the relationship between a living being, cultural adoption and the experience of space.[20]

Sean Wai Keung: Subverting stereotypes through food metaphors

Born in Yorkshire and currently based in Glasgow, Scotland, food motifs in Sean Wai Keung's work serve as a starting point for explorations of identity and migration. His pamphlet *You Are Mistaken* won the Rialto Open Pamphlet Competition 2016 and he also released *Be Happy* (2019) with Speculative Books, which explores racial identity, class and the idea of happiness in the digital era. His first full-length poetry collection, *sikfan glaschu*, was published by Verve Poetry Press in April 2021. 'Sikfan', meaning 'eat rice', is a widely used term for the Chinese-speaking community. Encompassing the poet's food and cultural encounters, Sean's collection starts with an epigraph that refers to the rituals of eating in the five years in Glaschu, Glasgow.

In 'tomb-sweeping day 2020 glaschu (with thoughts of my 婆婆 and 公公 in england)', Sean re-imagines what life was like for his grandparents who moved from Hong Kong in the 1950s to the UK, without fluency in the English language:

> i tried to imagine once what it would be like
> living over half your life without being fluent
> in the local language – how much more intelligent
> you would have to become at things such as social
> cues and body language – at reading expressions

The phrase 'I tried to imagine' highlights the feeling of incompleteness in the speaker that in a way one can never re-enter or access the actual experience that his grandparents had, which also reinforces the idea of how necessary this act of re-imagining is for the speaker.[21] At the same time, the speaker remarks on how intelligent his grandparents must be, being able to decipher meanings from 'social cues and body language', a way of 'reading' the world foreign to them. Later, the speaker portrays the way his grandparents communicate with each other in a non-language of familiarity, as they wind down after a day of work at the Chinese restaurant:

> because she knew that he had already put the change in the till
> and he knew that she had already flicked the switch on the fryers
> from the circle diagram to the one-line diagram
> and they both knew that in a few minutes time they would unlock
> the front door together before flipping the plastic sign
> from the red side reading *closed*
> to the blue one reading *open*

Figure 12 The marriage ceremony of Sean Wai Keung's grandparents in Liverpool. Courtesy of Sean Wai Keung.

The repetition of 'knew' reinforces the idea of the wealth of knowledge and the personal past of immigrants like his grandparents, which remains hidden and unacknowledged. At the same time, there is a deliberate sense of melancholy in the portrayal of the working-class conditions, marked by 'the plastic sign', 'the fryers' and 'the one-line diagram'.[22]

Pivotal to Sean's poetry is the interrogation of migrant identities, inter-generational understanding and loss. Ethnically Chinese, Sean's mother has lived in Hong Kong for much of her childhood, whereas his father is English, and they met in Hong Kong when he was working there. Going to Hong Kong from time to time to visit his extended family, 'Baaibaai' (拜拜.) is the poet's ode-like narrative on the constant farewells to one's ancestral home (in his case, Hong Kong, the former British colony now returned to China), which marks the divide between the first- and second-generation immigrants. As the speaker conveys in the poem, 'Baaibaai' is a Cantonese word, and 'how you informally say goodbye'.[23] The poet then maps out the specificity and the indefinite interval of his farewell to the city: 'The last time I was in Hong Kong I made a real effort to say baaibaai to everyone there I knew I would never see again for a long time.' However, he interprets the fact that these Hong Kong locals reply him using English, to be an indicator of 'how inept I was'.[24] The poem concludes with a sense of disappointment, as the speaker cannot reconcile the emotional closeness he feels for Hong Kong, with the physical distance between him and the city, or with his constant absence from the city he feels so strongly about: 'and while it does feel like I havent been back/to where I'm from in years now/ perhaps its for the best.'[25]

In his work, Sean addresses the intersection between race and class through the use of humour. In my interview with him, he points out his subverting stereotypes:

> Humour has often been the acceptable way for the underrepresented to put their issues out into the world. At the same time, it has often been the tool of the powerful against the underrepresented. [...] For me, it's a way to present vulnerability without being the victim. It's a seizing of a narrative that has been used against me and a way to use it against them, instead.[26]

In 'china sea', the speaker wonders about the authenticity of the restaurant, and the impossible distance between him and Hong Kong:

> and now here i am and im really not in hongkong
> but i am in a restaurant eating [*the hoose*

Figure 13 Sean Wai Keung in Hong Kong. Courtesy of Sean Wai Keung.

fried isnae worth it jist git the special im told] and there is
a giant plastic dragon hanging over me on the ceiling
and im thinking of beautiful clear water and tourist buses a world or two away.[27]

Here the enjambment together with the lowercase first person ('i') are both experimental and meaningful, and the humour acts to alleviate the pain of remembering a home quite out of reach.

Figure 14 Chinese restaurant (China Sea) in Glasgow. Courtesy of Sean Wai Keung.

From packaged ham to Skype conversations and tomb-sweepings ritual during Chung Yeung, Sean Wai Keung's poems negotiate the uncanny spaces of racial and cultural hybridity. His playful use of poetic language and forms serves as an act of performance and resistance against stereotypes.

Will Harris: A playful and philosophical engagement with race

Published by Granta in 2020, Will Harris' debut collection, *RENDANG*, won the Forward Prize for Best First Collection and was shortlisted for the T. S. Eliot Prize 2021. Will Harris' witty and experimental take on poetics changes the way we see poetry. A London-based, prize-winning Anglo-Indonesian-Chinese poet, and author of the pamphlet *All This Is Implied* (HappenStance, 2017) which was joint winner of the London Review Bookshop Pamphlet of the Year award, a book of essays *Mixed-Race Superman* (Peninsula Press, 2018), he also co-edited the Spring 2020 issue of *The Poetry Review* with Mary Jean Chan. His second collection, *Brother Poem*, will be published by Granta in 2023. Blending new poetic forms, language and narrative, Will Harris has developed a distinct poetic voice to capture 'the liminality of race through an intriguing, experimental process of cultural translation' and 'the complex and incongruous feelings of people from hyphenated or marginalised identities.'

The preface page positions *RENDANG* vis-à-vis various other terms starting with 'Ren-', drawing our attention to the power of naming and the similarity and differences between names. In 'Break', Harris shifts effortlessly from one 'break' or 'breaking' to the other – be it a line break, a song, a couple splitting up, an intermission – and by this meandering of thought on separation, redefine the meaning and experience of it within the narrative as well as through linguistic experimentation.[28]

Harris' poems delve into the complexity of identity, self-perception and race in a personal, imaginative way. Interspersed with surreal dreams, 'The White Jumper' follows a Joycesian stream-of-consciousness and opaque language: '[r]unning and jumping from one grassy/platform to another I stop'. The 'white jumper' constantly reappears, alluding to one's preoccupation with racial difference. As the speaker walks past 'Pret, Spaghetti House, Five Guys, Bella Italia', it is impossible not to notice the visibility of the Other.[29]

A dexterous prose poem, 'SAY', starts from a stone carved with the word SAY but is also thought to be about SAYLES, an old firm that 'sold refined sugar, with plantations in the Caribbean and a factory in Chiswick', hinting at the speaker's multicultural family history. It also suggests the global nature of production and consumption, that the concept of the local is never straightforward. Weaving storytelling with linguistic play, the speaker confronts his uneasy feelings towards the father and arrives at the belief that whether you 'speak up or scarcely whimper, /you speak with all you are'.[30]

The book ends with 'RENDANG', the title sequence. Embedded with dialogues, its fragmentary lyric form charts the speaker's casual encounters with Yathu, Hayley and other strangers in London and elsewhere. On the one hand, this is a poem on the speaker's shifting states of mind and inner fears ('I wanted morning but I feared/to sleep'). On the other, it is an artist's statement, as the writer addresses the contradictory nature of his subject matter:

RENDANG. I lay
The pages of this book
Around me. I talk to them.[31]

No, they respond. *No, no.*

In my interview with Harris for *Wasafiri*, he discusses his intention to challenge the reader's expectation or assumptions through playing with the book title:

I was imagining potential responses to my work from white readers, questions about my 'exotic' 'roots', expectations that I perform my otherness, that I offer some kind of 'insight' into a distant land. Food has always been a convenient way to essentialize people – I mean, it fosters the illusion that other cultures can literally be consumed. In some ways, the closeness you feel to an author when you 'consume' their work is also illusory. All you're reading are words, scarred and patterned and splattered by the trace of a million different small and large inter- and intra-cultural differences.[32]

Navigating the cosmic, the philosophical and the personal in surprising ways, *RENDANG* challenges the reader to confront their limited notion of perspective, prompting them to rediscover their own meanings on race, language, marginality and class.

Nina Mingya Powles: Nostalgia and visuality

Evocative and imbued with nostalgia, memories of love and hope, *Magnolia,* 木蘭, is a debut collection by Nina Mingya Powles, a young poet and publisher of Malaysian-Chinese heritage from New Zealand currently residing in London.

Born in 1993 in Aotearoa, New Zealand, and having lived in New Zealand, Shanghai, New York and now London, Nina Mingya Powles is a Malaysian-Chinese writer. Her earlier poetry chapbooks including *Girls of the Drift* (2014) and *Luminescent* (2017) were published by Seraph Press, and her debut UK poetry collection, *Magnolia* 木蘭, was published by Nine Arches Press in 2020. Shortlisted for the Forward Prize – Felix Dennis Prize Best First Collection in 2020, the collection captures her mixed-race identity and a fascination with the Chinese culture and language through experimental, multilingual poetics. In 2018, Nina was one of three winners of the Women Poets' Prize. Powles is the author of two non-fiction books including a food memoir, *Tiny Moons: A Year of Eating in Shanghai* (Emma Press 2019) and *Small Bodies of Water* (Canongate 2021), the latter a collection of personal essays reflecting on 'a girlhood spent growing up between two cultures and what it means to belong', which received the inaugural Nan Shepherd Prize for Nature Writing'. She holds an MA in Creative Writing (Distinction) from Victoria University of Wellington. Nina is also the founding editor of Bitter Melon, an independent press that publishes limited-edition pamphlets by Asian poets.[33]

In *Magnolia,* 木蘭, Powles translates her longing to be understood or accepted into vivid glimpses of a personal world. Her poems are marked by their strikingly visual, sensuous and ephemeral quality, inviting the reader into a world rich in colours, materiality and textures.

Many of Powles' poems are dream-like pondering and cultural translation about the fluidity of home and cultural identity. In her memoir, *Tiny Moons: A Year of Eating in Shanghai,* Powles stated: '[H]ome has always been complicated.'[34] Born in 1993 in Wellington, New Zealand, in 1997 she moved with her family to New York because of her parents' jobs as diplomats at the time, then back to New Zealand. In 2005, the family moved to Shanghai and spent three years there, and in 2018 Powles moved to live in London with her partner where she has lived since. According to her, the epiphany about these journeys arrives only in retrospect: 'I hated having to leave behind everything every few years, but in retrospect I feel incredibly lucky to have had a childhood like that. As a result I feel tethered to multiple places in the world, especially Wellington, my birthplace, Shanghai, and London, where I live now.'[35]

Inspired by her constant journeys across the East and West, Powles' poetry captures a multicultural, experimental narrative of memories and nostalgia. Unlike some earlier immigrant literatures in the UK that focus on the socio-economic conditions and struggles of the immigrants to assimilate, Powles celebrates the beauty in the identity of the minority, which is much more focused on cultural translation and on embracing cultural hybridity. For example, in 'Mid-Autumn Moon Festival 2016', the poet conveys the significance of the festival to the Chinese community through the use of such evocative, well-crafted language:

> At dusk we sit outside cutting mooncakes
> into quarters, with a plastic knife, peering
> at their insides: candied peanut or purple yam,
> matcha or red bean?[36]

Observing the festival, the two young people are seated 'outside'; yet, they can't help but become curious about what lies 'inside' these mooncakes. They reach for the meaning of words with the help of technology:

> We look up the Chinese name
> for persimmon on my phone, 柿子, we taste the word
> we cut it open, wondering at how it sounds
> so like the word for lion, 狮子, lion fruit
> like a tiny roaring sun, shiny lion fruit.

By incorporating, breaking down and comparing the Chinese characters, the speaker immerses herself in the complexity of meanings and possibilities, capturing the intimate relationship between self-hood and language. In an interview with Powles, she remarks on her complicated relationship with the Chinese language, and her eagerness not just in learning or embracing the language, but to reinvent, to capture through research and re-imagination the power of 'a new realm of language':

> I did grow up with the sounds and tones of Cantonese, Mandarin and Hakka, but mostly I grew up with English. I went to Chinese school on weekends and hated it; after a while my mum gave up trying to teach me. So although those languages were always deeply familiar to me, I didn't grow up speaking them. When I was older and started learning Mandarin as an adult – I would have loved to learn Cantonese, and still would, but there wasn't a university course for Cantonese – I found that the sentences' melodies, the natural inflections, and the the four tones were familiar to my body. Like that feeling when the image of a room flashes up in your mind and you know instinctively you've been there before in a dream, or as a very young child. Learning a language is a bodily thing, for me, much like poetry. [...] I always found this hard to explain when the inevitable question "Why are you studying Chinese?" came up in class. I didn't know how to say: "I want to be able to talk to my Po Po and

Gung Gung; I want to feel more rooted in my body; I want to enter new realms of language and incorporate this unknown part of myself into my poetry."[37]

Powles' formative linguistic encounters are so fundamental to her poetry, to the extent that this multilingual experience in her has forged her poetics. Section two of the book, 'Field Notes on a Downpour', is a textured long poem that captures the multiple, shifting dimensions of a bilingual speaker.

> Some things make perfect sense, like the fact that wave (波) is made of skin (皮)
> and
> water (氵) but most things do not.[38]

This above line highlights the exploration of what lies hidden as well as what's visible in the language passed on to her from her mother. On the one hand, the poem questions the meaning of each individual word, but the suggestion that 'most things do not' make sense seems to infer the speaker's difficulty to understand China as a place and its practices. In another part of the poem, the speaker confesses:

> There is always something disappearing here. The skyline goes dark at 10:30p.m.
> Old buildings are crushed to pieces and replaced by shopping malls. The subway
> map rewrites itself at night.

Refusing to explain what the above means and juxtaposing these observations along with terms that have more lucid meanings, the poet recounts the constant gap between what is said and what is meant, between what can be explained and what can't, when she lived in China. In many ways, in Nina Powles' poetry, the feeling of belonging and unbelonging is equally significant dimensions of the diasporic individual's identity and very often both sides of the coin.

Marked by the freedom and hybridity in the use of form, her work contests with the formal boundaries between different poetic forms. They beckon the reader to look at both the mixed-race speaker's body and the mind. In 'A city of forbidden shrines', Powles offers a glimpse into an in-between space where one can 'almost' grasp the meanings:

> I was almost born in the lunar month of padded clothing
> [...]
>
> almost spent a girlhood watching sandstorms
>   tearing through the almost golden sunlight
>
> I almost scraped dust off my knees each day for fifteen years
>   almost painted paper tigers each year to burn

I can almost hold all the meanings of 家 in my mouth
      without swallowing [*home, family, domestic*
a *measure word* for every almost-place I've ever been][39]

In the title poem of the collection, 'Girl Warrior, or: Watching *Mulan* (1998) in Chinese with English Subtitles', the poet offers a rethinking of the classic tale of *Hua Mulan* via its Disney animation version. A prose poem that consists of fragmented recollections, the speaker alludes to her enjoyment and limited understanding of the movie *Mulan*, an ancient Chinese myth about a girl who disguises herself as a man and takes her father's place in the army:

When I watch *Mulan* in Chinese with English subtitles/I understand
only some of the words

My focus shifts to certain details/how Mulan drags a very large
cannon across the snow/with very small wrists[40]

This cinematic representation of the film scenes allows the reader to share the eagerness to embrace a culture that belongs to, and eludes, her. The poet annotates a version of the Mulan story that is not so much 'authentic' to the original, but rather one that is more meaningful to herself or her world. In this context, her work leads us to appreciate why, according to Bhabba, any 'hierarchical claims to the inherent originality or "purity" of cultures are untenable, even before we resort to empirical historical instances that demonstrate their hybridity'. In other words, Powles' poem inhabits what Bhabba calls a 'Third Space', though unrepresentable in itself, which constitutes the discursive conditions of enunciation that ensure that the meaning and symbols of culture have no primordial unity or fixity – that even the same signs can be appropriated, translated, rehistoricized and read anew.

To a certain extent, it is also a poem about the translation of her identity and her relationship with both the Chinese and English worlds. In *The Penguin Book of Prose Poem*, Noel-Todd remarks on the value of the prose poem – with its 'wayward relationship to its own form' – in becoming the 'defining poetic invention of modernity'.[41]

Inspired by Mulan's feminist spirit and boldness in the film scenes, the speaker in the last part of the poem turns to her own inner strength, asserting who she really is and what she is capable of:

I paint my lips/
I draw avalanches/

I light fires inside dream palaces/
I cut my hair over the bathroom sink/

The adoption of the present tense here is very poignant as it calls into question the threshold between fiction and reality. There is full conviction that one is perfectly at liberty to 'draw avalanches' as well as 'light fires inside dream palaces'.[42]

Throughout the collection, food rituals – the preparation of food and the consumption of it – become a cultural space and language.[43] Through evoking different food memories, from a spring onion pancake recipe to the local way of eating dumplings in aged vinegar in 'Black Vinegar Blood', Powles beckons the reader into her diasporic space and time.

In 'Styrofoam love poem', the poet pictures with stark humour the ambiguity of the 'Chinese dream' in the form of instant cup noodles, a household staple for Chinese communities:

my skin gets its shine from Maggi noodle packets/ golden fairy
dust that glows when touching water/ fluorescent lines around the edge
/ a girlhood seen through sheets of rainbow plastic

Tinged with feelings of guilt, the speaker explores in metaphorical terms the symptom of a society deeply entrenched in consumerism, and the individual's act as a potential threat to the environment:

chemical green authentic ramen flavour/ special purple packaged pho/mama's instant hokkien mee/ dollar fifty flaming hearts/ hands in the shape of a bowl to carry this cup of/ burning liquid salt and foam/ mouthful of a yellow winter morning/ you shouldn't eat this shit it gives you cancer/ melts your stomach lining/ 99% of all this plastic comes from China/ if we consume it all maybe we'll never die/ never break down/ I'll never be your low-carb paleo queen/ I'll spike your drink with MSG/ find me floating in a sea of dehydrated stars/ on the surface of my steam shine dream/ my plastic Chinese dream[44]

Through its inventive forms and a richly textured and nuanced language, *Magnolia, 木蘭*, is an eloquent debut collection that offers multiple layers of meaning about home, identity, language and womanhood. With an assured, imaginative voice that embraces multilingual expressions and hybridity of forms, Powles reveals the convergence and gaps that exist between the personal and the universal, the authentic and the foreign, and a willingness to translate one's complex, multicultural identity into being.

Figure 15 Chinese breakfast ('dou fu nao') that Nina Mingya Powles had with her mother in Beijing, 2018. Courtesy of Nina Mingya Powles.

Figure 16 Traditional Chinese dumplings that Nina Mingya Powles had with her mother in Beijing, 2018. Courtesy of Nina Mingya Powles.

Jennifer Lee Tsai: Inter-generational history, taboos and womanhood

Born in Bebington to Chinese parents and grew up in Liverpool, Jennifer Lee Tsai is a fellow of The Complete Works III, a Ledbury Poetry Critic and a Contributing Editor to *Ambit*. Her work has been published in the *Bloodaxe Anthology Ten: Poets of the New Generation* (2017) edited by Karen McCarthy Woolf, and her debut poetry pamphlet, *Kismet,* was published by ignitionpress in 2019. She is a winner of the Northern Writers Award 2020 and a PhD candidate in Creative Writing at the University of Liverpool. Jennifer Lee Tsai's poetry explores with sensitivity the gaps between generations, cultures and belief systems.

A key trait in Lee Tsai's poetry is her deftness in weaving geography and historical consciousness into the poetic narrative. An elegy for the poet's father, 'Between Two Worlds' depicts the in-between state of the living and the dead. Resisting the painful reality, the speaker's mind turns to the Tibetans who believe that after death, 'the blood in the centre of the heart forms three drops', observing how the family will survive grief: 'the TV blaring in the background,/the sound of laughter,/my mother and brother carrying on the family business'. Filled with darkness and hope, *Kismet* conjures a world where the divide between the living and the dead becomes indistinct, where inner strength and love can transcend fears and bring healing.[45]

Lee Tsai's poems are unapologetically political. 'Breathing', for example, is a striking poem that celebrates hope, courage and humanism despite the threat of oppression. It draws from Song Dong's *Breathing* showing a paralysed man in Tiananmen Square on New Year's Eve's fear: '[H]e breathes over the petrified lake/in Houhai Park. Nothing gives.' Despite the stillness of it all, he is not dead but capable of starting again, if anyone can rescue him: '[a] patch of frost thaws/only to freeze again when he rises'. The ambiguous nature of time and pace in the poem correlates with the poet's interest in Julia Kristeva's notion of 'Women's Time', and 'the ways that time operates in our personal consciousness, personal sphere or dream space, which is an individual understanding of time'.[46]

In *Kismet*, Lee Tsai questions gender stereotypes in Chinese communities. In '1961', we catch a glimpse of working-class women from the local Hakka community, the aunt who 'lights incense, replenishes the bowls of oranges and white chrysanthemums on the ancestral altar', an elegy in memory of her grandmother's suicide in 1961. In 'Going Home', a long poem in parts, Lee Tsai subverts the moon metaphor, alluding to the resistance of Chang Er against her husband's plans. 'Love Token' captures the morbid, elliptical thoughts of a self-professed 'witchy vagrant locked inside an endless hall of mirrors' who inhabits 'the wrong place at the wrong time, my wasted youth traded for a ghostly ride in a fairground.' Such is a version of self where 'a Chopin nocturne plays inside my head every time' and yet is capable of such power it can 'smash through the glass'.[47]

According to Lee Tsai, poetry writing is a way to 'reclaim fragments, to use them in new arrangements, an act of recovery'.[48] To a large extent, a diasporic person will always experience a sense of fracture or duality in their identity. For example, in 'Self-Portrait at Four Years Old', a prose poem, Lee Tsai writes about the realization of her emerging, dual identities as both a Chinese and British person:

> I am the smallest one in class/the only Oriental at a primary school in Birkenhead/ At four years old, I learn to read better than a child twice my age/My first school uniform/grey cardigan knitted by an aunt/grey skirt, grey like an English sky.[49]

Here, the poet calls herself 'the smallest' and 'the only Oriental' in the class, exposing the difficulty of self-acceptance and the poet's awareness of the problematic stereotypes that emerge from growing up in a culturally homogeneous setting. The prose poem form, with the use of slashes to punctuate the poem, is especially powerful and apt in reinforcing the sense of fracture. In her loneliness ('I don't tell her that I never feel like smiling at school/I am learning to be silent'), the speaker turns to the fairy tales for reassurance or an escapist fantasy, only to realize her otherness, prompting her question to her mother:

> At home, I read fairy tales with my mother/ Goldilocks and the Three Bears/ Rapunzel/ Cinderella/ Sleeping Beauty/ Snow White and the Seven Dwarfs/ Only Snow White has black hair/ Her eyes are brown, like mine/ but her skin is white/ What colour is my skin, mama?

These unresolved questions of identity make their way into the imaginary space of fairy tales. The open ending – 'I put on my best smile for the camera' – eludes the reader, suggesting the speaker's ambivalence, displacement and a performative self that is open to change.[50]

In my interview with her, Lee Tsai admits that her reading of French feminist critiques about female identities has encouraged her to explore and interrogate 'notions of otherness, spirituality and embodiment, the invitation to write the body, the idea of a feminine writing, to focus on the unconscious'.[51] In writing about difficult experiences to do with shame, abuse and childhood trauma as well as the complexities of desire, Lee Tsai is drawn to Catherine Clément's idea that '[s]omewhere every culture has an imaginary zone for what it excludes', conveyed in her seminal essay 'The Guilty One', especially by the possibility to write about the repressed female figures of the 'Imaginary', 'which include the seductress, sorceresses/witches, mystics, heretics and hysterics'.[52]

This tendency to portray the multiplicity of the female self is then a way of resisting stereotypes and translating otherness.

Natalie Linh Bolderston: Poetic testimony, tenderness and survival

Born in Stoke-on-Trent to Vietnamese-Chinese parents in 1995, Natalie Linh Bolderston is winner of the Eric Gregory Award, the Rebecca Swift Women Poets' Prize, and member of the Roundhouse Poetry Collective and the 2020–21 London Library Emerging Writers Programme. Her pamphlet, *The Protection of Ghosts*, published by V Press in 2019, is a poetic testimony about her ancestry and her family's migration experience coming to England as refugees in 1978. She works as an editor for an academic publisher, Rowland and Littlefield.

The poet's family moved to England in 1978, and in the same year Vietnam invaded Cambodia. In 'My mother's nightmares', atrocities return to haunt: 'Taste like seawater and vomit, handfuls of spat blood. The sky is a paper bruise, and it is always 1978. A gunshot forces her to carry the dead in her womb. The speaker struggles to understand her own nightmare, the fear of losing her mother: 'There is a garden where her skin is drying on the line, a handful of her hair/on the lawn'. In the last section, we return to the present, where both mother and daughter are survivors who 'both know there are some things we can only/consider with our eyes closed'.

A glossary-like poem that alternates between the voices of Bá Ngoai (grandmother) and the mother, 'Divinations on Survival' pushes boundaries with form. Bolderston's poetry transforms history into the personal, a seamless flux of voices and multilingual expressions.[53]

Her poem, 'Middle Name with Diacritics', has been shortlisted for the Forward Prizes 2021 for Best Single Poem. Breaking down her name character by character, the poet reconstructs the narrative of her family's migration and the wisdom she acquires through the experience:

Linh hồn [soul]

4. Ancestors/who stitch your prayers into houses/with the floors missing
5. The name of four teenage girls/in my mother's refugee camp
6. The part of me/often left out or misspelled/that moves quietly
   through the world
   [...]

Ra lịnh [to command]

5. Names given up/because home did not rest easily/on unyielding tongues
6. My mother's medicated bloodstream/that tells her/her pain does not exist/
   that her bones/have not yet lived through/all they can endure[54]

Drawing from Bolderston's discussion of her poem, we appreciate the way she 're-centres' the narrative: 'I chose to write about this using my middle name because it's part of my identity – the only part of my name that acknowledges my Vietnamese heritage. However, it is often left out, misspelled, or anglicised. Therefore, I wanted to re-centre it while also centring the culture and history of the country where it comes from.'[55] Bearing it in mind, one understands more easily the taboo and unspoken feelings in the speaker and the daunting experience of representing a culture, to inherit the pain and pass on the story, and to find ways to represent one's history and language even if – as a second generation – tongues can be 'unyielding': 'Names given up/because home did not rest easily / on unyielding tongues.'[56] According to Hayden White's 'The Value of Narrativity in the Representation of Reality', narrative is how we 'translate knowing into telling, the problem of fashioning human experience into a form assimilable to structures of meaning that are generally human rather than culture-specific.'[57] In Bolderston's poetry, form becomes a way of processing and framing trauma. Tender yet unflinching, these poems tell of survivors of atrocities, armed with knowledge and love.

L. Kiew: The politics of an opaque language

A Chinese-Malaysian poet living in London, L. Kiew's pamphlet, *The Unquiet*, published by Offroad Books in 2019, is an excellent example of British-Malaysian-Chinese multilingual poetry on the complexity of home. Born and grew up in Malaysia until the age of ten, Kiew came to the UK to study at a boarding school, going back to Malaysia only in the school holidays. Her parents worked as university lecturers in science while her father was the first one in his family to go to university and complete a PhD. She holds an MSc in Creative Writing and Literary Studies from Edinburgh University and was a 2019/20 London Library Emerging Writer. L. Kiew earns her living as an accountant.[58]

Kiew's poems often prompt the reader to confront dialects in their transliterated, untranslated form, inviting the reader to grapple with incomplete or opaque meanings. Her ambivalent sense of belonging is expressed in the spontaneous shifts between Hokkien, Teochew and English. In 'Learning to be mixi', the speaker conveys a young girl's mixed feelings at leaving home for boarding school: 'It was so panas/but aircon in airport/bite like cat.' While home dialect feels like 'a blush licked/my face, campur-campur/speech bursting the ice wall', school days in England amount to attempts to suppress what's natural:

> I was buckled in, and taken off
> to England, the boarding school
> (not like Enid Blyton, not at all) and
> Cambridge, the colleges,
> the backs and the hate,
> suppressing the suffix-lah,
> being proper and nice,
> cutting my tongue with that ice.

The speaker is disappointed by an England that deviates from the books she has read. Moreover, the learning child remains a passive figure that is 'buckled in'.

In 'Swallow', the metaphorical bird suffers from 'overeating from the dictionary – nouns sticky as langsat, a kilo of adjuncts, a kati of adverbs'. Regional dialects are repeated, juxtaposed with unfamiliar words (e.g. 'plangent', 'minatory') and remain deliberately unexplained. The poet's incisive vocabulary; the brisk, run-on lines; sparse punctuations and disrupted syntax are revealing but disturbing. In her interview with fellow poet and critic Alice Hiller, Kiew explains her reflective writing practice on language, particularly her emphasis on giving the reader an immersive experience of the spoken linguistic environment through unglossed dialect, punctuation and choice of form:

> I chose romanisation for *The Unquiet* because actually for me there is an interesting politics around the learning of characters, especially now when the only way to be able to learn them would be through Mandarin. And the primacy of Mandarin is a kind of construct that has come out of the rise of communism in China, and the development that they describe as Mandarin being the common language. That wasn't the case previously. You can write all Chinese dialects in characters but when you do that, what tends to happen is that most readers will

then attempt to read them as Mandarin, which they are not. I didn't want that at all. I wanted to foreground the primacy of dialect in that space.

Hence, through regarding the politics in form, Kiew's poems explore the mind's complexities and the undercurrents in relationships. In 'Balik kampang', the wish to return home where her father in a sarong will be waiting, dissolves into the thought of a child in rush-hour traffic, with 'no one left to/take her anxious hand'. In 'Dinner', a couple's struggle to conceive is hidden in metaphors of 'frozen meat', 'chopped rind', 'Your cold cut sandwiches/on Saturdays', while the unusual syntax and the motif of bleeding in 'Though I love you, I wipe the bowl. The sink's red' conveys internal suffering.

Laura Jane Lee: an inter-generational racial imaginary

Published by Outspoken Press in 2021, Laura Jane Lee's *flinch & air* offers a bold perspective that connecting an individual's subjectivity with the family history, politics and society.[59] Through retracing inter-generational stories of courage, shame and humiliation, the poet brings to the forefront a voice that is personal, gendered and political. Thinking of her grandmother (Chu Ching or 'por por') who grew up being the only girl in the family of four children, Lee coins a new pronoun 'wee' to capture the reimagined, merging narratives of her grandmother's life and her own, imagining the plurality of that female experience. In the poem, the hostility of a patriarchal society is captured in the metaphor of the weather, where the female is subjugated:

> wee darling,
> that strangled night when the moth-black
> rained with hushed
> men-shouts, and high-strung the lightning
> roughed our
> little mud-hut, you, wee
> thing, how you slept whilst
> creatures rang whinnying in the hollow-
> weather [...]

Using the deliberately short lines and words such as 'little' and 'wee thing' to portray the female figure, there is a contrast between the merciless weather and the vulnerable child ('as if /strange, strange, strange the /thundershower milked you of all /rousing'), a situatedness that can only generate the language of protest, of 'howling' when the mother returns.[60]

Jinhao Xie: Mapping the longing

A poet born in Chengdu and now based in London, Jinhao Xie's poetry touches on themes of culture, identity and the mundane. Published in *Poetry Review*, Poetry Foundation, *Bath Magg* and anthologized in *Slam: you're gonna wanna hear this* published by Pan Macmillan, their poems often expose one's vulnerability and ambivalent desire(s) as one oscillates between familial and romantic relationships. For example, in 'moonlight' published on Poetry Foundation, Xie uses the voice of an unreliable narrator to revisit personal trauma. The poem highlights intimacy and understanding between the brothers ('I hold hands with my brother', 'his stubborn heart laughs with mine' and 'my brother is the moon: watching over me'), only to reveal that the trauma is deliberately suppressed and eclipsed ('my future and his past is nothing but / a smudge').[61] Throughout the poem, there is a repetition of the word 'graphite' which 'glides past his cheeks' and remains unexplained, but connects with the deliberate re-imagining or denial of domestic violence ('*how our laughter blooms, in dad's punch.*') By experimenting with the notion of distance and intimacy within a lyrical voice, and by reinventing language to capture the fluidity or ambivalence in meaning, the poet taps into the aesthetics of ambiguity, construing what Caroline Bird said about writing the truth using 'A Surreal Joke' as an example: 'this poem is true but contains no facts.'

Named after Wong Kar-wai's 2000 film with the same title–a film that explores sexuality, heartbreak and loneliness through the protagonist's complicated extra-marital love that explores sexuality, heartbreak and loneliness through the protagonist's complicated extra-marital love. In this poem, the speaker explores aptures desire in a metaphorical languuage, expressing a bewildering sense of longing and inability to reconcile between different experiences in love:

> she reminds you of the ocean
> you once begged to be drowned in.
>
> 3 a.m. club, dj playing destiny's child
> *survivor*, defending your heartbeat.
> late night shake up the next morning.
> The crowd fades, scattered rain
> stains the street. cats' footprints.[62]

The deliberate use of the lowercase letters and rather disjointed phrases or lines (separated by full stops), alludes to a sense of fissure or disconnection in the lover's body. The impressionistic poem concludes with the dreamlike manifesto: 'Every jellyfish dream of being/an androgynous nymph.' In 'Gender and Grammar in Chinese: With Implications for Language Universals', Catherine Farris investigates how the use of pronouns in the Chinese language differs from the English, and the implications it has in changing the way one perceives or understands gender representations.[63] Moreover, Farris also challenges us to consider the ways different social terms in Chinese will overly mark the feminine, hence exposing the society's assumption that the generic term implies male presence.[64] Since Xie is a native speaker of Mandarin and Chengdu hua, I see this encapsulating 'androgynous nymph' and jellyfish metaphor not only as a refraction of the poet's non-binary identity, but a way of reinventing language to transcend the confines of both the Chinese and English language and the underlying ideologies. As evidenced in the above poem, Xie's poetry demonstrates the fluidity and playfulness inherent in an emerging aesthetics of non-gendered language.

Notes

1   *Free Verse* (2006) <https://www.spreadtheword.org.uk/free-verse-report/> [Last accessed 20 September 2022].

2   'The Complete Works Diversity in UK Poetry Conference', Goldsmiths, <https://www.gold.ac.uk/calendar/?id=11157> [Last accessed 20 September 2022].

3   Gemma Robinson, James Proctor and Jackie Kay (eds), *Out of Bounds: British Black and Asian Poets* (Tarset: Bloodaxe Books, 2012). *TEN: Poets from Spread the Word* edited by Bernadine Evaraisto and Dhaljit Nagra (Tarset: Bloodaxe Books, 2010) <https://www.bloodaxebooks.com/ecs/product/ten-new-poets-from-spread-the-word-974>.

4   Institute of English Studies <https://ies.sas.ac.uk/whats/conferences-and-symposia/previous-conferences#conferences-2017> [Last accessed 20 September 2022].

5   'Ledbury Poetry Critics', Centre for New and International Writing, University of Liverpool, <https://www.liverpool.ac.uk/new-and-international-writing/emerging-critics/> [Accessed 15 November 2021]. Please refer to Conference report on Race and Poetics and Poetry, RAPAPUK (2016), <https://www.poetryfoundation.org/harriet-books/2016/06/race-and-poetry-and-poetics-in-the-uk-conference-report-published> Last accessed 12 January 2022.

6   'Poetics of Home Festival', <https://poeticsofhome.co.uk/> [Accessed 1 March 2022].

7   See besean (2020), <https://www.besean.co.uk/> [Last accessed 20 September 2022].

8   Huen, Antony, '*As Slow as Possible*, and *Letters Home*', *HKRB,* 10 August 2018, <https://hkrbooks.com/2020/08/10/as-slow-as-possible-and-letters-home/> [Accessed 3 January 2022].

9   Kit Fan, *As Slow as Possible* (Todmodern: Arc Publications, 2018), 55.

10 Ibid., 21.

11 Ibid.

12 Ibid., 27.

13 Ibid.

14 Kwek, Moving House (Carcanet, 2020).

15 Kwek, *Moving House*, 64.

16 Kwek, *Moving House*, 31–315.

17 Kwek, *Moving House*, 66.

18 Cynthia Miller, *Honorifics* (Rugby: Nine Arches Press, 2021), 22–3.

19 Miller, *Honorifics*, 48.

20 Ibid., 26, 27.

21 See his grandparents' marriage ceremony in Liverpool and the image of China Sea restaurant in Glasgow, Figures 13 and 14.

22 Sean Wai Keung, *Sikfan Glaschu* (Birmingham: Verve Poetry Press, 2021), 42–3.

23 Ibid.

24 Ibid.

25 Sean Wai Keung, *Sikfan Glaschu*, 30–1.

26 Jennifer Wong, 'Jennifer Wong Interviews Sean Wai Keung', *Asian Cha*, 23 January 2021, <https://chajournal.blog/2021/01/23/sean-wai-keung/> [Accessed 9 January 2022].

27 Sean Wai Keung, *Sikfan Glaschu*, 68–9.

28 Jennifer Wong, 'Rediscovering Self, Race, and Class through Cultural Translation: An Interview with Will Harris', *Wasafiri,* 37.3 (2022), 44–8.

29 Will Harris, *Rendang*, 17, 19.

30 Harris, *Rendang*, 61.

31 Harris, *Rendang*, 74.

32 Ibid.

33 New Zealand Academy of Literature, 'Nina Mingya Powles', <https://www.anzliterature.com/member/nina-mingya-powles/> [Accessed 7 January 2021].

34 Nina Mingya Powles, *Tiny Moons: A Year of Eating in Shanghai* (The Emma Press, 2019), 27.

35 Jennifer Wong, 'A conversation with Nina Mingya Powles' (2021), mss. See Appendix, 210.

36 Nina Mingya Powles, *Magnolia* (Rugby: Nine Arches Press, 2020), 19.

37 Jennifer Wong, 'A conversation with Nina Mingya Powles' (2021), mss. See Appendix, 210.

38 Powles, *Magnolia*, 50.

39 Nina Mingya Powles, *Magnolia* (Rugby: Nine Arches Press), 64.

40 Powles, *Magnolia*, 11–12.

41 Noel-Tod, Jeremy, *The Penguin Book of the Prose Poem* (London and New York: Penguin Hardback Classics).

42 Powles, *Magnolia*, 13.

43 See Figures 15 ('toufu nao' breakfast) and 16 (dumplings) documenting the poet's breakfast with her mother in Beijing, 2018.

44 Powles, *Magnolia*, 58.

45 Lee Tsai, *Kismet* (ignitionpress, 2019), 20–1.

46 Joe Carrick-Varty, 'Interview with Jennifer Lee Tsai', *bath magg*, <https://www.bathmagg.com/interview3/> [Accessed 9 November 2021].

47 Lee Tsai, *Kismet*, 24.

48 Jennifer Lee Tsai at Poetics of Home Festival panel on family history, moderated by founding editor of *Wasafiri*, Prof. Susheila Nasta, on October 2021, <https://www.youtube.com/watch?v=wfeJcC7bZkQ> [Accessed 9 November 2021].

49 Lee Tsai, *Kismet*, 1.

50 Joe Carrick-Varty, 'Interview with Jennifer Lee Tsai', *bath magg*, <https://www.bathmagg.com/interview3/> [Accessed 9 November 2021].

51 Jennifer Wong, 'An interview with Jennifer Lee Tsai', Appendix, 214.

52 Ibid.

53 Natalie Linh Bolderston, *The Protection of Ghosts* (V. Press, 2019), 9.

54 Natalie Linh Bolderston, 'Middle Name with Diacritics', <https://www.forwardartsfoundation.org/forward-prizes-for-poetry-2/forward-prizes-in-conversation-with-natalie-linh-bolderston/> [Accessed 9 January 2022].

55 Ibid.

56 Ibid.

57 Hayden White, 'The Value of Narrativity in the Representation of Reality', *Critical Inquiry*, 7.1 (1980), 5.

58 Alice Hiller, 'Interview with L. Kiew', 28 June 2019, <https://alicehiller.info/2019/06/28/i-am-a-different-person-in-one-language-than-i-am-in-another-l-kiew-on-combining-teo-chew-hokkien-and-english-in-the-unquiet-then-rewriting-privilege-by-letting-words-become-beas/> [Accessed 9 January 2022].

59 Laura Jane Lee, *flinch & air* (London: Outspoken Press, 2021), 5.

60 Ibid.

61 Jinhao Xie, 'moonlight' in *POETRY* (2021), 354.

62 Jinhao Xie, 'In the Mood for Love', *Poetry Review*, 110.1 (2020), 11.

63 Catherine S. Farris, 'Gender and Grammar in Chinese: With Implications for Language Universals', *Modern China*, 14.3 (1988), 278–80.

64 Farris, 'Gender and Grammar', 278–80.

8

Anglophone poetry in Hong Kong: Cosmopolitanism and a split notion of home

A British colony until 1997, the Anglophone literature in Hong Kong has always been marked by a unique sense of cosmopolitanism. Over time, the subject matter and demographics of poets writing poetry in English in Hong Kong have evolved. While the expatriate poets in Hong Kong have been writing in English (e.g. Akin Jeje, Andy Barker, John Wall Barger, Mary Jane Newton, Konstandinos Mahoney and Nashua Gallagher, Pauline Burton, Kavita Jindal, David McKirdy, Tim Kaiser, Martin Alexander, Kate Rogers, Gillian Bickley, Madeleine Marie Slavick and Viki Holmes), there have also been a number of local Chinese poets who chose to write and publish their works in English. To some extent, the unique socio-political and cultural position of Hong Kong means that they are writing within China but at the same time writing outside the Mainland. Compared to the literary production in Mainland China that is predominantly Giving its hybrid, linguistic and postcolonial setting, Hong Kong's Anglophone poetry is marked by cosmopolitanism and a complex sense of belonging. In this chapter, I have included a brief overview on some of the local poets writing from Hong Kong as a way to contrast with the works by Chinese poets writing in the UK and the United States.

In *Colony, Nation and Globalisation: Not At Home in Singapore*, Eddie Tay points out that, when contextualizing a text and its author, what is 'transnational' and what is 'national' or native is often not exclusive to each other:

> At the outset I have argued that there is transactional and transnational representation at work in Anglophone work by Singapore and Malaysian-born authors who are based in the two countries. The recent emergence of literary texts written by authors outside of Singapore and Malaysia extends this transnational politics of representation. This tells us there is a need to consider how these transnational categories shape themes in literary texts. The national, it would seem, is already transnational.[1]

While he has applied this to the discourse on the Anglophone work by Singapore and Malaysian-born authors, it seems that a similar approach is also relevant when appreciating the racial, cultural positioning and in-betweenness of Anglophone Hong Kong poets.

Published in 2003, *City Voices: Contemporary Hong Kong Voices in English: Hong Kong Writing in English 1945 to the Present*, edited by Michael Ingham and Xu Xi, is one of the most well-known cross-genre anthologies celebrating Anglophone Hong Kong writing. The anthology traces a growing *local* literary scene from the early writing of the 1950s through the creative surge of the 1990s and the millennium. But what is the *local* in Hong Kong? Louie Kam argued for the unique position of Hong Kong as a 'transit camp' and an East-meets-West literary marketplace:

> It was a city of exiles, populated by people who had come, for the most part, from the mainland of China in search of business opportunities or political refuge, and the wind that had blown them to the colony might just as easily carry them further in due course, to other cities in Southeast Asia, to Australia or North America. Hong Kong was a transit camp of the Chinese diaspora, a city of sojourners, economic migrants and refugees, and not a place to develop sentimental ties.[2]

As Douglas Kerr points out in 'Louise Ho and the Local Turn: The Place of English Poetry in Hong Kong', many of the Hong Kong poets write about an 'identity out of difference', a difference 'from *both* the colonial *and* the national culture that in turn differentiates Hong Kong from most other examples of postcolonial identity formation'.

In Howard Choy's discussion of Hong Kong films, Choy remarked that Hong Kong people are caught between the 'dual nationality of overseas British and Chinese nationals' and that the city itself is a 'heterotopia' of sorts, marked by its otherness of space.[3] Choy acknowledges about the geopolitical marginality and cultural hybridity of Hong Kong. Tu Wei-ming, in his book *The Living Tree*, explores the cultural and spiritual beliefs shared across a diasporic space and argues that Hong Kong is, 'at least in spirit, part of the Chinese diaspora'.[4]

Ha Jin pronounced that he could sense a freedom in using the foreign language which he had never felt in his native tongue: 'I had written a few poems in Chinese, but I wasn't happy with them. The Chinese language is very literary and highbrow and detached from the spoken word. It doesn't have the flexibility that English has. So I slowly began to squeeze the Chinese literary mentality out of my mind.'[5]

Leung Ping-kwan: Writing from a multicultural locality

Leung Ping-kwan (1949–2013), one of the best-known Hong Kong poets, wrote mainly in the Chinese language (Traditional Chinese) under the pen name 'Ye Si 也斯'. Because of the complex status of Cantonese, which is spoken but rarely written, he sees the role of a poet in Hong Kong to be 'distanced from all that grandiose and heroic voice'.[6] In other words, Leung feels no need to make his Chinese 'standard' or to 'represent' Hong Kong. Born in Guangdong in 1949 but grew up in Hong Kong, Leung is the author of many collections including bilingual editions such as *City at the End of Time* (1992), *Foodscape* (1997), *Clothink* (1998), *Travelling with a Bitter Melon* (2002), *Shifting Borders* (2009), *Amblings* (2010) and *Fly Heads and Bird Claws* (2012), which were published in Hong Kong. His publications included different genres such as poems, essays, short stories, novels, as well as translation, literary and cultural criticism.[7] As Elaine Ho pointed out in 'Remembrance' published in *Asian Cha*, Leung 'played a major role in introducing an entire generation the French *nouveau roman*, Latin American magic realist fiction and American underground literature', which showed his experience with the multicultural and diasporic spaces as a poet.[8]

This openness was an expression of the curiosity he had about the world – the world he lived in, he travelled to, he read about. This curiosity developed texture and density as it led him to probe the details of everyday living and find in them unexpected provocations to thought. Nothing seems too trivial or too local as subject matter. He longs to 'read the world from the perspective of simple objects, rather than from the viewpoint of monuments or heroes; I want my poems about things to be a dialogue with the world, to learn and be inspired by the shapes, smells and colours of things.'[9] Through his portrayal of the local food, history, streetscape and culture, we derive a Hong Kong identity that is marked by a sense of the local, a sense of being Chinese culturally and the feeling of being in a cosmopolitan place. For example, in 'Ode to a Bittermelon' (1988), food becomes an important motif in appreciating the uniqueness of home:

> The loudest song's not necessarily passionate;
> the bitterest pain stays in the heart.
> Is it because you've seen lots of false sunlight,
> too much thunder and lightning, hurt and hurting,
> too many indifferent and temperamental days?
> Your silence is much to be admired;
> you keep the bitter taste to yourself.[10]

Unusual-looking and bitter in taste, bitter melon is unique to Chinese food cuisine. Here, 'the bitterest pain' seems to be more than just about the taste of the melon.[11]

In Rey Chow's essay on Leung Ping-kwan's work, she highlighted the food connections across his poems, tracing the importance of food motifs in his writing *Foodscape* (食事地誌) where poem titles refer to many of the local dishes and ingredients found in Hong Kong, such as the Hakka stew in '*Pun Choi* on New Year's Eve (除夕盤菜)', 'Salted Shrimp Paste (鹹蝦醬)', 'Soup with Dried Chinese Cabbage (菜乾湯)'.[12] Combining the lyrical and the narrative, Leung's poetry celebrates both local and transnational culture. A widely travelled writer, Leung also alludes to an inclusive global culture where cultures meet, while at the same time demonstrates his historical consciousness. For example, in 'At Hotel Bela Vista', he mentions the African Chicken, a famous main course in Portugal cuisine, alluding to the influence of Portugal culture on Macau as a former Portuguese colony.

In an interview with *La Revue des Ressources*, Leung mentioned how his sociopolitical awareness has informed his poems:

> Cultural encounters could be very rewarding, but sometimes the encounters could also be mixed with political or economical forces, and sometimes the two cultures do not encounter on equal footing. People could enrich oneself through cultural excounters, but sometimes they worried of losing themselves, and justifiable to think so too.[13]

Other than the appeal to the sensory in these food poems, I argue that Leung captures a sense of the Hong Kong people's distinct in-between identity within the Chinese diaspora and experience of space and their multiple or even divided sense of belongings. In his early poem 'Cityscape' translated by Brian Holton, the speaker in the poem is – strangely – masked:

> The city is always the colour of neon
> Secret messages hidden there
> The pity is only, you're wearing a mask

Written in response to the poet's own travel photo, it shows Tsang Chou-choi, the late Hong Kong street artist's style of graffiti on the wall, while the window reveals a cityscape.[14] The poem ends with the lines 'Yesterday and us, we've come face to face/But however we try, we can never recall today'.

Therefore, when we arrive at Leung's famous poem 'Mussels from Brussels', we can appreciate the poet's understanding about home, as he reflects on his dinner with a Chinese film director.[15]

> And yet in the universe
> There are different kinds of mussels, always will be […]

[...] Chinese mussels strayed from home,
thousands of miles away, will still taste of
the ponds and lakes that bred them. All mussels have their own history
There isn't a mussel thoroughly metaphysical.[16]

As Elaine Ho pointed out, Leung was well known for his comments on the complexity to show the divide between 'Chinese literature' and 'Hong Kong literature':

> [H]ow Hong Kong Chinese literature had been marginalised, both by mainland Chinese writers and scholars who could only see it as peripheral and by western readers who could not see 'China' beyond the mainland. But the pressures of authenticity and identity did not disorient or compress him so that he became exclusionary or provincial. From first to last, he remained open to literatures from different places and in different languages.[17]

The early pioneers: Louise Ho and Agnes Lam

On the one hand, many poets in Hong Kong write in Chinese and were translated into English by local or overseas translators. At the same time, the 1990s saw the publication of some of the pioneering, first-generation Anglophone poets of Chinese ethnicity, for example, Louise Ho, Shirley Lim and Agnes Lam. Although many of these poets have lived in Hong Kong for most of their lives, their works betray a continued contesting definition of 'home' and identity of the Hong Kong writer. For example, Louise Ho, a pre-eminent Hong Kong-born poet, often explores in her work the unstable identity of Hong Kong people: that they are inhabitants of the East and of the West, feeling belonged to both worlds and yet constantly displaced. Born in Hong Kong and having lived in French-speaking Mauritius and in Hong Kong where she taught at the Chinese University of Hong Kong, Louise Ho is one of the early pioneers of Hong Kong poetry in English. In her widely anthologized poem 'Home to Hong Kong', she articulates the possibility to arrive at a sense of belonging even when away from one's home or one's own community, making connections with people from other nationalities:

A Chinese
        Invited an Irishman To a Japanese meal
By the Spanish Steps
        In the middle of Rome
Having come from Boston
On the way home.

In the poem, while 'home' will be arrived at as a destination, the speaker feels a sense of belonging even when travelling abroad, meeting an Irishman, situated between places. Imagistic and often full of irony, Ho's work examines the fluidity of social space in Hong Kong, a place steeped in its tapestry of history and colonial memories. The sense of geography – particularly the foreigners' presence in Hong Kong – reflects Hong Kong as a place of diverse cultures and cultural encounters while the enjambement suggests the split identity or narrative of Hong Kong.

A well-known pioneer of Anglophone poetry in Hong Kong and author of several collections inspired by Hong Kong and its relationship with other places and cultures, Agnes Lam also reflects on this cosmopolitanism of place in her poetry. Born and brought up in Hong Kong, Agnes Lam left home at nineteen to study in Singapore, before going to the United States to study for her PhD in linguistics. Later, she spent six years teaching in Singapore before returning to Hong Kong. Many of her poems are intimate portraits of the local people working and living across different social spheres and classes, and explore Hong Kong in historical and social transition.

In 'Apology', written in 1998, the speaker recollects her visit to teach in Beijing, where her counterpart – a local Mainland academic – apologizes for offering only a modest conditions of the accommodation: 'We came to your guest house/and you expressed regret/about my room condition.' While she appreciates her Mainland friend's concern, the speaker establishes a sense of affinity by suggesting:

> But there is no need
> to apologize, my friend.
> I too am Chinese.
> This too is my country.
>
> If you must apologize,
> Then should I?[18]

Through seemingly simple, pare down language, the poet articulates the difficult, conflicting feelings of a Hong Konger towards Mainland citizens (often referred to as 'tung bao' in Cantonese or 'tong bao' (同胞) in Mandarin). The speaker then foresees her need to apologize for her class privilege and position as a Hong Konger ('for my navy Ferragamo shoes') and most of all, she questions herself about her entitlement to – vis-à-vis her Mainland counterpart – freedom of choice as a scholar: 'Freedom of choice to cross academic borders, travel intellectual distances?' The poem ends with an unsettling metaphor:

Moving back
Thirty years, when
leeches were sucking your
Blood as you were
bending to plant grain,
I was feeding in Hong Kong
On the harvest from China.[19]

A Hong Kong reader will likely be familiar to the local historiography, which includes a history of stereotypes of Mainlanders and their 'crude, laughable mainland Chinese practices'.[20]

Lam's 'The rape of a nation' describes one's experience of revisiting the historical past through watching a film on a violated nation. In the poem, the trauma of soldiers 'burning, raping, killing/in a land not their own' is relived. The speaker betrays a sense of passivity in that 'nothing was done to me':

I was doing nothing.
Nothing was done to me.
But I felt the desperation of both
The penetrators and the victims.[21]

Written on 22 June 1997 (dated by the author), however, in a critical transition moment of Hong Kong between the end of the colonial era and Hong Kong's return to China (1st July 1997), the poem seems to suggest a more complex reflection on nationhood, identity and collective anxiety.[22] The anxiety can be gleaned from the ending of the poem in which many questions appear unanswered, stemming from the images of violence:

Was it from another time?
Another space?
was it just television?
Or a hallucination? A prophecy?
A fragment of collective memory?[23]

The questions at the end of the poem seem to refer both to the history of foreign aggression against the nation, and suggest the collective anxiety towards the return of Hong Kong to China after centuries of British colonial rule.

Eddie Tay: Moving between languages

In many ways, Eddie Tay demonstrates his identity as a multicultural poet in the Chinese diaspora. Born and grew up in Singapore, Eddie Tay moved to Hong Kong in 2004, and is now Associate Professor at the English Department of the Chinese University in Hong Kong, where he teaches creative writing and poetry. His poetry crystallizes personal and collective memories, the struggles and triumphs of the working class. His first poetry collection, *remnants*, consists of renditions of mythic and colonial history of Malaya as well as a homage to the Tang Dynasty poets Li Bai, Du Fu and Li He. His second volume, *A Lover's Soliloquy* (2005), extends his interests in Tang Dynasty poetry through renditions of the erotic poetry of Li Shang-yin. His third collection, *The Mental Life of Cities*, won the 2012 Singapore Literature Prize. In it, he experiments with bilingual (English-Chinese) poetry to articulate one's dwelling in multiple languages (Cantonese, Mandarin and English) and a hybrid representation of home.

Tay's first home language is Hokkien, the language spoken in Taiwan as well as in the Fujian province of China. He is also a fluent speaker of Mandarin and English as well as knowing some Cantonese.[24] Tay's experience helps us appreciate the complexity of the Anglophone Chinese poet, as there is often a spectrum of cultural and linguistic relationality. In 'A Second Language', the speaker articulates an ambivalent position, an in-betweenness about his ethnic roots:

> I have never read proverbs on bamboo
> never felt the flourish of my name
> in Chinese characters with the grip
> and stroke of a brush. No calligraphy records on my geneaolgy.[25]

In discussing Tay's poetry that often alludes to the complexity of language or languages, it is very helpful to bear in mind what Rey Chow in *Not Like a Native Speaker* calls the Hong Kong community's engagement with the Chinese language, a 'monolingualization for purpose of nationalism', in which 'writing and sound (or, more precisely, a select set of sounds) are made to correspond as though they were a real unity, as though they were one'. While most native Hong Kong people speak the Cantonese dialect, Cantonese remains a spoken dialect, while the written Chinese language will adhere more to a standardized form.

> Well before her entry into English, therefore, the Hong Kong school-child must learn to negotiate between her native tongue and a naturalized, because officialized, Chinese language that is alien in vocabulary, sound, syntax, and idiom. The simple act of learning to write in Chinese – the supposedly native or

indigenous language – means, for this child, de facto suppressing or switching off an intimate oral and aural code the way things are said and heard in the medium of her primary speech – so as to conform to the correct, because standardized, manner of modern Chinese writing (based on Mandarin/Putonghua speakers' oral and aural code). Given this necessity of transcoding already actively in play in the linguistically plural terrain of the native culture, one can surmise the compound, if ever inarticulate, nature of interference involved in the child's languaging experience once she crosses the next symbolic threshold into the colonial school system and begins acquiring English.[26]

Living and working in this linguistically as well as culturally hybrid environment, there is – inevitably – a sense of one's otherness and the obliteration of the 'native' or the authentic, as one continues to search for or claim an anchoring language. In Tay's 'My Thought Fox' in *The Mental Life of the Cities* (2010), he offers a portrait of himself as becoming the Hong Kong school child, looking and learning the same Chinese words that his son is learning:

In this shoebox of an apartment
I look at the characters with *pinyin*
pasted on the door

口,手,鼻,眼,腳,耳。(mouth, hand, nose, eye, foot, ear)

It is eleven degrees Celsius,
a Hong Kong winter,
and I am a snail in its shell.[27]

[…]

I google Ted Hughes,
Scan his line online for inspiration,
And read the latest on Obama.

My thought fox will not arrive.

I check my e-mail.

I hear cooing and sighing
my baby is awake.[28]

In the poem, the speaker – as a father, a writer, a Hong Konger – articulates the parallel worlds of physical and virtual space he shifts uneasily between. Dwelling in his own home like 'a snail in its shell' he is observing and participating in the world as a global citizen. On the one hand, home is where his family responsibilities are located ('I hear cooing and sighing/my baby is awake'); on the other, he is a poetic citizen across the digital space, looking for inspiration from Ted Hughes's work online.

Divided into sections and accompanied with the poet's street photography work, Tay's fourth collection, *Dreaming Cities*, explores the artist's musings on urban life in his home cities. Published in 2016, the book dwells on language, human geography and hybridity, and especially his sense of (un)belongings against the urban backdrops of Hong Kong and Singapore. While the poet has divided up the narratives on Hong Kong and Singapore into different sections in the book, in poems such as 'stations of the cross', the speaker compares highlighting the sojourner's idea of home as a matter of personal circumstance and choice:

> And shall I ask the skin paper stone
> of a question
>
> is the light better in hong kong
> when I think
>
> is the airport shinier in Singapore
> with me priced as a passenger
>
> When will I go home

The speaker is shocked at being viewed as just another passenger as he moves from one home to another. The rhetorical questions are ironic, as these criteria are hardly valid factors in deciding where to stay. In the collection, home – in the form of urban space – is constantly re-imagined. In 'groundwork', the metaphors 'power in granite' and 'thick sulphur of this city' suggest tension in the society:

> There is power in granite
> Not of your choice,
> earth-deposits of a history of money.
>
> We imagine ourselves to be trees
> In the thick sulphur of this city
> where no one needs to speak.
>
> Maybe you're waiting to tell a story
> Of an underground government
> Of broken bodies.[29]

With deep irony, the speaker reveals that the power in granite is 'not of your choice', comparing people to trees that breathe in sulphurous air and the unnatural sense of silence ('no one needs to speak') in the society. Despite the suppression and metaphorical language, however, the speaker expresses a longing for a language or to break from this 'waiting', to account for the trauma of the 'broken bodies'.

Shirley Lim: Crossing Malaysia, Hong Kong and the United States

Born in in Malacca in 1944 to Malay and Chinese parents, Shirley Geok-lin Lim was raised by her Chinese father in colonial Malacca and attended missionary schools. She wrote poetry in the English language, and later read English at the University of Malaya: experience which, as Neil Khor pointed out, shaped the poet's poetic vision.[30]

From Lim's work and life journeys, we can see that a diasporic poet's sense of community can be multiple and not necessarily tied down to her birthplace. Lim earned her BA from the University of Malaya and her PhD from Brandeis University. She has lived in various places including Malaysia, Hong Kong, Singapore and California. A leading scholar in Asian-American literature, Lim also writes and publishes poetry. She is the author of ten collections. For the purpose of this book, I would like to highlight her contribution to the representation of home and identity in Anglophone Hong Kong poetry as a sojourner poet in Hong Kong, drawing particularly from her diverse range of work, namely poems from *Walking Backwards, Do You Live In* and *Embracing the Angel*.[31]

A writer and research professor from the University of California, Santa Barbara, Lim worked in Hong Kong for a number of years, from 1999 to 2001, when she became the Chair of the Department of English at the University of Hong Kong, and later for various lengths of time as Visiting Professor at other Hong Kong universities, including Baptist University, Polytechnic University and City University of Hong Kong. Students from her creative writing courses published the University of Hong Kong's own creative writing journal, *Yuan Yang*, and City University of Hong Kong's *Halfway Home*. Published in 2010, *Walking Backwards* can best illustrate her pondering over her identity as a sojourner living and working in Hong Kong at the turn of the millennia. For example, in her poem, 'Passport', the speaker conveys her own ambivalence of being half-Chinese or Asian, being raised by her Chinese father:

> I am walking backwards into China
> Where everyone looks like me
> And no one is astonished by my passport
> Declares I am foreign, only
> Envious at my good luck.

Confessing her inability to converse in the local dialect(s) ('Without a tongue of China'), she is reminded of separation from her grandparents, as she imagines that the locals surrounding her to be her family: 'On Causeway Bay, ten thousand/ cousins walk beside me, a hundred thousand brothers and sisters.')[32] At the same time, the line '[a]nd no one is astonished by my passport/Declares I am foreign, only/Envious at my good luck'. Hence, the speaker alludes to the possibility that she can be both the exiled foreigner and the local at the same time, who looks the same but is not the same as the locals, made different because of her passport.

In 'The Source', Lim portrays the China she experiences as 'the source that I have not studied'. Playing on a mother-and-child relationship, the speaker goes on to convey: 'China was the milk that was too heavy/that made one gag. Vomit. Like the scent/Of stinky tofu.' In the second half of the poem, she portrays China as a 'great lump/Of decay where no one is happy' while she wonders 'Was China in Malacca, a misfit, dumb/Country; and I its misfit child,/Bastard and deaf, handicapped and wild.'[33] Combining the use of stark humour with Chinese food stereotypes, Lim exposes feelings of disillusionment and unbelonging of a child unable to appreciate the 'source' of her sense of place.

In *Do You Live In?* published in 2015 – a year after the 2014 protests in Hong Kong – Lim examines the relationship between the society and the government, as well as the social movement led by the new generation that is changing Hong Kong. Lim worked in Hong Kong as a Distinguished Visiting Professor in the English Department at the City University of Hong Kong, witnessed Hong Kong's Umbrella Movement organized by local secondary and university students, which lasted from 26 September to 15 December 2014.

In 'Our People's Wish', a poem that draws on Wendy Cope's identity poem 'Lonely Hearts', Lim mocks the foreigner's naive question for the Hong Kongers: 'Do you live in Hong Kong? Is it you?'[34] The poet asks a difficult rhetorical question, whether there can be a political leader who is satisfactory to the PRC government and yet be able to make the people's wishes come true: 'Can someone make the people's wish come true?/A democrat the PRC can love./Do you live in Central? Is it you?'[35] Throughout the poem, the speaker asks in an ironic tone, looking for a certain 'you' who could lead Hong Kong out of political turmoil. The poem conveys despair at the prospect that such a candidate cannot exist, as the speaker witnesses how 'this dream now pursues the dragon now, with tear gas, plastic cuffs'.[36] The poem ends with the questions deliberately unanswered.

In 'The Children's Movement', the speaker highlights the social a consequence of the older generation's expectation of obedience:

> [… } In all your years
> you've obeyed father and mother,
> pushing your questions down, each day
> deeper, into the dungeon of your making.
> Each year has brought you new sweets,
> Gifted for your tray full of past years'
> treats, many untasted […][37]

The speaker laments that the older generation's expectations have led to the mind's dungeon full of 'questions' and that these questions 'have crouched like rats growing larger,/Fiercer the longer unfed'. At the end of the poem, the speaker has an epiphany in which he or she arrives at the paradoxical allegiance that 'love is disobedience, disobedience love,/and the dungeon doors open for you/and your questions to walk through'. The poem captures one's hunger for answers and the resurrection of questions that have been hidden from view in the dungeon for too long.

Evocative, honest and thought-provoking, Lim's poetry offers a nuanced yet politically engaged perspective of an immigrant and global citizen, as she asks poignant questions about identity, society and gender.

Nicholas Wong: A poetics of desires

Born and grew up in Hong Kong, and now a senior lecturer in creative writing at the Education University of Hong Kong, Nicholas Wong's poetry explores the idea of sexual desires, language and colonialism. Published in 2015, Wong became the first Asian poet to receive the Lambda Literary Award for his debut collection *Crevasse*, which interrogates the in-betweenness of the self located in the local culture of Hong Kong and the desire for the West. The collection is prefaced with an epigraph from Maurice Merleau-Ponty, a French phenomenological philosopher who notes the impossibility of observing one's own physical body and, therefore, the necessity of a 'second' or 'unobservable' body from which to view one's own. Bearing this metaphysical enquiry in mind, I see the 'body' central to Wong's collection as a place for one's sexual as well as political longing.

In Wong's second collection, *Besiege Me*, published by Noemi Press in 2021 and a finalist for the Lambda Literary Award 2022, language becomes a way to embrace as well as to evade the political, and the meaning of words cannot be taken for granted.[38] Through irony, subterfuge and experimental forms, the reader is drawn into the speaker's consciousness and experience of a lonely and dystopian world, where one craves for authenticity and intimacy. For example, in 'Children of China' – a surreal prose poem – oppression is compared to a baby's helpless dependence on the mother: 'We wake, forced to taste/your colostrum.' Here the speaker expresses his dislike for the 'aimlessly loud & lewd' character of the nation, which is filled with greed and ruthlessness: 'That is to say, *more is orgasmic.*' Throughout the poem someone – anonymous yet obvious – denies the speaker's thoughts: '*It isn't funny,* you said, *because funny only applies to things I admit have happened.*'

Irony is at the heart of *Besiege Me*. In 'Advice from a Pro-Beijing Lobbyist', Cantonese exclamations mix with Hong Kong-style English offering advice on how one can behave and align with party thinking.

> See? There's freedom. It's ok ga to like Americans
> like SpongeBob, so long as you can find ways to caulk
> the sky until the city furls in its discipline, dry from serrated
> democrats and the shape of floods gum loh.

By conjuring a body of parts, Wong alludes to the oxymoronic nature of the nation-state where there are 'more foot masseuses than feet. More eye surgeons than witnesses'.[39] Through this clever merging of different dialects and languages, Wong explores parallel historical narratives and exposes how language dictates the hierarchy and structure of power. In his Lambda interview, Wong reveals the impetus for his book:

> Since then, a lot has happened in Hong Kong [...] and in Taiwan (legalization of same-sex marriage in 2019). On a personal level, my parents and Bradley (my son-like corgi, who passed around the same time last year) have been showing obvious signs of aging. *Besiege Me* was born out of all these, a form of sadistic gagging.[40]

Figure 17 Hong Kong street scene during November 2019 with the word 'Hongkonger' painted onto the public infrastructure.

Some poems with the same titles such as 'Dark adaptation' and 'Work (interrupted)' appear in different versions throughout the collection, capturing a sense of mystery and threat. In one 'Dark Adaptation', alluding to a future in 2052, we are introduced to a strangely didactic poem in the form a sinister game of 'fill in the blanks', with politically nuanced omissions for the reader to complete:

This is how it was in the beginning: some eggs knew
what to do with _____ if _____ did not break them.

It was always a battle between the __
& the ____ that kept rising behind the door.

By drawing our attention to the formation and encryption of a text, Wong depicts writing and reading as highly political acts, thereby revealing the power of poetry as testimony. In an interview with Sarah Howe, Wong reveals cites Asian-American and avant-garde American poetry as his major influences: 'my teachers were Americans and my reading list was totally American. These days I'm actually more drawn to Asian-American poets. There's Solmaz Sharif. That book, *Look*, is amazing.[41] Wong's poem such as the above demonstrates his keenness to push boundaries with form and voice that resonates with the work by American poets such as Sharif.

The final poem, 'Apologia of the Besieged City', features an unnamed, abusive lover who scorns the needy 'blind puppies' that cling to him (or her) for love and intimacy. These puppies can be understood as allegories for a frightened citizenry:

Imagine the vibe in bed. Imagine how hard
it is for me to love them back. They're blind puppies
when we fuck. They wriggle around to find
an available nipple to nurse.

The speaker understands that these puppies have no other way to gain independence, for they are vulnerable and must always cling on to the motherland.

Surreal and bold in its myth-making and the representation of place as a merging site between fiction and reality, this collection offers us fresh understanding about the metaphorical potential of innovative poetry, where power conflicts and personal suffering can be portrayed via deeply political, disguised truths.

Tammy Ho: Poetry as activism

Born and grew up in Hong Kong, Tammy Ho is known for her poetry that engages with multilingualism, displacement and political activism. She is the founding editor of the popular online *Cha: An Asian Literary* Journal and a co-editor of the academic journal *Hong Kong Studies*. Ho has a PhD in English from King's College London, and is now Associate Professor at Hong Kong Baptist

University. Her first poetry collection, *Hula Hooping* (Chameleon Press, 2015) – winner of the Young Artist Award in Literary Arts from the Hong Kong Arts Development Council – explores family love, womanhood and the working class in Hong Kong. In this chapter, I will focus on her second poetry collection *Too Too Too Too* (2018) and her recent poems that mark her shift as an activist poet, especially her work that revolves around the conflicting meaning of home in Hong Kong.

In her interview with The Leeds Centre for New Chinese Writing, Ho reflects on her conviction about the role of the writer in engaging with current topical issues:

> When I do write poetry, I mainly focus on social, political and topical issues. I also think that there are subjects that cannot wait. They need to be written down and read *now*. Writing may not be able to effect much (immediate) change, but it is at least *something*. And in some cases, writing is an act of defiance, resistance, protest.[42]

Published by the leading Singapore-based publisher Books Actually in 2018, Ho's collection, *Too Too Too Too*, interrogates the value of truth, conscience and the role of history. Responding to the urgent, topical issues of the time – from the political tensions during the Occupy Central movement in 2014 to the subsequent witnessing of the Umbrella Movement – some of Ho's poems reflect the changing political climate and the ineradicable nature of collective memories. Through the use of the surreal, Ho deliberately unsettles the reader by rereading or representing Hong Kong as a home as well as a site of displacement. First published in September 2016, 'Beijing Standard Time' starts with a line from Louis MacNeice's *Autumn Journal* as an epigraph: '[w]here the waters of life are free of the ice-blockade of hunger/And thought is as free as the sun', while the first stanza begins with a direct question about one's authority in delineating time:

> Do you own the sun?
> Perhaps you do – you do dictate time.[43]
> Everywhere across this vast land,
> Your time is *the* time.

Opting for the pronoun 'you', the poem takes on an ironic tone, and draws our attention to the relationship between 'you' and the speaker. The policy of adopting a single time zone across China to enhance national unity is reflected here as a surreal experience of displacement, where the people in Xinjiang – which the poet calls 'China's westernmost province' – will need to adopt the same time zone as Beijing, even if it is a land situated far away from the nation's capital. The poem ends with the following irony about the shift of 'blame':

> Can you blame them? Following
> nature's laws is only natural.
> And besides, the day is long,
> And the emperor is already asleep.[44]

The speaker articulates the local communities' inability to adjust to the single time zone when the people in Beijing would be literally asleep by the time it is morning in Xinjiang.[45] The poem also reveals the instability of place in the Chinese diaspora: that the everyday experience differs across regions.

In 'We Are What We Are Made Of', a poetic response to the creation of the Lennon Wall in Hong Kong during the protests in 2014, the poet notes the paradox of people's 'beginning' that starts from yesterday, when the Lennon Wall appeared, changing the city's landscape: 'Beginning from yesterday/walls are covered in squared colours,/street names changed.' [46]

> Beginning
> from June 2019, people
> in a city look at each other:
> million faces, million thoughts,
> united in water, practice, slogans.
> Beginning from now,
> there is no turning back, no stopping.

The poem alludes to the 2019 protests in Hong Kong amidst the debates on the amendments of the extradition bill.[47] By suggesting that the 'people/in the city look at each other', the poet highlights the collective nature of unease and realization of change, while the imagery of walls covered by 'squared colours' (colourful sticky notes) and 'puffs of smoke' (teargas) that signals the beginning of conflicts, and the necessity for the poet to reflect on the current, topical issue using a metaphorical language. The phrase 'united in water, practice, slogans' alludes to the protest slogan 'be water' – originally a quote from Bruce Lee – which signifies that 'the protesters' actions should be adaptable, tactical, fast and spontaneous – the way water flows through cracks in a structure'.[48]

At the end of the poem, the speaker draws our attention to the determination and enigmatic identity of the 'we':

We are what we are made of:
desperation and unbeatable will.
This is the beginning of the open
secret that we don't ever quit.

Again, as with some of Ho's more recent poems, there is a continued sense of engagement with 'we', and the allusion to 'desperation and unbeatable will' also captures conflict and resistance. As we discuss in the chapter, compared with Nicholas Wong's political poetry, Ho's poems are much more activist and direct.

In 'Two zero four seven', the poet draws from W. H. Auden's 'Stop All the Clocks' in articulating the contradictory experience of local time in Hong Kong:

Stop all the clocks, hong kong people,
That which we hold dear about this city

Is likely to end in 2047.

The title 'Two zero four seven' alludes to the fifty years of 'One Country Two Systems' in Hong Kong. The deliberate caesura seems to point out the abrupt change to what we 'hold dear about this city'.

Again, in Ho's poem, language becomes contentious matter:

Let 2047 be displayed
On tall buildings and spoken of often,

Before our shared euphemism
becomes another censored year.[49]

Ho's the need to 'speak' articulates a sense of liminality unique to Hong Kong as a place, as it is neither here nor there, not a city nor a country:

Getting back to the question 'Can we say Hong Kong *literature?*' it might be useful to look at Hong Kong literature as something more than texts written by Hong Kong writers or with Hong Kong flavour. But it has to be acknowledged that in the larger political and cultural context, merely talking about Hong Kong culture and literature could be challenging, as the city's identity is often elided, pushed as it is to the Chinese periphery.[50]

A passionate advocate of Hong Kong literature, Ho has set up Hong Kong's English-language *Asian Cha* journal to showcase Hong Kong writers. Along with Michael O'Sullivan, Eddie Tay and Michael Tsang, she launched a peer-reviewed bilingual journal *Hong Kong Studies* in 2018, highlighting original, intersectional and cross-disciplinary research on Hong Kong affairs from multiple fields in the humanities and the social sciences.[51]

Ho's list poem 'How the narratives of Hong Kong are written with China in sight' interrogates the idea of 'truth' in Hong Kong. The first few statements are deeply sarcastic, playing on the abstract political phrase of 'One Country Two Systems' that is supposed to be the bedrock of postcolonial Hong Kong, and the incredulity of propaganda against the West:

1. Call me One Country. Two Systems.
2. It is a truth universally acknowledged that democracy fighters in Hong Kong must be genomically modified by the West.[52]

Later in the poem, the speaker incorporates various quotes from the works by Dickens, Beckett and Nabokov, etc., to mock at the curious, complicated relationship between Hong Kong and China: 'Happy cities are all alike; every unhappy city is unhappy in its own way. Hong Kong is unhappy because it wants happiness too much.' Some of the statements are more subtle or slanted allusions: although a reference to the first line of Toni Morrison's *Beloved*, '689 is spiteful' actually refers to Chun-ying Leung, the former Chief Executive of Hong Kong, elected to the post with 689 votes.[53] In borrowing the literary language from the West to talk about the changes in Hong Kong, Ho has created an oblique language that is playful, experimental and necessary, exploring the silences and taboos around the postcoloniality of the city.

Antony Huen: Identity politics through ekphrasis and multilingual poetry

A poet, critic and lecturer, Huen is also widely published in literary journals in the UK and in Hong Kong. A PhD graduate from the University of York and now a research academic at the Metropolitan University of Hong Kong, his poems have appeared on *Ink, Sweat & Tears*, *The Oxonian Review*, *Wasafiri*, and *Hong Kong Review of Books*.

One of Huen's key strengths is the playful interrogation or engagement with language(s). In 'Cantonese Proverbs' published in *amberflora*, for example, he explored with humour and precision the fertile meanings between languages:[54]

In the island city, you're a double-
headed snake, with the dark face towards me.

Checking you out, I drop my bucket
of crabs, as if I ran into a ghost.
[...]
You're removing the plank you've used
to reach the mainland.[55]

Cryptic and amusing, the phrases and lines are translated from the Chinese proverbs familiar to the Cantonese-speaking community. 'Dropping a bucket of crabs (倒瀉籮蟹)' means the chaos resulting from rushing things through, while 'removing the plank you've used/to reach the mainland' is a carefully constructed sentence building on the phrase 'removing the planks'(過橋抽板), but the speaker adds his own interpretation of the proverb to make fun of one's disconnect from the 'Mainland'.[56] By deliberately translating the proverbs very literally, Huen displaces both the native speaker and the foreigner, creating a hybrid language or space where both of them become outsiders.[57] While the very visual images are seemingly disconnected from each other, the act of translating one's thoughts into Cantonese can be read as an act of resistance, a carving out of a 'safe' refuge or language for the self, and to allow one's thoughts to remain eclipsed, and which cannot be easily decoded by the Mandarin-speaking community.

Writing in response to the images of the Chinese University of Hong Kong, 'In the Woods', Huen's commissioned poem for the Singapore-Hong Kong Digital Travel Bubble project hosted by Sing Lit Station offers a glimpse of the idyllic university campus ('lamp posts are half-covered in moss,/Birds are only seen in the signs'), except for the hint of the speaker's sentiments hinted in the first couplet: 'there's no sign of the white smoke/hanging over the rest of my city' reveals what the speaker is trying to evade.[58]

Jason Eng Hun Lee: displacement and hyphenated identities

Born in the UK, having spent his childhood in Malaysia and now lecturer at the Baptist University of Hong Kong, Jason Eng Lee's debut collection *Beds in the East* (Eyewear 2019) is an ambitious book that interrogates diasporic lives, hyphenated identities and the notion of displacement.

Lee has a keen eye for form and voice. In 'Sons of the Soil', the speaker reflects on the struggles of the indigenous in Malaysia ('their backs breaking / over blood-sapping rubber trees'), and one's legitimacy and sense of citizenship: 'What deeds or earth-born titles have they received, /These *bumipetera* friends of mine?' Derived from the Sanskrit and absorbed into the Malay, the term *bumipetera* refers to 'sons of the earth' and is loaded with political meaning, and brings to mind the inter-ethnic hostilities in Malaysia since the 1970s.[59]

In Lee's poems, personal and collective history are often narratives in parallel. For example, 'School Parade', the poet explores ambivalent feelings and resistance against British colonial rule of Malaysia from the perspectives of a young mixed race person: 'Throughout August we learned of *Merdeka* / how the British were fought and overthrown /by all our patriotic forefathers'. What seems at first a 'celebration' turns into a matter of 'chasing madness', with students 'conspiring to evade /service to school and its oppressive rule'. In '45 Belgrave Square', the visit to the Malaysian High Commission in London ends with the speaker's rights to Malaysia revoked because '[y]ou don't have the right stamp'.[60]

A sense of nostalgia and drama permeates the collection. With a nod to Matthew Arnold's 'Dover Beach', the elegiac poem 'Islands' examines one's connections with the ancestors and the need to belong ('Their arcane faces contort in my mind /and whisper for me to beach myself'), ending with the vision about diasporic existence that demands courage and self-reinvention:

They too will resist the lull of rocks
And rise up from the ocean's womb
Standing on the edge of something new.[61]

In 'Three Lions Pub', conflicted, hyphenated identities are given a political and satirical spin, where the speaker is confronted with racist comments in a pub ('*He ain't Chinese. /He's Malaysian. All look the same to me.*'), as he defends his uneasy identity as a mixed race person, 'a half-baked Englishman'. The football match being screened at the pub offers a loaded subtext about patriotism, competition and class divides, while highlighting the tension between the local and diasporic spaces.[62]

With a confident voice, an attentive use of the narrative form and exuberant poetic language, *Beds in the East* captures the conflicting states of diasporic existence and challenges the reader with unsettling questions about one's racial positioning and allegiances.

Tim Tim Cheng: finding home in eco-poetry

Born and grew up in Hong Kong and having studied MA in creative writing at the University of Edinburgh, Tim Tim Cheng is the author of a forthcoming pamphlet *tapping at glass* from Verve Poetry Press in 2023. Tim Tim Cheng's poetry is known for engaging with the notion of home and place via slanted, politically-engaged allusions and metaphorical, nuanced language. Published in *Berfrois*, 'The Sand I Stand on Is Not My Own' conveys a sense of existence through the metaphor of the coast:

> Graveyards regurgitate bones
> by the shore as vessels bob, spitting curves
> of dirt stolen, smuggled and sold from nations
> to nations for a nation of proud promises
> that break the ones in existence. The sand
> I stand on is not my own but a congregation
> of distances.[63]

Here we are confronted with reminders of death and a feeling of betrayal ('smuggled and sold from nations / to nations for a nation of proud promises') by a nameless nation. The speaker acknowledges her position as an outsider ('The sand/I stand on is not my own'). Through capturing an unfamiliar, surreal landscape in a frozen moment of time, this dense, one-stanza poem portrays a complex and suppressed identity in the midst of instability.

Conclusion

As Jason Polley argues, Hong Kong remains 'a place in translation and transition' and it is precisely this 'very incoherence that binds Hongkongers, the incoherence that establishes the place as actually coherent'.[64]

At the same time, it is important to recognise the highly cosmopolitan, liminal nature of contemporary Hong Kong poetry, with poets ranging from expatriate writers such as Canada-born poets Kate Rogers and Akin Jeje who are non-Chinese yet writing about Hong Kong; to a new generation of young, local 'Hongkonger' poets such as Louise Leung, Felix Chow and Tim Tim Cheng who explore more with local culture, language, topical issues and history.[65] Connected to but distinct from the UK and Hong Kong, the writing community has demonstrated the complexity of writing creatively and publishing in the English (colonial) language, in response to the tidal historical as well as socio-cultural changes of the city before and after the Handover of 1997. From the differing, shifting views between a Hong Konger and a Mainland Chinese person, to the surreal depiction of the dependent, suckling babies of China, Anglophone Hong Kong poets articulate their ambivalent sense of belonging, as they interrogate the coherence of their location and identity.

Notes

1   Eddie Tay, *Colony, Nation and Globalisation: Not At Home in Singapore* (Hong Kong and Singapore: NUS Press and Hong Kong University Press, 2011).

2   Louie Kam, 'Louise Ho and the Local Turn: The Place of English Poetry in Hong Kong', in *Hong Kong Culture: Word and Image* (Hong Kong: Hong Kong University Press, 2010), 3.

3   Howard Y. F. Choy, 'Schizophrenic Hong Kong: Postcolonial Identity Crisis in the *Infernal Affairs* Trilogy', *Transtext(e)s Transcultures: Journal of Global Chinese Studies*, 3 (2007), 52–66.

4   Tu Wei-ming, 'Cultural China: The Periphery as the Center', in *The Living Tree: The Changing Meaning of Being Chinese Today*, edited by Tu Wei-ming (Stanford: Stanford University Press, 1994), 13–15, 15.

5   Kenny Ng, 'The Migrant Voice: Writing Diaspora between Sinophone and Anglophone Scripts', *Journal of Modern Literature in Chinese*, 1.14 (2017), 139.

6   Dung Kai-cheung, *The Archaeology of an Imaginary City* (New York: Columbia University Press, 2012), 5.

7   P. K. Leung, 'Behind the Pen', <http://leungpingkwan.com/> [Accessed 9 November 2021].

8   Elaine Ho, 'Leung Ping Kwan', *Asian Cha*, <https://www.asiancha.com/content/view/1434/400/> [Accessed 9 November 2021].

9   Ping-kwan Leung, *Lotus Leaves: Selected Poems of Leung Ping Kwan*, edited and translated by John Minford (Hong Kong: Chinese University Press, 2021).

10 P. K. Leung, *City at the End of Time* (Hong Kong: Hong Kong University Press, 2012), 146. Also, see Ames Siu Yan-ho, 'Colonial Food in Poetry: Hong Kong and Macau in Leung Ping-kwan's Food Poetry', in *Tasting Cultures: Thoughts for Food* (Leiden: Brill, 2015), 27.

11 Rey Chow, 'Leung Ping-kwan: 'Shuqing and Reveries of Space', in *The Oxford Handbook of Modern Literatures*, edited by Carlos Rojas and Andrea Bachner (Oxford: Oxford University Press, 2016), 568–70.

12 Rey Chow, 'Thinking with Food, Writing off Center: Notes on Two Hong Kong Authors', in *Global Chinese Literature: Critical Essays*, edited by Jing Tsu and David Der-wei Wang (Leiden and Boston: Brill, 2010), 134.

13 Régis Poulet, *La Revue des Resources*, 6 November 2016, <https://www.larevuedesressources.org/hong-kong-metaphor-of-the-contemporary-world,619.html> [Accessed 5 March 2020].

14 See P. K. Leung, 'Cityscape', *Hong Kong Memory*, <https://www.hkmemory.hk/MHK/collections/Yasi/all_items/images/201607/t20160705_79562.html> [Accessed 20 November 2021].

15 C. T. Au, *The Hong Kong Modernism of Leung Ping-kwan* (Maryland: Rowan & Littefield, 2019), 107.

16 P. K. Leung, 'Mussels from Brussels', translated by Martha Cheung from *Travelling with a Bitter Melon*, 232–5.

17 Elaine Ho, 'Leung Ping Kwan', *Asian Cha*, 20 (2013), <https://www.asiancha.com/content/view/1434/400/> [Accessed 20 November 2021].

18 Agnes Lam, *A Pond in the Sky: Selected and New Poems* (Macau: ASM, 2013), 102–3.

19 Ibid., 104.

20 Flowerdew John, 'Discriminatory Discourse Directed towards Mainlanders', in *Critical Discourse Analysis in Historiography* (London: Palgrave Macmillan, London, 2012), 219.

21 Lam, *A Pond in the Sky*, 82.

22 Michael Tsang, 'Three Generations of Hong Kong English Poetry: Leung Ping-kwan, Agnes Lam and Jennifer Wong', *Asian Cha*, 2014, <https://www.asiancha.com/content/view/1773/453/> [Accessed 12 July 2021].

23 Lam, *A Pond in the Sky*, 82.

24 Eddie Tay, *Anything You Can Get Away with: Creative Practices* (Singapore: Delere Press, 2016), 33.

25 Eddie Tay, *Mental Life of Cities* (Hong Kong: Chameleon Press), 78.

26 Rey Chow, *Not Like a Native Speaker* (Columbia: Columbia University Press, 2014), 46–7.

27 Tay, *The Mental Life of Cities*, 44–5.

28 Ibid., 54–5.

29 Eddie Tay, *Dreaming Cities* (Singapore: Ethos Books, 2016), 14.

30 Neil Khor, 'Malacca's Straits Chinese Anglophone Poets and Their Experience of Malaysian Nationalism', *Archipel*, 76.1 (2008), 143–4.

31 Shirley Lim, 'Biography', SingLit tation, <http://www.poetry.sg/shirley-geok-lin-lim-bio> [Accessed 5 May 2021].

32 Shirley Lim, *Walking Backwards*, 35.

33 Ibid., 36.

34 Geok-lin Lim, Shirley, *Do You Live In?* (Singapore: Ethos Books, 2015), 82.

35 Ibid.

36 Ibid.

37 *Do You Live In?*, 76–8.

38 Willem Finn Harling, 'May We Present Besiege Me', 12 March 2021, <https://lambdaliterary.org/2021/03/nicholas-wong-besiege-me/> [Accessed 11 January 2022].

39 Nicholas Wong, *Besiege Me* (Noemi Press, 2021), 3.

40 Harling, 'May We Present Besiege Me'.

41 Sarah Howe, 'Sarah Howe in conversation with Nicholas Wong', *Wasafiri*, 32.3, 32–7.

42 Tammy Ho, 'Interview: Tammy Ho Lai-Ming', The Leeds Centre for New Chinese Writing, 2017, <https://writingchinese.leeds.ac.uk/2017/08/01/interview-tammy-ho-lai-ming/> [Accessed 5 May 2021].

43   Tammy Ho, *Too Too Too Too* (Math Paper Press), 54–5.

44   Ibid.

45   'Matt Schiavenza, 'China Only Has One Time Zone – and That's a Problem', *The Atlantic*, 2013, <https://www.theatlantic.com/china/archive/2013/11/china-only-has-one-time-zone-and-thats-a-problem/281136/> [Accessed 5 May 2021].

46   Tammy Ho, 'We Are What We Are Made of', *LA Review of Books,* 2019, <https://blog.lareviewofbooks.org/poetry/moment-everyone-revolution-poems-tammy-ho-lai-ming-hong-kong-crisis/> [Accessed 12 January 2021].

47   Reuters, 'Timeline: Key Dates in Hong Kong's Anti-government Protests', *Reuters News*, 30 May 2020, <https://www.reuters.com/article/us-hongkong-protests-timeline-idUSKBN23608O> [Accessed 7 December 2021].

48   Jeff Hou, Hong Kong's Sticky-note Revolution', *The Conversation*, 2020, <https://www.smithsonianmag.com/travel/hong-kongs-sticky-note-revolution-180974042/> [Accessed 3 March 2021].

49   Ho, *Too Too Too Too*, 57.

50   Tammy Ho, 'Can We Say Hong Kong?', *Asian Review of Books*, 3 February 2017, <https://asianreviewofbooks.com/content/can-we-say-hong-kong/> [Accessed 6 January 2021].

51   For details, refer to *Asian Cha* and *Hong Kong Studies* at <https://www.asiancha.com/wp/> and <http://www.eng.cuhk.edu.hk/HKStudies/> [Accessed 6 January 2021].

52   Ho, *Too Too Too Too*, 66–8.

53   Ibid.

54   Antony Huen, '<https://amberflora.com/issues/issue-10/antony-huen-cantonese-proverbs/> [Accessed 15 March 2022].

55   Ibid.

56   Ibid.

57   See writecantonese8, 'Cantonese Proverbs in One Picture', <https://www.google.com/amp/s/writecantonese8.wordpress.com/2014/02/25/cantonese-proverbs-in-one-picture/amp/> [Accessed 6 January 2022].

58   Antony Huen, 'In the Woods', <http://www.poetry.sg/travelbubble-3>, Poetry.sg [Accessed 12 March 2021].

59   Jason Eng Hun Lee, *Beds in the East* (London: Eyewear, 2019), 35–6.

60   Lee, *Beds in the East*, 26.

61   Lee, *Beds in the East*, 53.

62   Lee, *Beds in the East*, 65.

63   Tim Tim Cheng, 'The Sand I Stand On Is Not My Own', *Berfrois* (2021) [Last accessed 6 November 2022].

64   Jasob Polley, Vinton Poon and Lian-Hee Wee, *Cultural Conflict in Hong Kong: Angles on a Coherent Imaginary* (Singapore: Palgrave Macmillan, 2018), 5.

65   Author of *Out of Place* (Toronto: Aeolus House, 2017), Kate Rogers was born
     and has lived and written in Hong Kong for decades. Author of *Smoked*
     Pearl (Hong Kong: Proverse Press, 2010), Akin Jeje was born to Nigerian
     and Kenyan parents in the US in the early 1970s, having lived and worked in
     diverse locations from Nigeria, the UK, Canada, Hong Kong and the US, whose
     works deal with multiculturalism as well as Hong Kong cosmopolitanism. See
     <https://www.worldliteraturetoday.org/author/kate-rogers> and <https://www.
     proversepublishing.com/authors/jeje_akin> [Accessed 22 September 2022].

Epilogue

In this book, I have chosen to focus on a select range of works by the Anglophone Chinese diaspora poets (except Bei Dao and Leung Ping-Kwan who write in Chinese) to offer a meaningful but by no means exhaustive cross-section of literature to shed light on the rich, burgeoning scene of the Chinese diasporic voices. It is meant to give merit and to map out the different approaches of these writers, and to make an attempt to understand the affinities and differences between the generations. Through understanding or analysing the variety and thematic concerns in their work, I hope to illustrate how the works of these writers are related, as well as continuously shaped by their local cultures, the interconnected history and community – whether they are native in that community or not, or have moved from one home to another. If anything, contextualising their work can help us to ask the relevant question and to challenge ourselves with the shifting concepts of 'diversity', 'race', 'identity' and 'difference', in an increasingly polycentric rather than Eurocentric world.

At the same time, it is evident that the landscape of contemporary poetry where the diasporic poets situate themselves is changing quite rapidly. In the United States, Chinese-Anglophone poets are very active in their literary output as part of the 'Asian-American' community. Race and identity remain salient topics in the works of many Asian-American writers such as Chen Chen, Jane Wong, Franny Choi, Jenny Xie and Sally Wen Mao; there is a growing emphasis on understanding the subjectivity and multiplicity of these voices beyond the immigrant narrative. In the past two decades, the works by the pre-eminent Chinese diasporic poets e.g. Marilyn Chin, Li-Young Lee, Arthur Sze, John Yau, Timothy Liu, Mei-mei Berssenbrugge and Victoria Chang from a crucial part of both the Asian-American and the American literary canon, while their works have been included in major American poetry anthologies including the Norton Anthology of Poetry and the *Best American Poetry* anthologies.[1] Meanwhile, Asian-American anthologies continue to serve as helpful guides to appreciate or discover newer voices. The anthology entitled *Chinese American Voices: From the Gold Rush to the Present* (2006), edited by Judy Yung, Gordon Chang and Him Mark Lai, provides glimpses into the historical contexts of such generations of Chinese immigrants through primary documents and stories by Chinese Americans, from letters, speeches, oral histories, personal memoirs, poems, essays to folksongs.[2] Many of the works by the more established poets are now taught in classrooms. Victoria Chang's deeply moving, formally striking collection, *OBIT* (Copper Canyon Press 2020), which draws from her grief for the loss of her mother and which 'teaches us how to speak grief, a language in which the unsayable and the mundane coexis – a ghostly, yet deeply material syntax' – was shortlisted in the prestigious Griffin Prize award.[3] Arthur Sze – who has written for nearly five decades – won the 2019 National Book Award in Poetry, with his tenth collection, *Sight Lines* (Copper Canyon Press 2019).[4] Quite a number of these writers have enrolled in mentorship programmes such as the Asian American Writers Workshop (AAWW) and the cohorts of Kundiman fellows.

Yet, is the international award culture a fair gauge of the lasting value of these works? In particular, how do readers, judges and critics avoid the temptation of turning more readily to poems with the more recognizable ethnic markers or 'exotic' signifiers, instead of judging their merits in terms of their voice, formal craft, experimentation and poetics?

In the recent years, with the emphasis on 'diversity' and promoting 'under-represented voices' and 'BAME' voices in the UK, initiatives to explore or showcase writing by Chinese diasporic writers have become more evident. These include the Bi'an writers network and the Bi'an writers awards founded by Mary Cooper back in 2018. The inaugural, online Poetics of Home Chinese Diaspora Poetry Festival, funded by Arts Council England (Lottery Fund), was held in October 2021, in which up to thirty poets of Chinese or East Asian heritage read from their work and engaged in discussions with UK-based and Asia-based scholars. Meanwhile, a writers collective called the BESEA poets (British East Asian) collective has been formed by Christy Ku. Moreover, the research-focused British Chinese Studies Network founded by Dr Alex Tickell (Open University) and Dr Lucienne Loh (Liverpool University) organized network events, reading groups and research seminars, and held its first conference in 2021.[5] These activities have all helped to increase one's understanding of Asian poets through more in-depth dialogues.[6] Meanwhile there are also various writers' talks showcasing the works by diasporic writers at universities such as the Leeds Centre for New Chinese Writing, while at the University of St Andrews, Prof. Gregory Lee has introduced a new MA Chinese Studies degree dedicated to the modern and contemporary culture in the Chinese-speaking world and to preserve Hong Kong studies and the city's paraphrenalia in the midst of political uncertainties in Hong Kong.[7] In March 2022, Eric Yip, a Hong Kong-born, nineteen-year-old poet who majors in Economics at Cambridge University, won the National Poetry Competition in the UK and his work now attracted much attention within the country as well as internationally.[8] As mentioned by the competition judge Fiona Benson, 'Fricatives' is a poem that tells of 'an uneasy assimilation, and of government surveillance'.[9] The fact that it received the enthusiastic support from the diasporic community not just in the UK but in Hong Kong (given that it is becoming increasingly difficult to express certain topics freely back home) can indicate greater reception of and interest in the new generation of diasporic voices.

In Hong Kong, writers such as Nicholas Wong have received recognition for their work such as the Lambda Literary awards. As discussed earlier, the UK-educated, Hong Kong-based scholar Antony Huen's award-winning essay has enriched as well as complicated our understanding of the connections between contemporary British poetry and cultural memory.[10] Some younger Hong Kong poets such as Cheng Tim Tim and Wendelin Law have moved to the UK to pursue further studies in creative writing. In Hong Kong, initiatives such as the annual Hong Kong Literary Festival and the international writer in residence scheme at Baptist University of Hong Kong have helped to promote exchange between writing communities in and outside Hong Kong.[11] Funded by the Education University of Hong Kong and led by Nicholas Wong, Writing Plus – an online platform filled with free learning materials designed by local and overseas Hong Kong poets, writers and translators on their own works, together with the dedicated section on contemporary Hong Kong poetry – has blurred the geographical boundary between the poets writing in and outside Asia.[12] Generally, given the current political climate, it remains to be seen as to how the creative writing scene in Hong Kong may change in the coming years.

In his essay, 'The "Old Hong Kong" and "A Gold-Sifting Bird": Hong Kong and Chinese Ekphrasis in Contemporary British Poetry', winner of *Wasafiri*'s inaugural essay prize in 2022, Antony Huen argued that there the Hong Kong School of poets have sought to, through imaginative language and ekphrasis, represent the 'increasingly troubled geopolitical relations between Hong Kong, mainland China, and the UK'.[13]

In the UK and the United States, both major and indie publishers – including pamphlet and chapbook publishers – are also increasingly aware of the range of poets writing across this diasporic community and have sought to publish them. In Oxford, PhD student and writer Jiaqi Kang – together with Lis Chi Siegel, Iris Lang and Michelle Tay – founded a creative magazine focusing on the Sino diaspora called *Sine Theta* (sinθ) in 2016.[14]

In the long run, it is certainly vital to ensure that the interest to publish these diverse diasporic voices among poetry publishers in the UK and the United States represents sustained rather than short-lived efforts, in order to address the needs of the changing readership. While various mentorships and poetry collectives in the UK such as the Ledbury Poetry Critics, Scottish BAME network, Barbican Young Poets and South Bank New Poets Collective, the AAWW and the Kundiman fellowship in the United States are instrumental in giving visibility to writers operating in such community(ies), it is also crucial to encourage the independence and sustainable development or growth of these writers beyond prizes, mentorships and poetry collectives. In the publishing scene, one needs to avoid letting the major publishers rely too heavily on the established structures, networks or hierarchies when deciding who to publish, or publishing the works from these communities being tokenistic in achieving 'diversity'. Meanwhile, recent poetry anthologies such as *To Gather Your Leaving* anthology (Ethos Books 2019) edited by Singaporean Australian writer Boey Kim Cheng, Arin Alycia Fong and Justin Chia which cross-examines and highlights Asian diaspora poetry as a new literary tradition that across America, Australia, the UK and Europe gives more visibility to the literary output arising from the global Asian diaspora regardless of the citizenship of the poets.[15]

At the same time, it is important to recognise the highly cosmopolitan, liminal nature of contemporary Hong Kong poetry, with poets ranging from expatriate writers such as Canada-born poets Kate Rogers and Akin Jeje who are non-Chinese yet writing about Hong Kong; to a new generation of young, local 'Hongkonger' poets (Nicolette Wong, Louise Leung, Felix Chow and Tim Cheng) who explore more with local culture, language, topical issues and history. Connected to but distinct from the UK and Hong Kong, the writing community has demonstrated the complexity of writing creatively and publishing in the English (colonial) language, in response to the tidal historical as well as socio-cultural changes of the city before and after the Handover of 1997.

To a large extent, identity – race, gender, class, sexuality – is a social construct. As leading Malaysian writer Tash Aw articulates in his essay 'Fluidity and Resistance: Ideas of Belonging in a Fractured World', the dilemma of the twenty-first century is to consider the different ways of looking at and accepting multiple identities, and to embrace the pluralities of existence: 'the identities –

racial, cultural, and class – imprinted upon me by birth and upbringing, or the ones I have chosen?'[16] Isn't it more natural and more powerful to 'insist on the difficult pluralities of our existence than to deny them'?[17]

Notes

1   See David Lehman (ed.), *Best American Poetry* (New York: Simon and Schuster, 2021) and Margaret Ferguson, Tim Kendall and Mary Jo Salter (eds), *The Norton Anthology of Poetry* (London and New York: W. W. Norton, 2018).

2   Judy Yung, Gordon Chang and Him Mark Lai (eds), *Chinese American Voices: from the Gold Rush to the Present* (Berkeley and Los Angeles, CA: University of California, 2006).

3   Griffin Prize, *'Language'*, 18 April 2021, <https://www.griffinpoetryprize.com/language-from-obit/> [Accessed 5 March 2020].

4   'Arthur Sze's *Sight Lines* wins 2019 National Book Award in Poetry, Copper Canyon Press, <https://www.coppercanyonpress.org/arthur-szes-sight-lines-wins-2019-national-book-award-in-poetry/.> [Accessed 1 April 2022]

5   British Chinese Studies Network, <https://www.open.ac.uk/arts/research/postcolonial/british-chinese-studies-network> [Accessed 6 March 2022].

6   See Poetics of Home Festival <https://poeticsofhome.co.uk/> and BESEA <https://www.besean.co.uk/esea-heritage-month> [Accessed 5 March 2020].

7   Isabelle Steger, 'Guardians of Hong Kong Culture Spring Up from California to Singapore', *Bloomberg*, 27 January 2022, <https://www.bloomberg.com/news/features/2022-01-27/preserving-hong-kong-media-and-arts-culture-from-abroad> [Accessed 5 March 2020].

8   'Fricatives', Poetry Society, 1 April 2022, <https://poems.poetrysociety.org.uk/poems/fricatives/> [Accessed 5 March 2022].

9   Sarah Shaffi, 'National Poetry Competition Has Its Youngest Ever Winner', *The Guardian*, 1 April 2022, <https://www.theguardian.com/books/2022/mar/31/national-poetry-competition-youngest-ever-winner-eric-yip-fricatives> [Accessed 1 April 2022].

10   Régis Poulet, *La Revue des Resources*, 6 November 2016, <https://www.larevuedesressources.org/hong-kong-metaphor-of-the-contemporary-world,619.html> [Accessed 5 March 2020].

11   Eddie Tay, *Anything You Can Get Away with: Creative Practices* (Singapore: Delere Press, 2018).

12   Yannie Chan, *The Loop*, 15 September 2021, <https://www.theloophk.com/hong-kong-poet-nicholas-wong-launches-online-literary-platform-writing-plus/> For

more, see the platform Writing Plus at <https://www.writingplus.hk/> [Accessed 5 March 2020].

13   Ibid.

14   Valerie Wu, 'Redefining Asian Identity: Art and Literature across the Chinese Diaspora', *US-China Today*, 19 May 2021, <https://uschinatoday.org/features/2021/05/19/redefining-asian-identity-art-and-literature-across-the-chinese-diaspora/> [Accessed 25 May 2021].

15   Boey Kim Cheng, Alycia Fong and Justin Chia, *To Gather Your Leaving* (Singapore: Ethos Books, 2019).

16   Helena Lee, *East Side Voices: Essays Celebrating East & Southeast Asian Identity in Britain* (London: Hachette Books, 2022), 120.

17   Ibid., 127.

Appendix: Author interviews

An interview with Li-Young Lee
(7 May 2017)

Wong, Jennifer, 'Redeeming Desire: A Conversation with Li-Young Lee', *World Literature Today*, 92.1 (2018), [Accessed 20 April 2018].

JW. You have travelled to and lived in different 'places'. How do you see the meaning of home and being away? Have you ever felt at home with where you are and who you are, and if you do what gives rise to that condition or state of mind? How does the idea of being at home or not at home, or the notion of 'place', change your writing?

LYL. 'Home' is a word and, like any word, it's subject to a paradox all words seem subject to, a paradox I find interesting for a number of reasons, including its correspondence to certain principles of yin and yang, known to the Chinese as *tai ji*, or the great polarity, and known in the West as the Word, or Logos, the dynamism of polar opposites. The logic of that paradox goes something like this: the fewer definitions a word has, the more defined that word is, the more definition it commands, and the clearer are the meanings attributed to that word, and the less likelihood that crisis surrounds those meanings. But also the less likelihood that subtleties and potentialities might congregate about that word.

On the other hand, the more definitions a word has, the less defined that word is, the less definition that word secures and, subsequently, the greater the number of possible meanings that accrue to that word, the greater the number of subtleties and potentialities that buzz about that word, and the greater the likelihood that crisis attends that word. Of course, I'm thinking in general, and about a word in isolation, and these conditions are mediated by context and use, by a word's entering into relationship with other words. But it turns out, for me, the word 'home' is, on the one hand, not very well defined by a country or place or any particular structure, but on the other hand, that word is the site of immense subtlety, potency and crisis. Maybe it is for everyone, but I wouldn't know. The fact is, my siblings and I basically grew up knowing that our parents were completely unable to protect us from harm. Whatever 'home' they might have provided for us, God bless them, was completely vulnerable to spontaneous, wanton and unjustified violence, from which we had no legal or other forms of protections. You see, Jennifer, I was born to scapegoats. My mother and father and the families they came from were violently scapegoated in China, where my parents were born. After escaping China, my parents started a family from scratch in Jakarta, Indonesia, where I was born, and where my parents found themselves to be the open targets of violent scapegoating yet again, this time with their own children at hazard.

After escaping Indonesia and finally arriving as refugees in the United States, a country at war at that time with an Asian country, we were scapegoated here, in less murderously violent ways, but still undeniably subjected to that particular practice of victimage, from which my parents, being themselves victims, could in no way shield us. So, what might 'home' mean in such circumstances? Everything, except safety. Everything, except security. Everything, except membership that confers privileges or protection. Everything, except a place one may return to for rest or sanctuary. I think that anyone who hasn't experienced being scapegoated would have no inkling of what I'm talking about. And yet, when I look at the world we live in today, I see that my family and I aren't a special case, but standard and the majority. Globally speaking, all I see is the sign of the scapegoat. There are scapegoats everywhere on this planet. We live under the sign of the scapegoat, everyone scapegoating everyone. In fact, I've written a poem about it called 'Goat's Head'. What can 'home' mean to anyone these days except crisis? Our earth-home itself is suffering massive crisis. Maybe the word 'home' is more important than ever to contemplate. But I can't seem to get my head around it.

JW. How do you see your identity as a writer, especially a Chinese writer? Should ethnicity be remembered or ignored when readers appreciate your work?

LYL. It seems to me that your question is possibly, at its root, a question about reading sameness and difference. Now, I'm not sure I have anything clarifying to say about this subject, and I fear that what I do say might only mystify understanding further, but let me give it a shot. I feel that reading sameness and difference(s) is very important. That is, keeping in mind the specificity of an artist, which includes ethnicity, gender, etc., as well as other socio-historically determined categories of identity, only enriches our reading of that artist.

I don't believe, for instance, that reading T. S. Eliot in forgetfulness of his race or ethnicity helps me to read him better. It actually deepens my appreciation of him to put him in the context of what all the other white males of his historical moment were doing with their lives. He was writing 'The Four Quartets'. Take some guy like him in every way but one. What was that guy doing? But you see, as in my example, reading difference necessarily means simultaneously reading sameness. Take, as another example, the artist Carmen Amaya. I think understanding her work in the context of her being Roman and born in the slums of Barcelona deepen my appreciation of her, and yet, none of that can completely explain her indisputable greatness as an artist. The facts of her life don't altogether account for her sublimity, her depth, her power. There are many who share her circumstances. She's the same as many. But they're not Carmen Amaya. She's different. There are many privileged sons of bankers who don't become Paul Cézanne. And being homosexual and Spanish didn't not influence Lorca, but neither does either of those facts account for the greatness of his work. Let me also say that I feel there are differences of greater, or even ultimate importance, that we must never lose sight of, even as we keep within our radar the more obvious differences of race, gender, class, etc.

One of those differences of ultimate importance is the difference of poetry itself. Poetry is marked by its difference from other instances of language. If that difference isn't strong enough in a poem, the other differences don't make for interesting enough reading. Not for me, at least. Because there is a sameness that finally erases all differences except the most salient differences, it seems to me. It is a sameness that is so powerfully levelling that it makes all of our talk of differences seem almost (almost, I said) like Chicago criminal gangs squabbling about the nature of their differences in regards to the different colours they fly. That sameness is this: we, all of us, are and each and every one of us is a member of one of the most violent, destructive, desirous, disputatious, creative, innovative, loving, tender, hateful, brute, reflective, imitative, cowardly, irrational, reasoning, unconscious, insensitive and visionary species on the planet. And we have without exception, from the beginning of time, regardless of race or gender or sexuality, maintained our societies, nations, cultures and human groups by murder, expulsion, exploitation and ritual violence, as well as campfire songs, stories and recipes for dumplings. There is no human group that can claim difference from this, our collective anthropological profile. And it is in the context of this very profile that I believe poetry must be written, not just in the context of our specific profiles.

JW. So your father was a Christian and you were brought up in Christian teachings. Is spirituality a very important element in your work and in your expression of identity? Also, the search for meaning in your poetry, the questioning the world as the place to be… I wonder if you have thought of a more utopian place to be?

LYL. Yes, my father was a Christian minister when he was alive. His intense interest in the Judeo-Christian tradition, primarily its literature, the Old and New Testaments, seems to me now so clearly motivated and inspired by his lifelong experience of being a victim in some of human history's more violent scapegoating episodes. It's obvious to me now that his reading of the Bible allowed him to see and understand the scapegoating phenomenon, which he as a man and we as a family personally suffered. The Old and New Testaments so clearly and movingly depict the history of humanity's natural inclination to resort to scapegoating in order to discharge pent-up hostilities and aggression, and how that tendency even got instituted as the cultural practice from which the very word scapegoating comes, and how that practice is, it can be argued, the ritual of rituals, the seminal ritual out from which all practice of sacrifice, ritual murder and expulsion grew, as well as the phenomenon that most potently expresses humankind's tendency towards sacrificial and exclusionary thinking, a kind of thinking practised to this day, a kind of thinking that answers human violence with violence, that uses violence as a way to curb violence, uses war to end wars, and so on. Perhaps it's an objectification of sublimation, I'm not sure.

   The genius of the Bible is its critique of this development in several different kinds of inter-personal manifestations, beginning with the rivalry of Cain and Abel, moving through the human near-sacrifice of Isaac, the expulsion of Joseph, the formal instituting of the practice of the scapegoat expulsion, war and straight through and into the scapegoating of Jesus. In this way, the Bible is true, profoundly so. Reading it literally as history seems ridiculous to me, but to read it as my father read it, as a revelation of our human evolution and our struggle with our own violent nature and our denial of that, our own violent countenance and the cost of that denial, seems indispensable to me. Especially given the state of the world today. Of course, my father also had a lifelong and deep interest in many Daoist sacred texts as well, including the *Dao De Jing* and the *I Jing*. In fact, and this might answer some of your other questions regarding East and West and having to choose one, I was noticing something interesting about the *I Jing* and Ovid's *Metamorphoses*.

JW. Do you feel you have to choose between Western poetics and Chinese/Asian poetics, and why?

LYL. First of all, though, regarding your question of having to choose East or West, I don't understand why we have to choose. In fact, I believe we don't have to choose. We do, however, we must, I believe, if we want to live, synthesize the best of both worlds, since both worlds have so much living and necessary knowledge to offer. I don't know from what mistaken sense of loyalty or mis-guided sense of affiliation anyone comes to the feeling of having to choose. Maybe that need itself, that feeling of having to choose, is a residue of sacrificial/scapegoating thinking, a flavour of thinking that implies or suggests that something must always be expelled, something must always be sacrificed. I think, in order for us to be more fully human, and in order for us to answer to today's challenges, the best of East and West are going to have to be fully synthesized. I don't perceive any natural conflict between East and West. I don't believe, as Heraclitus believed, that some sort of natural conflict and strife must exist between any two potent terms, and that only out of such strife does creation come about. He should have studied *tai ji,* poor guy. His sense of the Logos is one of war and strife. In *tai ji,* the only true creation comes out of harmonious conciliation and reconciliation between equal and opposite powers, which were never dual to begin with.

Which brings me back to the *I Jing* and Ovid's *Metamorphoses,* two books in humankind's early history, separated only by around 500 years, the Chinese book pre-dating the Roman poem. Both books were originally entitled *The Book of Transformations* or *The Book of Changes.* Both books are attempts to understand humankind's primordial beginnings. But the Latin book is full of murder, rape and suicide, depicting and enacting the very logic of sacrificial thought, while the Chinese book is full of wisdom, compassion, hope and comfort, giving advice about how to escape the traps of violence and sacrificial thought. One book, Ovid's, while a joy to read and not without substantial rewards, ultimately mystifies the reader by projecting human lineaments onto the divine, thereby obscuring the very divine, primordial processes it seeks to uncover. Meanwhile, the Chinese book, also an absolute delight to study, serves to demystify the reader's confusion about humanity's place in the universe by stripping away all human projections from the face of primordial reality and revealing trans-human, non-species-specific forces at work. Furthermore, it offers ways in which human beings can cooperate and harmonize with these forces in order to evolve towards deeper and more comprehensive modes of being. One is a book describing and enacting the logic of violence. The other is a book describing and enacting the logic of peace.

I'm not suggesting the East is any better than the West. Obviously, the East is as violent and materialistic as the West, and vice versa. I'm just remarking these two specific instances in our collective human literary history, reading their samenesses and differences. And as a way to answer your question of whether I believe in utopia or whether I want to live in some other world, all I have to say is that books like the *I Jing* and the Old and New Testaments convince me that the greatest human mission, encoded in the very fabric of human being, is inextricably entangled with the most meaning and power poetry can possess, and that these principles manifest together, mission, meaning and power, in concert through that human literary work whose impulse is de-mystification, revelation and the uncovering of humanity's primordial condition, its unbroken connection to the divine, and its conscious evolution away from violence and death, and towards peace and life.

This difference between literary works, some towards the logic of violence and the science of death, and others towards the logic of peace and the science of life, is another crucial difference for me, more important to me than some of the other differences we've named. This difference, and knowing this difference, and knowing how to read for this difference, is more important to me than all of the other differences: East and West, spiritual and material, mainstream and non-mainstream, Chinese and not Chinese, etc. These other differences are only important to me to the extent that they help me understand what I consider the supreme and this crucial difference: words that lead to peace and more life, or words that lead to more violence and death.

My allegiance to a logic of peace and a science of life is more important to me than any other allegiance, including home, country, family, race, class, gender, sexual preference, poetic school, you name it. What could any of those words mean if we all kill each other off or destroy the planet beyond repair?

An interview with Marilyn Chin
(24 August 2016)

Jennifer Wong, 'Jennifer Wong talks to Marilyn Chin', *Asian Review of Books*, 28 August 2020 <https://asianreviewofbooks.com/content/marilyn-chin-talks-to-jennifer-wong/> [Last accessed 6 June 2022].

Ideas of home

JW. You have been to a lot of places for your writing and residencies, and you have lived in different places: you spent your childhood in Hong Kong and moved to America. How do you see home and being away. Does it have a temporary or permanent impact on your work?

MC. I am very restless. I was born in Hong Kong, raised in Portland, Oregon. I went to undergraduate school in Iowa, and then lived in Bay Area in California. I have lived in California. I then got a teaching position in San Diego. I have been all over. I have lots of friends in Boston and New York City. I taught in the low-residency programme in Hong Kong's City University before it was closed. Any of these places are my home. Simultaneously I am in exile. When I was a child in Hong Kong, I used to think London is my capital. But then I realized I have a different kind of passport: I am not allowed to go to London. We are colonial subjects there, right? Home was where my mother and grandma were. But my mother and grandmother were gone now, and so I feel homeless in many ways, but yet I am constantly traveling.

JW. Your poetry engages with language(s) on many levels. What language does your family speak?

MC. My family spoke Toisan. They escaped from the Mainland before 1949, and they moved to Hong Kong. They came from peasant-like background. I was raised by my grandmother who spoke Toisan, a very ancient language. I see myself as part of the minority tribe. I align myself more with people like Kafka, with his weird dialect. I see myself as an outsider on many levels even if we are Han.

Writing and identity

JW. As for your interest in the Chinese literary tradition and forms. When and where does that come from?

MC. When we were young, we have to memorize those texts from Tu Fu and others. And my grandmother used to carry me on my back and chant to me Chinese poems and sayings. The first kind of poetry I heard was Chinese poetry, and so ingrained in my ear, even though English is my main language. The Chinese poem was ingrained in me when I was very young. You can hear the Cantonese language in my work. The Chineseness is in the DNA of my work. I can't divorce it from my work. I can't say I forget it, it's there. Bei Dao's generation was not trained in that tradition. They didn't go to university to study *wenyanwen* or ancient poetry. They were imitating the West. I tried to read Chinese poetry every day, because I think it's important for my aesthetics.

JW. Living in America, you embrace different sets of values. How does that impact on your writing?

MC. I feel that it has to do with Du Bois's idea of double consciousness: you inherit a set of values at home, and have to embrace another set of values when you walk out of home. You are appreciated if you are more assertive at school. On the contrary, you are supposed to be obedient at home. It's about balancing the two worlds. My poetry is about negotiating many worlds, the past and the present, as well as the East and the West. 'Inner cultivation' and outer despair. The sublime and the ridiculous.

JW. Your work is anchored by a strong feminist language.

MC. I am always fighting against the stereotype of the subservient female maiden. I want to shake up the assumptions about being a Chinese-American woman. We all must champion women's and children's rights in the world. The little brown girl is still the most vulnerable person in the room. It's important that I keep those feminist ideals and give voice to that girl who is still trembling within me. I have suffered hunger, abandonment, fear, violence early in my life. The self must represent something larger than the self.

There is always this wild girl peeking through the sageness. To say something controversial and to disrupt the surface. I am sixty now. I am a seasoned poet and writer.

I believe that I am a poet of the body and of the mind and of the soul! To mimic Whitman.

JW. Do you think that poetry has the responsibility of representing the minority and is representation essentially problematic?

MC. Writers must always speak out against racism and injustice.

When I went to the Iowa workshop in the early eighties, political poems were not valued. Some of my fellow writers were skeptical about my poems. But I have been engaged with social protests since the seventies and eighties. In those days, the minority artists worked together in a lively coalition to fight against the ugly dominant monster of racism. and I was active in the San Francisco Bay area protests. I am proud to call myself an activist.

On the other hand, I do write all kinds of poems. Henry Louis Gates told me that I must assert that I am first and foremost a poet, not just an activist poet. My work encompasses activist poetry but also does a lot more than protest. I am reinventing bicultural forms. I am an innovator: the creator of the Chinese-American quatrain, of the lyric manifesto, of erotic haiku and remix sonnets! In terms of the responsibility of a poet, it is important to engage in political and social issues, yes! This is a racist world! We must speak against all kinds of injustice.

JW. Do you think there are enough activist poets in America?

MC. Because Black lives are at stake every day, almost every person of colour has to respond to these issues. But for a long time some Asian-Americans didn't want to write about being Asian-Americans, didn't want to write a racially-marked poetry. I think that the pendulum has swung toward writing poetry with a social consciousness.

The two main issues in American history are slavery and the destruction of native Americans, historical events that have left a profound mark on American history. On even a larger scale, I would say more than ever, now in the era of Trump. We must fight against demagogues all over the world. This open hatred against immigrants! Against dark-skinned peoples … The language of building a wall, 'bad hombres', China-shaming! The demagogues are manufacturing fear and hate, Islamophobia, and generally, phobia against anybody who is 'different' and might take your job.

There is in discrimination against the model minority (Asian-Americans), motivated by the fear that Asian-Americans are taking over the opportunities in education and employment. On a more universal scale, I would say that there is the hatred against immigrants. Right now this becomes an urgent issue even in Europe, evidenced in the impact of Brexit. I think that area is under-addressed.

In the same way there is also resentment against China's economic power taking over the world. These are all current concerns originating from the eternal struggles of race and class.

I echo Adrienne Rich's idea that the personal is political. My poetics is rooted in my personal history, and from there I examine the world around me. I see myself not just as a Chinese-American, but as a global citizen. I care about America but also about what happens in the world.

JW. Your poems such as 'Sonnetnese', 'From a Notebook of an Ex-Revolutionary' interrogate the relationship between the past and the present, offering a somewhat postmodern, postcolonial reading of history and ancestry. What role does poetry play in understanding or articulating history of your homeland?

MC. One has to engage with the different aspects of history. For example, 'Sonnetnese' and 'From a Notebook of an Ex-Revolutionary' are both provocative parodies. I think the Chinese are still grappling with that part of history. Maybe the Western reader will not be able to access those poems fully. I want to embrace my Chinese-ness and yet it is very foreign and intriguing to me.

Very early in my career, I wrote about bamboo, not with an 'orientalist' sentiment but because I have seen bamboo scaffolding that is used in building giant skyscrapers in Hong Kong and I have seen a person fall off and die … Only someone who was raised in Asia could 'know' about bamboo scaffolding. Chinese history, Hong Kong history course through my blood.

JW. Would you say that your play on poetic forms is becoming more experimental in your recent collection?

MC. I think it's important to reinvent with poetry. It's about making form and contents work in a spectacular way. I try to challenge myself. I don't like to get too comfortable with a certain kind of poetry. I like to keep experimenting. It's important to love your genre and the possibilities. There's so much to explore for those poets with bilingual and multicultural backgrounds as well.

Some of my poems are more narrative and some are more experimental. My 'Twenty Five Haiku' was published in *Poetry Foundation* magazine. Some people loved it for its transgressiveness while there are also haiku purists who dislike it. I have kept to the seventeen-syllable form but I subverted and perverted the frog image. A satirical play against the patriarchy! I wrote a quasi-Chinese verse entitled 'Quiet the Dog, Tether the Pony', in which I took away all the punctuations. It reads like a Chinese translation but it is also an elliptical, postmodern poem. I took the title from Yeats. Yet it is a very Chinese poem because of the eclipsed pronouns.

JW. Do you see yourself as an American poet?

MC. I am an 'American' poet! Not because I subscribe to a certain American esthetic. I write in English and not in Chinese. I'm a force to be reckoned with. I have my 'chops' and I have written a serious, strong and diverse oeuvre of works. I belong to the American legacy and deserve a place in it. I look back at my career with pride. And I believe that I am presently at my height of creativity and am writing some bad-ass prose and poetry, right now, as we speak!

But the young girl who read my poem 'The Floral Apron' for the BBC to represent Hong Kong at the London Olympics wants to claim me as well. It's important to have a transnational readership. To not have borders, to have one's poetry travel well.

I celebrate my Americanness. I celebrate my Chinese-ness. I celebrate my transnational identity.

JW. You capture and weld the familiar and the alien, and your work offers refreshing insights on the power of naming and believing. In Hard Love Province, *for example, coinages like 'Cougar Sinonymous', 'Fathersong', 'Deterritorialized', 'Kalifornia' etc. suggest a new way of rewriting place(s), positions and identities. What is your rationale for naming things differently?*

MC. I think it's important to reinvent with poetry. It's about making form and contents work in a spectacular way. I try to challenge myself. I don't like to get too comfortable with a certain kind of poetry. I like to keep experimenting. It's important to love your genre and the possibilities. There's so much to explore for we poets with bilingual and multicultural backgrounds. It's up to poets to reinvent words! Internet memes, tweet-speak between hashtags … the world wants to shorten and limit the word count.

We poets need to enrich the vocab. And it's fun! Sinonymous embraces 'sin' and 'sinologist' and 'anonymous' in the same breath! 'Kalifornia' pays homage to my beloved state and the fierce Goddess. I'm a freaking wordsmith, I can't help it, I'm a poet!

At the same time, it is hard to categorize or pigeonhole my writing in a coherent way. Although I call myself an activist writer, I also play on forms and traditions. I amalgamate poems. I also play with the postmodern narratives, even poems that are more akin to songs and speech acts.

JW. You are a poet and an academic. Do you think that your engagement with the academic world impacts on your poetry?

MC. I retired from my tenured job early partly because I would like to devote more time to writing poetry. The ancients did that too, they retreated to the countryside and 'cleanse from the mud' of the academy and 'palace art'. They retreated into the woods to hear their own voice again. Of course, these were rich privileged aristocratic poets. Some were forced exiles like Du Fu, who wrote some of his best works in his later years. In angst, of course. He felt abandoned. However, as we all know, he became the greatest poet of China.

I taught in academia for over twenty-five years. Early on, I was informed by theorists such as Cixous, Said, Spivak, Gates and mostly postcolonial and feminist theorists. I learned a lot from the Black arts movement. I loved reading Black feminist thinkers on my own (outside of academia) – Audre Lorde, Barbara Smith, Angela Davis, June Jordan, bell hooks, etc. Tough women poets/thinkers like Gloria Anzaldua and Tri Min Ha. And, of course, Adrienne Rich.

I never let theory or academic jargon laminate my creative work. I think it's popular now to privilege a theoretical or conceptual framework first and have the poem be subordinate to the framework. I always value the poem first. The poem itself must be 'brilliant' and distinctive to survive the test of time. Well, we could argue about what it means to be 'brilliant.' Adrienne Rich believes 'the poem must serve' the people. Somehow, I don't want my poems to be relevant to only a few readers in academia.

I never write essays. I don't want to over-analyze ... the process could take the magic out of the creative fire. Being an academic also means that I am very self-critical. I scrutinize each word and I have worked up a hundred drafts for some poems.

JW. Who do you write for?

MC. I write for the best reader possible. I don't want to write down to my reader. Someone who is well-read, possibly knows some Chinese or interested in Chinese poetry. I hope my work will prompt someone to consider or study more about Chinese poetry. It's not a good idea to write down to your reader.

An interview with Hannah Lowe
(29 May 2017)

Jennifer Wong, 'On Home, Belongingness and Multicultural Britain: A Conversation with Hannah Lowe', *World Literature Today*, 92.2 (2018), <https://www.worldliteraturetoday.org/2018/march/home-belongingness-and-multicultural-britain-conversation-hannah-lowe-jennifer-wong> [Last accessed 6 June 2022].

JW. Your home culture is a mix of different places. How do you see the meaning of home and of being away?

HL. I didn't grow up in a different place and then migrate to England. I still live very near the place where I was born and have always seen England as my home. Beyond that, I see London, where I live, almost as a separate state from the rest of England or the UK, although I don't meant that in a separatist way, more a sense of feeling very strongly rooted to the city, to its multicultural makeup, and to a kind of urban living. But in a mixed-race household, with parents of different cultures, there's always an awareness of what exists beyond the local. Even when I was a child – though I didn't know where Jamaica or China were, or why my dad had come to Britain from Jamaica, or why his father had come to Jamaica from China – they were always anchors in my understanding of myself.

JW. How does the notion of place change your writing?

HL. In writing *Chick*, my first collection, I wasn't consciously trying to make an announcement of my mixed-race identity (it's probably important here to understand that I don't look obviously mixed-race). I wanted to write about my father and his life and his unorthodox occupation as a gambler in London's East End. But inevitably, the writing explored living in a multicultural household and my father's migration, my Black and Chinese grandparents, and my own sense of identity. It was a wonderful surprise that people responded so well to the book, and that acceptance also felt like a permission. Before then, I worried that people might see me as an imposter, because I look white and particularly because I haven't been a victim of direct racism, if that is considered to be a collective and determining factor of being Black or mixed. I still have these anxieties, but I also can't turn away from the material I find compelling and important. *Chan*, the collection that followed *Chick*, is much more focused on mixed-race themes and addresses racism, migration, and settlement more directly.

JW. You talked about homeland, that it is an anchor of some sort even if it is not comfortable territory.

HL. One of the reasons it might not be comfortable concerns appearances, and the associated experiences, as I've already mentioned. I don't feel I can go to Jamaica and announce myself as Jamaican, partly because I look more like the colonizer than the colonized! Nor do I feel it would be easy to go to China and announce I am Chinese. I wouldn't expect to be accepted on those terms, and moreover, I've been born and raised in Britain. I'm British. And yet I do feel deeply rooted to those places, because of my lineage, and I want to write about them.

JW. Do you think there is an ideal or utopian place where you belong?

HL. No, although it's an interesting question. I feel like, as far as possible, this is where I belong, right here, in north London, England, but I expect there are people who feel much more English than I do. I have an ambivalence about Englishness and no nationalistic feeling whatsoever. England is home because of its familiarity. I love the cultural life here, but I feel alienated from the dominant political modes of the UK at the moment, and from the class system, which is so deeply entrenched here, and certainly from the legacies of the British Empire.

JW. In your view, how has Brexit changed the people's sympathies or attitudes toward the representation of multiculturalism and immigrant identities?

HL. I think Brexit is a very complicated political event, but I read it as mostly a contest centered on class – the working classes hugely disenfranchised by austerity versus the middle and upper classes, and this mapped out over regions, so the traditional white working-class terrains of the North East, for example, pushing against the increasing wealth and cosmopolitanism of the South East. I don't think many people actually understood what the European Union does, but the idea of leaving Europe gained enormous momentum last year, with immigration being positioned by Brexiteers as a major reason. I heard an insidious, nostalgic nationalism being articulated in places – the idea that Britain could be restored to the former glory of the empire. I don't think we, as a nation, have ever been shamed about the empire in the way that, say, Germany has been about the Nazi years, and I think this lack of redress and reconciliation is a problem. I was horrified to hear the empire being regaled during the Brexit campaigns.

Multiculturalism was championed by the New Labour government at the end of the 1990s, in direct contradiction of Thatcher's concept of Britain as a monocultural nation. It's never been without its problems, but the sentiment of celebrating Britain's plurality was a good one. In the light of Brexit, I feel quite pessimistic about how Britain may reconfigure this identity, and representations of migrant identities (in poetry, fiction, film, and so on) will be a part of this dialogue. I hope these will challenge any notion of monoculturalism or the propagation of a Britain hermetically sealed off from other nations.

JW. The 'Borderliner' sequence of poems in Chan *articulates the impossibility of decoding cultural hybridity entirely. It is as if one's identity is always evolving based on acquisition of new knowledges. Can you shed light on your use and experiment with the poetic voices in the sequence (e.g., 'Genealogy' and 'Milk River / Yellow River')? Are they meant to continue each other and remap a larger consciousness?*

HL. Those particular poems reflect a tension between collective and individual consciousness, something I try to capture by juxtaposing two narratives, using bold/nonbold typography, the meaning of which varies across the poems but is sometimes intended to signal the tension between narratives that are well known, seemingly objective and/or 'historical', written in bold text, and those that are subjective, personal, unknown, silenced, or suppressed.

JW. How do you 'return' to a place that you never in fact left, and whose codes and culture you do not have immediate access to? What kinds of belonging can be enacted in these contexts, if there is any belonging at all?

HL. So in 'Milk River / Yellow River', I retell the public history of the Hakka Chinese, who have migrated far and wide from China, including to Jamaica. In Jamaica, the Hakka people are very proud of their ancestry, and the community is tight-knit, prosperous, Christian, quite morally upright. But my own grandfather, who was Hakka, was by all accounts none of these things! He lived a rather nomadic and financially reckless life, fathered many children by different black women, neglected those women and children. He beat my father so badly that my father once held a gun to his head while he slept, but he was too frightened of him to kill him. So the poems contrast these two narratives, the public-historical and the personal-historical, and invite the reader to see the tension there.

The poems are continuations of each other. The same ideas are at work in 'Genealogy', which retells the story of being taken by members of the Chinese Benevolent Association to the Chinese temple in Kingston and Chinese cemetery, where members helped me find my grandfather's grave. This was such a surprise to me, as I hadn't even known there was a cemetery, let alone that he was buried there. But there was a mild expectation that I had come to pay 'filial duty' to my grandfather, which the poem attempts to complicate by articulating my personal knowledge of him as a man who beat his children and perhaps wasn't worthy of my respect. The tension in the poem is supposed to emerge through speaking this secret knowledge – the fact I can say it in the poem but certainly not at the graveside.

JW. How do you perceive or understand your Chinese roots?

HL. My relationship to China has always been filtered through my father, who saw himself as a Jamaican, but I'm not sure whether that was at the exclusion of his Chinese identity or an absorption of it. What I would say was that he had a very troubled relationship with his Chinese father, who was both his caregiver and his abuser. His father ran a Chinese grocery store in Jamaica, like many other Chinese-Jamaicans, but he was also a prolific gambler who lost his business several times, and so my father's childhood was an unstable and nomadic existence, moving from one Chinese grocery to another. His father beat him brutally, the scars of which were still visible on my dad's body as an old man. So my dad rarely spoke about my grandfather, and for good reason.

I am sure my dad could speak the Hakka dialect that his father would have spoken, but he never did. He rarely mentioned his father but transmitted 'China' through his cooking, which he was very proud of, and which was a big part of our family life. When I remember my childhood home, I recall there was a certain Chinese aesthetic there, in the artwork, the porcelain, the fabrics – almost as though Chinese was never spoken but inscribed. But China, for me, always comes filtered through Jamaica – I am more familiar with the Chinese Jamaican community, having traveled there and spent time with them, than I am with China, which I have yet to visit.

JW. In articulating place, do you ever find it hard when you fuse symbols and myths from another place?

HL. What interests me about being 'diasporic,' as someone of the second generation, is not so much the knowledge you have of that place, because how can you know a place you haven't seen or lived in? I'm much more interested in how as a child and adult I have imagined those places, and those imaginings may have had little rooting to reality. As a writer, there's a great energy in that idea.

JW. In your poems you unravel the magic and dreams rooted in the past: going back to the past to shed light on the present. As compared with your first collection, Chan *reveals a more collective, historical past where individuals emerge. How do you see the relevance of history in the negotiation of a diasporic identity?*

HL. Until recently, the 'old country' has always been my focus. I've been fixated on what my father's life must have been in rural Jamaica of the 1930s or what the China that my grandfather left at the beginning of last century was like – so in that sense 'history' is crucial to the negotiation of diasporic identity, and I think plenty of people have written about the 'imaginary homeland' in different manifestations. In writing *Chan*, I read historical texts, such as histories of Jamaican decolonization, and of Jamaican culture and music – books like Ian Thomson's *The Dead Yard*, which gives quite a bleak view of Jamaica, I think, but what comes through in this book are the stories of individuals, and I suppose that's always for me where history lifts off the page, when I encounter the individual narratives and struggles of people against their circumstances – and this is what I try to re-create in *Chan*, through various storytelling poems and monologues.

But the present-day Jamaica is also a focus in *Chan*. I try to capture some of the anxieties I felt in traveling back to a place I had a tenuous claim to, and in going there to ask questions that might not have been particularly welcome. Both my father's remaining sister and brother are presented as ambivalent to my questions about my grandfather, since there was no love lost between them and their father. Similarly, I wanted to know about the secretive gambling dens that had once existed in Chinatown in Kingston, where he had played mahjong, but my feeling was that this wasn't a side of the Chinese presence that anyone wanted to show me. I think this is also part of the negotiation of diasporic identity – how do you 'return' to a place that you never in fact left, and whose codes and culture you do not have immediate access to? What kinds of belonging can be enacted in these contexts, if there is any belonging at all?

JW. *In poems like 'In' or 'Distressed British Seamen,' your poetic representation of England is blended with fiction and reality, hope and disillusionment. How do you see the relationship between nation/state and one's identity? Do you feel there is a necessary attachment and tension of allegiances?*

HL. The names of the distressed British seamen in *Chan* are borrowed from real people, listed on the *Ormonde* passenger list, and the term 'Distressed British Seaman' refers to any seamen who find themselves without a ship in a foreign port. In wartime, this might be because a ship has been bombed, but a source I found indicated that in peacetime the reasons might be less heroic – 'womanizing', brawling, drinking, imprisonment and so on. I became quite fascinated with these possibilities but also with seafarers themselves, who in some ways lived quite cosmopolitan lives, traveling between continents, working with foreign seamen, and often living in very mixed communities in port towns. One of the DBS is in fact called Saeed, an Arabic name. When the first DBS announces, 'I knew Black men at Tiger Bay – sea dog / from Cape Verde, Somali skippers. Now this lot / quiz me: England this or England that?' he is saying the *Ormonde* passengers are not the first Black people he's seen, because Britain is already a hybrid nation, and many of the sea-faring communities have a decades-long presence. So in other words, I intended for the fictional seamen of *Chan* to have an ambivalent relationship to the nation constructed on white monocultural terms.

JW. What writers do you like?

HL. That's a big question! My first love was for Black women writers such as Toni Morrison and Alice Walker. Their novels are the ones I fell for as an undergraduate and still go back to. In terms of poetry, the first poet to really speak to me was Philip Levine, the American poet who writes about the working-class and immigrant communities of Detroit. And since then, there are many poets I have discovered and loved: Derek Walcott, Jack Gilbert, Marie Howe, Sharon Olds … oh, the list is endless, but you might notice I have a big thing for the Americans.

An interview with Sarah Howe
(22 July 2015 and 4 August 2015)

On the meaning of home

JW. What do you think about being at home and being away? If you have experienced it, do you feel it has any temporary or permanent impact on your work?

SH. Home is where my family is. So I suppose it could be a portable concept, when you migrate for a longer tranche of time. Home is somewhere that can come with you. If pressed, I guess I think of England and especially London, the suburbs of London, where I spent the latter part of my childhood, as home. I started writing in earnest about ten years ago, which is also roughly when the thought process that would become *Loop of Jade* began. The catalyst was when I spent some time in America to study at Harvard – it must have had to do with being away, with leaving the familiar. It was the question of belonging and my own position in America, a place I'd never lived before, that engaged me back then. That sense of dislocation took me back to the feeling of being a seven-year-old in Hong Kong preparing to move to a new continent, being told by my parents where my 'real' home was.

JW. You mentioned being away twice, and that England is now your home. In terms of emotional connection with the place, have you always felt at home where you are or who you are?

SH. I have always felt both inside and outside of places. I was always something of an outsider in Hong Kong for those first seven years of my life because of being half-English, half-white and not speaking Cantonese. I have to admit I wasn't old enough to be aware of the full strangeness of that predicament, except that I spent those years hearing my mother speak in a language that I don't understand. I suspect that sort of experience gets one thinking about the relationship between sound and meaning, and how easily it is severed. The real jolt was coming to England for junior school, because that was the first time I really had a sense of myself as a 'minority' person, whereas at my previous school in Hong Kong there had been quite a lot of Eurasian children like me. I remember children remarking on my strangeness as a recent arrival, and not being well-versed in English culture. That was a period of discomfort, and the only time in my life when I encountered racism with any real intensity: the 'slitty eyes' gestures and 'Ching Chong Chinaman' sung in the playground. At that age, I think I did wish I was wholly white, if only because that would make things easier. I did silly things in a childish effort to integrate, to not stand out. I remember being given a box of talc one Christmas and trying to pat it over my face in an attempt to lighten it, thinking I could blend in better at school. I had a very simplistic notion of how assimilation worked. But I also sensed it was something my parents, and especially my mother, were worried about – that my brother and I would be marked out as different – and so it was also an anxiety I picked up from them.

On identity as a writer

JW. Do you see your identity as a Chinese writer? Should ethnicity be ignored or taken into account when readers appreciate your work?

SH. This is something I thought about as the book came together, and as I began to contemplate how it might be packaged or marketed. For some time, I had a different title in mind, *Lullaby Too Rough*, from Shakespeare's *The Winter's Tale*: the phrase is quoted in a poem that didn't make it into the final manuscript. 'Lullaby too rough' is still connected with the book's underlying story, since the phrase comes from the speech delivered by the servant in Shakespeare's play, who has been instructed to abandon the baby girl, Perdita, on the beach. That scene plays in my mind because of how it chimes with my own mother's abandonment as a baby in China. I mention this because it shows that at one time I was thinking of a title for the book that wouldn't include any overt signs of Chineseness. Before the book was published, I could see how much sense 'Loop of Jade' would make as the title poem of the collection, knitting together as it does so many of the book's underlying themes. And yet I was nervous about having such an obvious – one might even say clichéd – ethnic marker as 'jade' in the title, because I feared how that would colour readers' preconceptions about the book. In the event, my editor and I decided that the phrase was, on balance, rescued from cliché by the strangeness of the 'loop of…' construction. As a symbol of inheritance and protection, the jade bracelet I was gifted by my adoptive grandmother as a baby was too potent a talisman to pass up.

On the question of whether I see myself as a Chinese writer, I guess that has to be answered in concert with whether I see myself as Chinese in a larger sense. In lots of ways even my mother is atypically Chinese, even before you get to me. Because she grew up as a tenuously adopted orphan, whose supposed parent would often disappear or melt away, neither she nor I have any extended Chinese family structure, a phenomenon I feel is of huge cultural significance among other families in Hong Kong. I just don't fit into that kind of familial and social fabric, which for my Chinese friends seems such an important element in their sense of self and origin. The question of whether I consider myself Chinese has become one bound up with my writing. After the first few years of being in England, by the time I got to secondary school, I did not think too consciously about my Chineseness at all. I started to think of myself as basically white, although obviously I do straddle the two categories. I am interested in how race is perceived. Sometimes people think I am white, sometimes Chinese, sometimes biracial, but those ventured categorizations are largely beyond my control. But when I travel in China and Hong Kong, I am definitely perceived as a foreigner, for reasons of linguistic incompetence if nothing else. Very occasionally Chinese people in England have asked me if I'm Japanese!

I don't think I would call myself a 'Chinese poet', as that doesn't feel like an identity I can lay claim to; 'British-Chinese poet' perhaps, but even that feels like an oversimplification. 'Hong Kong poet' is another lens through which I've begun to consider my work more recently. As a label it feels truer to some extent, if only because Hong Kong's own identity is so cosmopolitan, so bound up with migration, departure and return. I think Western eyes sometimes don't appreciate quite how various a category 'Chineseness' is – that to be from mainland China, or Hong Kong, or Taiwan, or Malaysia, each implies very different things, and that's even before you start getting into the diaspora. A Singaporean friend asked me recently why so many of my poems refer to mainland China, its history and myth, when my own background – my mother was born in Guangdong province in the south, but never visited China again after moving to Hong Kong as a baby – is so remote from Beijing and the centralized power in the north. I think my answer would be that my mum always saw herself as part of 'China' as a larger cultural entity, even as her politics were opposed to the central regime's. I think I picked up that sense of simultaneous connection and resistance from her.

JW. How you see the relationship between your writing and homeland?

SH. My poem, 'Crossing from Guangdong', is concerned with what it means to travel back to a place you might, as an immigrant, postulate as a sort of mythical point-of-origin, but where you haven't lived for most of your life. Especially its final section tries to dramatize the dawning realization that no matter how much of a homeland that place is in your mind, no matter how beautiful, the reality simply can't bear that weight of expectation.

JW. From your experience, is there some utopian or idealized version(s) of place?

SH. I think place is perhaps more susceptible to idealization than people are. I might be quite realistic, even disenchanted, when it comes to thinking about people I'm close to, but place bears a sort of instinctive emotional freight for me, which I've tried to both evoke and resist in my poems. I'm thinking about the roots of 'nostalgia' in the Greek *nostos*, or 'homecoming': it's the same word used of the sea journeys the Greek heroes like Odysseus made in the wake of the Trojan war, trying desperately to return home. *Loop of Jade* is a kind of homecoming. On the one hand, the book is concerned with journeys, and especially with the idea of crossing from one place to another: a sort of lateral movement. On the other hand, its poems recurrently evoke the idea of the loop, or circling, which often has more to do with time. The three long poems spaced across the book, 'Crossing from Guangdong', 'Loop of Jade' and 'Islands,' move backwards in time, beginning with my symbolic pilgrimage to Hong Kong and then looping back in time. 'Islands' is in fact spoken in the voice of a character very like my mother, recalling the places of her childhood.

On poetic language and writing journey

JW. Is it hard to write those poems in your mother's voice?

SH. I wrote 'Islands' quite early on. These poems are based on conversations I had with my mother, during the evenings, when stories of her childhood came pouring out. I love her very much, but we don't have conversations of that degree of intensity very often, and so those outpourings on her part became quite exceptional occasions for us. Although I had known she was an orphan from when I was very small, I didn't know about any of the specifics of her early life before those late-night conversations in my twenties. Some of the topography of Hong Kong in that poem is based on my own experiences, sensory details of the heat or smell, say, that I inserted from my own childhood memories. So in that sense it is a composite voice, which I think is to some extent unavoidable when writing dramatic monologue: the form calls for a degree of stylization, a heightening of image and register. The trick is, at the same time, not to let the 'poetic' nature of the voice become too obtrusive.

I was quite nervous when I showed her poems like 'Islands' and 'Loop of Jade' for the first time, asking her whether it would be alright for them to be published in that form. We are quite an awkward family, full of silences about important things even at the best of times, so I initially found it quite nerve-racking sharing the poems with her and my father. We've obviously had many conversations on that topic now, but I still don't know what she really thinks about these poems. She did say once that they felt strangely like fiction to her, despite the familiar events and fixtures. I imagine it must be a bit like watching a film of your life – the uncanny feeling that the actors are getting everyone you know slightly wrong. Another challenge was my wish to capture the way my mum speaks: the particular patterns, oddities and hesitations of her English, which come to the fore in the poem, 'Loop of Jade'. I wanted to capture the feeling of someone who is having to stop to translate in her head, then offering up an English word that will do, but somehow isn't quite right.

JW. When you write, who do you write for?

SH. I suppose my ideal reader would be one who approached the poems with a degree of openness, generosity and the willingness to revisit them more than once. I suppose I usually write to please myself, first and foremost, but in the past my imagined community of readers didn't reach all that far – mentors, workshop groups, trusted fellow poets, magazine editors (though when it came to imagining those magazines' readerships, I had more trouble). Of course my work won't be everyone's cup of tea, and there's no problem with that, but I would prefer to have faith in the reader and try to earn their trust in return. I work in a range of styles, some of which are more experimental, while others verge on the confessional. In recent years, I started to see this stylistic divide as yet another way in which my sense of straddling two worlds – and not wanting to be too settled or comfortable on either side – plays out in my work.

One last consideration is the extent to which, in the early stages at least, I was writing these poems with an implicitly Western reader in mind. This started to shift, however, in the last few years as I realized that Chinese people, British-Chinese people, Asian people more generally, were starting to turn up at my readings. I found the responsibility of this quite anxiety inducing: the notion that they were seeking out my work because it spoke particularly to them, because it dealt with experiences – experiences familiar to them – that felt unrepresented in the wider culture. I remember I was also quite nervous of being judged unfit to write about Chinese subjects at all, on account of being half-British. In the event, I think this fear spoke more to my own fears than it did to the feelings of those Asian audience members. It's very clear to me that *Loop of Jade* isn't some sort of dispatch from an 'authentic' China, but the record of a writer trying to forge some sort of tentative relationship with a culture that is very much not a given.

JW. How do you see the relationship between your ethnicity or roots and your writing?

SH. In the back of my mind, I sometimes thought I should stop writing poems to do with Chineseness, that I should draw a line at some point, for fear of being reductively labelled. There are a lot of poems in the book – perhaps even a majority, though I haven't totted up the pages – that have nothing to do with China at all, but were inspired by medieval Flemish paintings or English gardens. But you might not guess that from reading some reviews of *Loop of Jade*. I know of other ethnic minority poets who have felt the same fear of being pigeonholed.

JW. How do you see your diaspora or culturally hybrid identity?

SH. As far as diaspora is concerned, I have never particularly felt part of a 'community' of Chinese people in this country, simply because I didn't know that many Chinese people in the UK growing up. I had a couple of British-born-Chinese friends at secondary school, one of whom remains one of my closest friends. The composite monsters of my Borges encyclopaedia poems – Sirens, Sphinxes, the 'chimera' mouse that glows green thanks to the jellyfish genes spliced into its DNA – offered a helpful vehicle for thinking about cultural and racial hybridity. What it means to be assigned to categories or grids of identity – categories you might embrace or wish to resist – is what those poems are concerned with exploring.

JW. What are your views towards Chinese vs English poetics? Are you influenced by any Chinese poets?

SH. I am not anywhere near as well-read in Chinese poetry as I am in English, though I have read many anthologies and collections by individual Chinese poets in recent years. Increasingly I found I wanted to have access to the poems in the original instead of relying on translations – a dream that remains somewhat remote for me, even since I began studying Chinese in my late twenties. I have just enough Mandarin to follow along happily in parallel-text editions, albeit with constant reference to the dictionary, but not enough to judge the quality or nuance of the translations. Thinking about the points at which Chinese and English poetics have met in the past, *Loop of Jade* grapples explicitly with the legacy of Ezra Pound, and the question of how Chinese culture reached Europe in the age of Modernism. Pound's convoluted process of translating the Cathay poems – via the crib translations of Li Po made by Ernest Fellonosa, who didn't himself speak Chinese, but relied on Japanese scholars to act as intermediaries – the sheer inauthenticity of that process, the un-authoritative nature of his approach, were somehow liberating for me.

The fraught fantasy space of *Chinoiserie* – the Orient as imagined by a European willow-pattern plate or a modernist poet 'translating' Li Po – became an important entry-point for exploring my sense of racial and cultural in-betweeness. I'm fascinated by moments when you might suddenly glimpse the world through the eyes of an 'other' and be startled. *Loop of Jade* repeatedly stages moments like that. I have on my wall a copy of a woodcut by Hiroshige II whose original I saw once in Japan. It's part of a triptych depicting nineteenth-century London: the artist has heard about monuments like London Bridge and St Paul's, but they become an arched wooden bridge and tiered pagoda respectively, while the English society ladies sport Japanese parasols.

JW. Do you have any difficulty in articulating in the English language or in articulating your otherness?

SH. I feel very at home communicating in English. My degree of command in English probably demonstrates, to her mind, why my mother did not want to raise me as a bilingual person. Influenced by the scientific studies of the time, I think she was concerned with the possibility that a bilingual education would slow down language acquisition, or harm it overall, leaving me speaking an imperfect or accented English. I think she was afraid that I wouldn't fit into the target culture that she wanted me to be part of – that is, my father's culture. On another level, I don't believe she would ever articulate this to herself consciously, but I think she wanted to protect me from Chineseness in some sense, or at least from the harsher aspects of the culture she grew up in. I have always felt great discomfort or sadness or inadequacy being a part-Chinese person who cannot speak comfortably in Chinese. There is always this sense of loss, and I think it comes through strongly in this book. The book is an artefact designed, in some ways, to try to recover that lost heritage.

On culture and identity

JW. Are you concerned that there is a gap of understanding between East and the West, things being untranslated. Do you think it is easy or difficult to convey your meanings?

SH. I have always found that it made intuitive sense to me, the notion that human experience is not universal, not straightforwardly translatable across languages or borders – that the Western, or British, or American (and so on) way of seeing the world is far from being the only way. I suppose my background explains why I should feel like this. I confess to being troubled by the dominance of English as a 'world language'. It's hardly an original thought of mine, but the traditional Anglophone complacency about not particularly seeking out foreign works for translation, not valuing the labours of literary translators, just reinforces that sense of perspectival centrality. It has been an interesting experience for me learning Chinese as an adult and feeling intrigued, even wonderingly estranged, by the stark differences between how English and Chinese treat grammar. This gets us into the fascinating territory of cognitive linguistics, pointing especially towards Benjamin Whorf's contested work on linguistic relativity and the idea that the language you speak shapes your worldview, often popularly invoked by that hoary piece of apocrypha about Eskimos' fifty words for snow. As a poet I have some instinctive sympathy for Wittgenstein's suspicion that the 'limits of my language mean the limits of my world', though I recognize that this question is hardly settled among linguists and philosophers.

Where Chinese specifically is concerned, a couple of years back I read Perry Link's *An Anatomy of Chinese: Rhythm, Metaphor, Politics* (2013), which revisits George Lakoff and Mark Johnson's work on conceptual metaphor in various fascinating and innovative ways. For example, he revisits the question of how English and Chinese each express time concepts in terms of space, mapping past and future as up or down – that sort of thing. In the process, Link manages to debunk the longstanding claim that the two languages treat this spatialization of time concepts in fundamentally different ways, revealing the tendency of past Sinologists to exoticize Chinese in this respect. My poem '(k) Drawn with a very fine camelhair brush' tackles some related ground on the question of Sino-European relations and 'mistranslation'. But at a more personal level, the poems about my mother in *Loop of Jade* are also full of little 'false friends' type moments – like her use of the phrase 'boarding school' to describe the institution in Macau described in 'Loop of Jade' and 'Islands', even though 'boarding school' means something so radically different to English ears, with its associations of elitism and privilege. I spent my childhood watching my mum searching for a word in English, before settling on something I sensed she didn't feel was adequate to describe the Chinese phenomenon at hand – quite possibly because an exact English equivalent didn't exist.

To address your question in broader cultural and political terms, I am much more immersed in English media than Chinese media. I feel the way China is reported here suggests that there might be a continuation of Yellow Peril-type misunderstanding, which sometimes emerges when British people talk about China's emergent power in aggressive, even fearful terms. Thinking back to Niall Ferguson's recent TV series about China, I often found his way of interacting with his Chinese interviewees in that programme objectionable: his tone was so patronizing, even to the Chinese academics he spoke to. Moments like those feel to me like they reveal a continuing gap of understanding.

JW. I enjoyed your poem '(k) Drawn with a very fine camelhair brush'.

SH. Despite my lack of my command or fluency, I have been trying to incorporate Chinese snippets or characters that disrupt the surface of my poems, in an effort to convey there are different ways to understand the world than alphabetically. That poem, 'Drawn with a very fine camelhair brush', is a sort of a meditation on and quarrel with Ernest Fenollosa's famous essay, 'The Chinese Written Character as a Medium for Poetry'. As edited and published by Ezra Pound, it offered a sort of poetics of natural law rooted in the supposed characteristics of the Chinese writing system. My poem opens with a much older version of this same Utopian fantasy, as illustrated by the Jesuits Missionaries of the seventeenth century and the hopes they projected onto Chinese writing as they encountered it for the first time. Thanks to the visual immediacy of its ideograms, they speculated that Chinese might be the perfect Adamic tongue – the language originally given to man by God, which suffered no gap between sign and referent – thought lost since Eden and Babel. As Umberto Eco has shown, this 'universal language' was a sort of questing beast for European Renaissance thinkers – at different times, other candidates included Hebrew, Egyptian Hieroglyphs or various South American languages. Indeed, the Borges essay that gives *Loop of Jade* its epigraph touches on the historical search for this perfect language. 'Drawn with a very fine camelhair brush' plays a tricksy game with these ideas, on the one hand attempting to evoke this Western enchantment with the magical immediacy of Chinese, while on the other hand debunking it: the scholar-poet does lose his boat after all.

JW. It's interesting how you blend in the idea of enchantment, familiarity and mystery, and to go back to ancient sources or materials.

On relationship between family and writing

JW. How does your family impact on your identity?

SH. This is an important question for the book. I'd answer this is by talking about the 'loop of jade' that gives the book its name and the symbolic force it holds. It refers to the jade bracelet, sized for a baby's wrist, which my mother's adoptive mother bought for me when I was born. She had it blessed it at the temple at the same time as having my fortune told. As you know, such bracelets are meant to serve as a protective talisman for the toddling baby: the idea is that, should he or she fall, the jade will smash rather than the child being hurt. As an object that had a sort of direct, tactile contact with my family's past (it's practically the only object I have that passed through my adoptive Chinese grandmother's hands), this means I attribute to it some emotive value as an heirloom, despite its relative newness. For me it is a symbol of inheritance – a continuous circle, though one whose very purpose depends on the fact it can be broken – which I think aptly figures my own broken connection to my Chinese heritage. It was given to me by a Chinese grandmother I never really knew, and to whom I wasn't related by blood, because she was the woman who took in my mother as a baby. For me, that jade bracelet points both to the fracture in my family tree and to my efforts to reconnect with some sense of my Chinese ancestry.

JW. You are aware of this sense of connectedness to the past in addition to who you are.

SH. Yes, sometimes in quite strange ways: I have this uncanny sense whenever I go to Hong Kong or Guangdong that everyone I pass in the street could potentially be my family – long lost cousins, say. The fact that people from that part of the country do look so much like my mother – I sometimes think I see her in the crowd walking through a busy MTR station – gives rise in me to this sense of generalized kinship with the place that can't quite be pinned down. This is partly because the odds suggest that I probably do have a host of cousins, aunts, uncles or other relations still living in that part of China, and yet I can never know who they are. I think this feeling has shaped my poetry's encounters with the place.

On influences

JW. Are there any Chinese authors or Western authors who have influenced you?

SH. Most of the epigraphs in my book are from Western writers, with the exception of Mao and the collection of Buddhist koans – maybe there are more, but I can't remember off the top of my head. This probably does reflect my Western reference points and habits of thought. As for Chinese writers, I'm sure a book like *Wild Swans* has influenced me, as can be seen in a poem like 'Tame', whose very title is a sort of simultaneous homage and riposte to Jung

Chang's unavoidable volume. Xinran is also someone I have read quite a lot, especially on the question of Chinese mothers who have given away children, the twentieth-century and earlier history of that phenomenon. Yu Hua is also very interesting. His novels might well have influenced me in ways I'm not aware of – Zhang Yimou's film version of *To Live* was certainly a touchstone of my twenties, perhaps even more so than the original book. Yu Hua's recent essays in *China in Ten Words* really stuck in my mind – I've read that book several times. His thinking about how the political utterances of Chinese dissidents might need to be evasive in nature, working through metaphor and implication, has been important to me. However, with Chinese writers like these, I'm conscious how a historical moment like the Cultural Revolution looms very large in their work, but is not really a part of my own mother's story, since she was in Hong Kong through those years. And so in turn the Cultural Revolution isn't part of *Loop of Jade*'s imaginative landscape except quite tangentially, despite the disproportionately large role that subject matter usually plays in Western audiences' engagement with Chinese authors. Going back to non-fiction about Chinese culture, he's not Chinese of course, but the American journalist Peter Hessler's books have also been very important to me, especially *Oracle Bones*, which treats the excavated layers of Chinese history in a way I think had a noticeable impact on *Loop of Jade*.

JW. You have read quite a lot of Chinese fiction.

SH. I've been trying to, but not managing to get through as much as I'd like. I find it easier to get immersed in the stories and not worry so much about language and the translation, which is what I find when I'm reading Chinese poets in English.

JW. It is also quite noticeable that your work has been influenced by literature in the West.

SH. Yes, of course, that makes sense. This is particularly so considering the reading and writing I do because of my job as a scholar of English Renaissance literature, immersing myself in Shakespeare, Sidney, Donne and so on. I guess my writing illustrates the extent to which I am embedded in that tradition, but also writing against it in some ways.

JW. It is an interesting experiment of the poetic voice, even if the materials have to do with your family or personal life.

SH. My poem 'Yangtze', for example, echoes the tropes and landscapes of a Classical Chinese poem – in some ways its stance is that of a parody, albeit an admiring and affectionate one. But the poem also attempts to grapple with the challenges faced by a contemporary China caught up in fits of modernization that often prove traumatic. The clash of poetic styles – or in the case of 'Yangtze', the clash between style and subject matter – is a way for me to explore various thematic questions by indirect means. I thought hard in the last years of writing *Loop of Jade* about whether my work could be accused of indulging in a sort of decorative, exoticizing 'self-tokenization'. I think it boiled down to an anxiety about not being able to control how the poems would be read, yet not wanting to spell it all out too crassly for the reader. But in lots of ways, this particular worry goes to the heart of the questions to do with identity, politics and representation the book takes it upon itself to explore.

In borrowing their epigraph from the Borges 'Chinese encyclopaedia', that central suite of poems springs from a Western writer's self-conscious exercise in Orientalist projection, and the poems themselves dance a complex dance of advance and ironic withdrawal. In fact, I've been so heartened in recent months that readers of the book, especially its Chinese readers, do overwhelmingly seem to receive *Loop of Jade* in the way it was intended: neither as an exotic dispatch from an 'authentic' China, nor as a series of Western-imposed clichés, but as a work that troubles at both ideas.

JW. You have a lot of interest in Chinese classical literature, especially poetry. Who are the writers you enjoy?

SH. I can't say I am a scholar of that area, but I do have a great fondness for the usual-suspect Tang poets. I also absolutely love Eliot Weinberger's *19 Ways of Looking at Wang Wei*. It was a revelation to me, and extremely interesting because of the idea that translations need constantly to be remade for each generation. That book shaped the way I read Classical Chinese poetry. Among modern poets, I was reading for a long time poets like Yang Lian, Bei Dao, Gu Cheng, the Misty Poets, partly because they were – still are – the Chinese poets most prominently available in English translation in the UK. More recently I've been making more of an effort to seek out contemporary female Chinese poets, so a volume like Eleanor Goodman's wonderful translation of Wang Xiaoni's *Something Crosses My Mind* was a godsend.

JW. Do you think there is any Chineseness in your work or the work of other poets?

SH. It's an interesting question, to consider what might link Chinese poets from the mainland, Taiwan, Hong Kong with those from the diaspora, though I'm not sure I'm qualified to speculate. From my own perspective, there is not really a tradition of British-Chinese poetry to draw on yet. All of us who might be tentatively grouped under that label are such recent arrivals: me, you, Jane Yeh, Kit Fan and so on. None of the poets on that list were born in the UK. Hannah Lowe was born in England, but her Jamaican heritage also links her to quite another, equally rich strand in the history of Chinese diaspora. The situation in the UK is so different from America, where a whole burgeoning tradition of Asian-American poetry continues to thrive. It is interesting to think about why that sort of tradition didn't emerge earlier on in Britain, but is only just beginning (I hope!) to put down roots now.

An interview with Xichuan
(9 July 2014)

Differences between Chinese and Western literature

XC. Before 1989, the European writers were keen to experiment in their writings. After 1989, with the collapse of communist power in Eastern European countries, the era brought with it genuine problems that could not be evaded. What she said made me reflect on the difference between literature in the East and West. In the West, there is a constant interest in the experimentation with form and consciousness. Chinese literature, particularly before 1989, was much affected by realism in the West during the nineteenth century. On the contrary, there was not so much emphasis on experimentalism.

So the Chinese writer challenges not so much against form but against moral judgement. In general, those widely disseminated are the ones who confront the moral boundaries. Of course, there are also those who challenge politically. But in my opinion there are not many good writers in this arena. I feel that many writers have done better in offering moral critiques than political critiques.

We have lived in China for a long time. I once talked to an American photographer who did *100 Chinese Faces*. He asked me about the Cultural Revolution. In my travels to other countries, I noticed how many Chinese studies in the West have all depicted the Cultural Revolution as a terrible event. I was a child when it happened, and did not know how the other countries, so there is nothing to compare with. So to me, as a small child, the revolution was as natural as air. Life carried on, with or without the Revolution. Although it was a terrible event, but me and the other kids still played our games or fought among ourselves. There's also life alongside the revolution.

I once spoke with a female poet from South Africa, who said that South Africa is not all just about the Apartheid. She was born in South Africa. According to her, she still carried on with her family life, met with friends and so on, and had a romantic relationship, so there are many other things happening outside the system as well, no matter what the system is.

So this is a way how the West oversimplifies, and distils their understanding of China in terms of symbolic events. We also see the West in the same way. For example, we thought of America in terms of their President, democracy and so on. We thought of the UK in terms of the Queen, the prince, the royals... We don't really know the real life of the British. We always tend to oversimplify. While we are all aware of the many problems in China, I would highlight that the tolerance level of the Chinese people is different from the people in the West.

Moreover, if you live in China, it is almost impossible to expect the country to become like the West. For example, if I give a talk in the United States, they will write up a contract for it. In China, they will just give you the money. From these you can notice how different the systems are in the West and in China.

We live in a country where we speak a very different language. Our language uses shorter sentences and leap from one idea to another, whereas English is a language of logic. For example, Shelley's 'Ozymandias' is a poem made up of a very long sentence. This is almost impossible in Chinese. Charles Dickens also likes to use long sentences. While it is easier to escape from logic in Chinese as we do not use so many long sentences. As such, this is a question of language as well as politics. I once wrote an article on the subject of language, in which I analysed the differences between Chinese and English language.

On influences

XC. For example, I have read so many French poets back then, such as Baudelaire, Mallarme, Verlaine, Rimbaud, to the less brilliant poets such as Supervielle. There are also poets who are related to China such as Saint John Perce. These are all early-twentieth-century poets. There's also Segalen. From Germany, there are Rilke and Trakl whom I enjoy most. In Spain, I like Garcia Lorca,

Aleixandre and Machado. The most meaningful poets to me are still T. S. Eliot and Pound. Other than Cathay, Pound has translated the Confucian teachings such as *She Jing (Odes), Great Learning and Zhongyung.* Contrary to Ezra Pound, there's Borges. They are almost opposites, but I like both of them, the works of Borges characterized by its mathematical precision. I almost enjoy many Eastern European literature, such as Borovsky. I have also translated Milosz and the *Book of Conversations* by Borges, as well as the works by Pound and Gary Snyder. I read and enjoyed many American poets.

Sometimes, I find that I can talk about Western literature with American writers, but on the other hand, they cannot talk about Chinese literature in the same depth. It might have something to do with the speed and scope of our translation work. In China, there is an average of a hundred books of American literature translated into Chinese. On the other hand, only an average of two Chinese books are translated into English.

The works of immigrant writers are much valued in English-speaking countries, such as Salman Rushdie (India), Naipaul (Caribbean), Kazuo Ishiguro (Japan), and Booker Prize winners Ben Okri (Nigeria), Kiran Desai (India) and Arundhati Roy. These are people who write about other experiences and other ways of thinking. Some Chinese writers outside China, such as Yiyun Li and Ha Jin (US-based) and Guo Xiaolu (UK-based), have gained much attention.

On diasporic Chinese writers

XC. From my own observation, a Chinese writer who has relocated to America, let's say, can only talk about his country in past tense. For me, I live in the country and have experienced the country's changes in the last thirty years. For the writer who has moved abroad, these dramatic changes are such a distant matter for him. The only information he has about the country comes from the media and the internet, which is limited to certain topics or contents. For me, who live here, I can observe many other different things over the years. The historical logic cannot be reflected in the news or media contents the diasporic writer received.

On the other hand, I remember a reviewer mentioned that my writing is not based on a brief sojourn, but reflects what one knows from living in a place for a long time.

Typically, a Chinese writer abroad likes to write about the exotic.

A foreigner who comes to China is always looking for an ancient temple because he is a tourist. In fact, if a temple is a famous temple, the temple would have received a lot of donations and hence would have been renovated. The contradiction lies here. So the way you observe a temple is not to judge the temple by its exteriors, but to tell its history by looking for ancient trees onsite.

There is the risk of a Chinese diasporic writer to write about China from the perspective of a tourist, because of his readership. For example, there has been an article written by a Chinese professor criticizing Ha Jin's *Waiting* for eroticizing Chinese society because he writes about women with bound feet in a period when that foot-binding practice has been abolished already. So there is the question of readership. A Chinese poet living in Mainland China writes for a Chinese audience, while a Chinese writer who lives abroad is writing for an English-speaking readership. These are different audiences.

JW. Who are your favourite Chinese poets or who are the more representative poets?

XC. In my generation, there are Yu Jian, Ouyang Jianghe, Zhai Yongming and Wang Xiaoni. Younger poets, there are poets such as Lei Binyang, Duo Yu, Zang Di and Chen Xianfa. They have such distinct voices.

JW. What about women poets?

XC. Many Chinese women poets write extremely well. Zhou Zan, Zhai Yongming, Wang Xiaoni, Yin Lichuan, Yu Xiang and An Qi. So there are many.

JW. It is not easy to stand out as a poet in such a big country.

XC. Not easy at all. As an example, there is a population of two million in Wangjing [the district where the interview took place], while there is a population of five million in Denmark. So Denmark is twice the size of Wangjing.

JW. How is it possible to attract the Chinese readers?

XC. There is still of a problem of readership in China: some people are looking at their phones instead of reading books. Moreover, there is also the issue of different types of writers: some are publishing their works online, rather than in print form. So in China, you have to admit that your readership is quite different unless you were a bestseller.

[*Parts omitted as outside project scope*]

Identity of a poet and contemporary poetics

JW. What role do you think a poet has in society?

XC. Some writers like to write about their hometowns, or family stories or a certain generation. For me, it's not so much the theme that matters but the way of thinking. I can write about anything. A poet's work in China is to change people's way of thinking, to liberate them from set ways of thinking in the past, and this is also related to the idea of language. A country's change must start from one's way of thinking.

JW. How do you see the contemporary Chinese poetry scene and development?

XC. Nowadays, there are not too many contemporary poets with original, profound thinking. There is still room for improvement in this respect. Many of them are still prone to imitating, quoting or following other people's ideas or other theories. Their thinking does not originate from a reality.

JW. I find that some contemporary Chinese poetry is quite opaque, and there is also a lack of poetry criticisms or theories to analyse these poems for the readers.

XC. That's true. Michael Palmer, an American poet, said that American poets should read more Chinese poetry, although he felt that poets in America are unlikely to achieve that. What he said is quite true.

An interview with Shirley Lim
(5 February 2022)

JW. In many of your poems such as 'to Li Po', 'Modern Secrets', 'The Source'… you capture the relevance of Chinese identity – in terms of language, culture and myths. A global citizen and writer, how do you reflect on the complexity of your Asian/ Chineseness, and this constant shifting of identities across places (i.e. Malaysia, Hong Kong/Chinese, America)?

SL. My poems, composed across time and space – as a child into my twenties in Malaysia, adult professional in the United States, and sojourner-resident-visitor in Hong Kong, Taiwan and the PRC – reflect these identity shifts, insights, revisions and questions on the nature of 'Chineseness'. That is, the poems written over almost sixty years together compose how provisional 'Chinese' identity was and is, how its many situational constructions have proven destabilizing, and how writing, whether poem, fiction, memoir or critical analysis, can endlessly imagine and re-imagine any identity – for your interview, 'Chinese', but at other moments 'woman' or 'mother', for example. I have taken as subjective and objective truth that 'Being' is doing. We are what we act. The Existentialists radically shifted our understanding of 'Being': WHO and WHAT we are not static. If Being is an essence, that essence (humanity, femininity, etc.) is a condensation of Becoming, of transformation. Such self-reflexive and meta-critical meditations on identity shifts are represented in my poems, stories, cultural critiques and my memoir, *Among the White Moon Faces*.

On the woman as the other

JW. In your poems, you have explored a diverse range of emotions/conflicting feelings in a woman: as thinker/writer, as a woman, as a mother, daughter, etc.

SL. Your segue here from Chinese to gender identity underscores strong interest in the identity issues you read in my poems. The poems referenced in your summative analysis do address, represent, explore and problematize female thematics, through relational narratives, family figures and socio-political meditations. At the same time, your elisions suggest that experiences of womanhood, the female body and situational gender roles (wife, housekeeper, nurturer, teacher, 'poetess', and more) are so multiple, conflicting, sometimes overlapping or synchronous, that the single word 'woman' taps into deep civilizational histories of this entire half of the human race. Expressions, effacements and traces of this half threaded through immense literary traditions continue to fascinate me as a reader, scholar and writer.

JW. I am intrigued by 'A Woman Speaks of Grandchildren': what does the ending hypothesis signify? And what does this mean: '[I]t's terrible to be / seduced by filthy books / ... to delete the world'?

SL. I am pleased you've raised 'A Woman Speaks of Grandchildren' for parsing. It's a cross-polyphonic, dialectical poem, and I don't think anyone has offered an analysis of its voices.

I read the poem as unironic at one level, and as ironically entangled at another. How I understand it is where I am situated emotionally at the moment of my reading. The speaker, as the title notes, is already turned to maternal desire: she desires grandchildren. Her opening position hyperbolically attacks the other desire, for 'poetry' as a second-rate Icarus' ambition – a woman's 'broken flight', arrogance resulting in death, in contrast to the life-affirmative nurturance of motherhood.

The first stanza sets up the structure of opposing drives, deeply immersive and passionately held in one body. Maternal desire, the ideal of the 'good mother', is enacted in the social, sensual, nurturing domain of the female body (yeasty thighs, backside, fragrant rice and milk) to produce the posterity evidenced in grandchildren. In contrast, the second stanza is relentlessly negative against the life of the mind, rejecting books as 'filthy', 'seductive', producing through 'high thoughts' a painful asceticism (starve, eat your heart out) and coercive self-isolation, hence resulting in a life 'wasted … in libraries'.

Yet the third stanza's elaboration on this rejected ideal is lyrical, even romantic, drawing on fairy-tale imagery ('sea-king's palaces'). The imagery picks up the first stanza's snarky, satirical image of the poet as someone who is half-asleep, boring, a bird falling and drowning as she struggles to fly, but turns this negative poet-figure on its head. The solitary scholar-poet desires – 'wants' – a life of 'deep talk', spent in libraries' 'tall walls of words'. The diction – clear blue, swift bird, heart of light, airy towers – alludes to classic traditions in which Poetry is valorized, and in so doing it subverts the harsh criticism voiced earlier.

The short closing stanza thus reads as ambivalent resignation or as a synthesis to the stanzaic structures of thesis and antithesis. The woman can never be wholly a mind in flight, disembodied. What remains is the maternal, material world, but there she must give way to a futurity in which her voice is silenced even as her body has been productive: '[I] fall asleep among loud voices/of grandchildren.'

The poem speaks to the tensions I live with daily, between a domestic physical world with its many pleasures and the internal mental world of poetry that drives, illuminates and signifies an ineffable ideal. The dilemma it delineates is gender-demoralizing; to my mind, although family obligations may well obstruct many men from literary pursuits, no man would emblematize his struggles in pursuing a poet's vocation as caused by the desire for grandchildren.

JW. In 'I Look for Women', I am surprised by the imagery of the 'sufficient' swans. Is that a mocking reference to Yeats?

SL. Yes, the image of the swans alludes slyly to Yeats' 'Leda and Swan', and, behind Yeats' recycling of the original story in Ovid's *Metamorpxhoses*. My poem's layered allusions, however, are not mocking but express a hoped-for agency, in its seizing of the ancient narrative, to strip it off its patriarchal power, the original brutality of Zeus' lust for the beautiful Leda and the transformation of the deity-self to a swan who rapes her as she dries her body by the river. That male Godhead, the rapacious Swan, is erased and re-imagined as a host of female swans, gentle and secure in their self-sufficiency. As the poem's title frames the new swans' story, I look/hope for such self-sufficient women, i.e. free from heterosexual desires, agendas and cruelty. I used this poem as a prologue in my memoir, *Among the White Moon Faces: An Asian-American Memoir of Homelands,* to signal that among the memoir's purposes were its intentions to praise and celebrate such self-sufficient feminists, to memorialize the historical and autobiographical experiences of patriarchal injustices and disorders, and to narrate my own journey through the labyrinthine confusions of coming to womanhood.

JW. 'My Mother Wasn't' is also a complex poem where the daughter translates her difficult emotions and allegiances by mixing the real and the surreal.

SL. Very few readers have noted this poem, I suspect precisely because it is so complex. The title, 'My Mother Wasn't', underscores the poem's theme, which is to displace all conventional social constructions of the mother figure as a universal type for nurturance. Instead, as the first line states, 'My mother was Chye Neo,' a local, individualized female, whose name identifies her as a Peranakan girl. 'Neo', coming from the Hokkien dialect, signifies ladies in the Chinese Imperial court, and marks the high descent status of the female subject. The poem is structured on this oxymoron: the biographical mother, although not an archetype but a historically socialized individual bearing the expectations of class and race, is nonetheless a gendered subject whose life story is burdened by traditional patriarchal strictures: 'fate/ that married her at sixteen,/ a good eldest daughter'. For the daughter-narrator, that universal maternal archetype, 'the... vessel of childhood', is shattered when the mother abandons her children, taking away with her the secrets of her unique communal and individual attributes and stories, breaking irreparably the generational transmission of female bonds that secures individual and social psyches: 'Before I could learn... why/ I was a daughter/ not a son, she left.' The daughter is fated by her mother's abandonment to gender/sexual confusion.

While the first stanza offers a compressed story of the mother's domestic talents and unhappy marriage, the last two stanzas do shift from realistic particulars to what you insightfully term 'the surreal'. For the daughter, her mother's abandonment flashes back in dreams that play out her childhood trauma. The daughter's broken relationship with the mother can only be apprehended in the realm of the sur-real, in super-charged emotions expressed in fantastical action and imagery. The surreal taps the psychic unconscious, through dreamwork that is able to access repressed emotions that are socially unacceptable and so unspeakable. For me, the poem enacts symbolically the violence that lies under feminist struggles. It raises to consciousness what first and second wave feminists do not address: what happens when a woman prioritizes what Henrik Ibsen called through the character of Nora in *The Doll's House* her 'sacred duty' to self before duty to her children. In her dream, the daughter receives her mother with hostility: 'I will not forgive till I have made you pay.' The poem underscores that abandoning maternal duty for self-actualization is not a triumph over patriarchy. I read Nora as a male-constructed heroine whose values are set in masculine terms; Nora's slamming the door as emblematizing a clarion call for freedom from patriarchal domesticity, to my mind, is a reductive gender reversal between adults. But for the girl-children left behind in the father's house, the loss of protective mother care suggests their total abandonment to uncontested patriarchy. The violence in the poem's last stanza, where the speaker confuses the mother's original situation, an early ill-fated marriage, with her own revenge theme, expressed in the animalistic image of the sow that eats its own young, enacts in its very incoherence the confusion of generational resentment that is seldom acknowledged.

The personal and the political

JW. In some of the poems in Do You Live In, *you explored the political values through interrogating the personal. In 'Children's Movement', 'National Day' and 'The Blood of the Children', your portrayal of the children brings back the idea of the family, or a family in quarrel, where the children are breaking away from the (seemingly patriarchal) family or the familial structures. Some of the poems compare the writer's and the children's actions, and bring in the speaker's longing for freedom (e.g. 'Teach the Free Man How to Praise'). Why do you choose to call them 'children'?*

SL. The answer is very simple. These poems address, describe and historicize the fact that these particular protestors were literally children, and sometimes young adults (YA). The scenes of children in their distinctive school uniforms camping out on the Hong Kong streets and avenues, holding classes so as not to miss on their studies, reading their textbooks and cleaning up their litter represented an image of the Hong Kong democracy movement as a unique form of disciplined struggle for a non-PRC future: if not for an independent HK, at least for the fulfilment of the 'one country two systems' promise. The poet-speaker is empathetic to the younger generation's idealism which in some ways is universal (e.g. 'Give me freedom or give me death' being a famed revolutionary slogan against tyranny and dictatorship). The title of the poem, 'Teach the Free Man How to Praise' is doubly allusive, alluding to W. H. Auden's eulogy, 'In Memory of W. B. Yeats', and to Yeats whose poems praising the Irish killed in the uprising against their British colonial rulers have served as a North Star to poets in similar anticolonial circumstances. I have always loved Yeats' 'Easter 1916'. Auden's eulogy celebrates the poetry of freedom struggles in both their failures and promise of future good with imperatives being strung on tense polarities:

> … sing of human unsuccess
> In a rapture of distress;
> In the deserts of the heart
> Let the healing fountain start,
> In the prison of his days
> Teach the free man how to praise.

This poem is self-reflective; it views its very articulation as an ironic exercise, the failure of the HK Democracy Movement already predictably 'unsuccessful' and the poem's voicing of the failure 'a rapture of distress'. What Auden's poem recognizes is how humanistic positivity evolves from its origins in the realities of human life as captive and barren, and that even 'in the prison of his days', the subject who learns 'to praise' is asserting the agency of 'the free man'. Dissent both realizes and signifies freedom. My poem plays on the complex dialectic of tyranny, failed protest and advancement towards a freer future that Auden's poem so masterfully expresses. The poem speaks in the moment of the HK Democracy Movement. But as a meta-poem, a play on Yeats' and Auden's visions of human struggles for liberty and against tyranny, it is not speaking only to that moment.

Literary influences

JW. From your early poems, you engage quite often with the Western canon (e.g. Coleridge, Marianne Moore, Whitman, Wallace Stevens). How do you see your own poetic lineage as an Asian poet?

SL. I do not fully understand what you mean by 'poetic lineage'. Your term sets up a biological/familial line of descent for me, identified as 'an Asian poet', whose engagement with 'the Western canon' needs explanation or may arguably be viewed as problematic. I resist casting poetry, its praxis, workings on collectivities and individuals, as a biological or even 'natural' phenomenon. It is a profoundly human cultural enterprise rising from specific historical contexts. Archaeologists and art historians have discovered similarities and parallels in prehistoric cave art across territories and continents that establish a synchronicity in human creativity. The power of discovering correspondence in unlike subjects, of storytelling shaping tribal rituals and identities, recording and speaking as central performances marking important moments – preparing for a hunt or combat, spring planting, autumn harvest, initiation celebrations, public funereal laments and more – the few who achieved such song and language abilities were honoured for their remarkable services. Coleridge's imaginative turn to strange tales was influenced by his enjoyment of Arabian *Thousand and One Nights* that circulated in popular English versions in the eighteenth century. Ezra Pound's *Cantos* may be placed in a lineage with Chinese Tang poets and Confucianist Analects. Entering a solely English-only school at six, I was steeped in Mother Goose rhymes. With no Chinese literacy and schooled minimally in Bahasa, now Malaysia's national language, I was raised as an indubitably Anglophone reader and writer. The 'Western canon' is MY canon. However, I am a multicultural subject, and my images, stories, allusions, socio-political urgencies, and even the sounds and rhythms in many of my poems are not a repetition of Western canonical texts. Readers will have to approach my work as mashed-up, mélange, interior and external-worldly inflected poems.

Immigration and courage

JW. *Many of your immigrant poems ('Blossoming') explore courage and homecoming. I enjoy 'Riding into California', the way you play with the sense of ghostliness of an adopted country, the mutual distrust between the immigrant and the adopted country. The line 'The good thing about being Chinese on Amtrack/ is that no one sits next to you.' This is so powerful. Thinking of this poem and others such as 'I Defy You', would you also say that for you there is an intersection between the problem of race and the problem of class?*

Any views on the current discourse labelling minority poets as 'writers of colour'?

SL. Initially, when the identity marker 'of colour' began to be used in the domain of writing, I was taken aback, even intrigued. 'Of colour' was a sociological concept, useful to demarcate histories and practices that discriminated against groups constructed as non-Anglo-Saxon British/American 'whites'. Obviously if non-whites were subordinated to colonialist whites, then they could collectively be viewed as 'people of colour'.

An interview with Cynthia Miller
(10 August 2021)

JW. Tell us more about your childhood: How are your journeys across continents related to your writing life?

CM. I'm Malaysian American, and my mom is Malaysian Chinese. The themes of migration and languages which I wrote about reflect the way we grew up. We had a very international childhood. My parents worked in economic development, we moved around a lot. I was born in Malaysia, lived in Nepal for my early years; lived in Beijing when I was six and went to a school there. I have lived in the United States since I was eight for several years.

When I was fourteen years old, we moved to India, completed high school in New Delhi, then I continued with university. At that time, my parents moved to the Philippines for work reasons. Mom's family are based in Malaysia the whole time and still are, while Dad's family lives in the United States. These are my anchor points on different sides of the world. So it makes it quite complicated how I understand how home and belonging are.

JW. Did you grow up knowing both sides of the family?

CM. Yes, we used to go back every summer, spent months in Malaysia. My parents tried their best to keep in contact with our family as much as possible, whenever we went back to Malaysia.

JW. What languages/dialects do you speak and how do you relate to those language(s)?

CM. Mom's family spoke Hokkien, but me and my sister don't have the same access to that language. It's an odd sensation to be surrounded by a dialect that we don't have.

We have been to Beijing and so spoke Beijing Mandarin. It's an uneasy feeling, being a few layers removed from my mom's native language. I am very curious about the Hokkien dialect, and there's a sense of foreignness in how the language sits.

In Malaysia, I don't feel totally Malaysian, and although I am American I don't feel American either.

JW. Being partly Malaysian, how do you connect with Chinese culture?

CM. There's a connection with China culturally. We still share many of the deep-rooted traditions, especially Chinese New Year. It's about how diasporic communities preserve the traditions because 'home' is so far away.

JW. Where do you feel most at home?

CM. I see Edinburgh as my home now. I have lived in the UK longer than anywhere else so this is home for now.

JW. Do you feel that your poems are an act of cultural translation?

CM. One of my central poems is my attempt to translate the honorifics into something that I understand. In my writing, I tried to translate my lived experiences and half-remembered episodes into things that I understand. The process of translation involves me communicating with my mom to rediscover what those experiences or names mean. Andrew McMillan talks about 'writing towards the lack'. For her, it is writing towards the lack of that language. And so honorifics is such an important and charged term: your centre of gravity is the family; the way you understand the others and generations before you. I also wrote about my grandmother who passed away before I was born, which again reflects a lack that I was writing towards.

JW. In using dialects in your poetry, what do you expect from your reader? Do you think they need to know or look up the meaning of these words?

CM. I deliberately do not italicize the Chinese or Malay words. I don't have an appendix or glossary. The reader can look those up themselves. For me, these poems create a mosaic of language and culture where things don't quite fit. Moreover, I don't have an uneasy relationship with Chinese and Hokkien, and I feel that I am still reckoning these languages and identities.

JW. Who are your literary influences?

CM. I admire the work of Nuar Alsadir, her notion of time, how she captures memory and identity – Ocean Vuong. I also love the surreal and fantastic work of Jane Yeh. I also enjoy reading Vanessa Angélica Villarreal's experimental work.

JW. Do you have any writing advice for writers?

CM. I'd say look for inspiration in odd places; stay curious, and to locate the voices you like. I think it's also important to have persistence.

A conversation with Nina Mingya Powles (12 August 2021)

On the meaning of home

JW. What do you think about being at home and being away? If you have experienced it, do you feel it has any temporary or permanent impact on your work?

NMP. Growing up in several countries, moving every few years – which I've continued to do into adulthood – has certainly shaped everything about me, including my work. I know I'm incredibly lucky to have absorbed lots of different places as a young child. I think I grew up learning how to be a skilled observer: quiet, almost invisible. Coming from a mixed background, I sometimes feel like I'm invisible at times but hyper-visible in other settings, which is a strange mode to permanently exist in.

JW. Do you think there is an ideal or utopian place where you belong?

NMP. No, there isn't. When I first started writing I think I was trying to write towards this imagined place – a nostalgic, phantom vision of 'home'. I slowly realized home was not one physical location but a multitude of places, scents, memories, people. I could never entirely relate to my school friends who had grown up all in one place – they knew where they belonged. I was never so sure.

JW. Have you ever felt at home being where and who you are? If you do, what gives rise to this conviction?

NMP. I've lived in the flat where I live now, in London, for three years, which is the longest I've lived in one physical place since I was seventeen. Before that, I carried bits of home around with me wherever I went and determinedly created my own sense of home wherever I lived: with a box of kitchen things, some photos on the wall, a pile of poetry books atop a desk. Although the past two years have been destabilizing and distressing, they've also forced me to ground myself here. This period has forced me to put down roots: to grow a small weedy garden, to cultivate new friendships, to allow myself to think of this city as one of my homes. But if I had to pick one place? Wellington, New Zealand, is my home.

On identity as a writer

JW. Do you see your identity as a Chinese writer? Should ethnicity be ignored or taken into account when readers appreciate your work?

NMP. I'll never be able to answer this question definitively! Yes, sometimes I feel that I can claim this space – but always with the knowledge that most people don't see me as Chinese. I have Chinese heritage, therefore I am a Chinese writer just as I am a New Zealand writer, but I don't necessarily fit within (white) readers' imagined version of a 'Chinese writer'. And it is true that East Asia generally is an entirely exotic, imaginary place for many readers who encounter my work for the first time. That's when a reader's response might be to take my work as representative of a culture or ethnicity or, unfortunately, 'mixedness', when, of course, it isn't – it's only me, writing from my own perspective. That's all I hope to do. A reviewer once remarked on 'exotic' imagery in my poetry, and to them I want to say nothing at all. I have nothing to say to someone who reads my work that way. My work is not for them.

JW. How do you perceive or understand your Chinese roots?

NMP. For a long time I didn't consider my Chinese heritage a 'real' part of me; it was hidden, inaccessible, invisible. It's still mostly invisible to others, but it is wholly a part of me regardless. Dedicating time to learning Mandarin helped with this, but also the understanding that learning a language is an immense privilege. Having the time and money and energy to dedicate to learning a mother tongue is not something everyone is able to do. Mandarin has been my first point of access, but now I want to delve deeper into the dialectic languages that actually make up more of my roots than Mandarin does: Hakka, Cantonese.

JW. When you write, who do you write for?

NMP. In the early stages of a poem or an essay, I don't write for anyone but myself. Otherwise, I couldn't do it. Later, in the editing process, I might sometimes have an imagined reader in mind – a friend, or someone like me. I used to worry about translating myself for other people, but over time, learning from other poets and writers, I shook off that fear.

On diasporic imagination and writing about the family

JW. How do you approach the gap in understanding between the East and West? Do you think that there is anything lost in translation or can it be bridged?

NMP. I honestly don't know how to answer these kinds of questions, because it's difficult for me to objectively perceive of such a 'gap'. I am of mixed heritage: white and Malaysian Chinese. Recently I was introduced to someone who asked me about where I grew up. I told them that I was born in Aotearoa and moved to China when I was twelve. Their response: 'But the two cultures are so different. How did you cope with that?' Yes, a Chinese city is a vastly different place to scenic Wellington, but I know that's not what they were saying. As they spoke to me, looking at me directly, with my Chineseness all but invisible to them, what they meant was: Chinese people are so different, so other. I struggle to articulate myself in these moments because my very existence becomes momentarily paradoxical, inconceivable and invisible. I am tired of explaining my existence to people – of bridging that 'gap' in their imagination.

JW. How do you understand authenticity? To me, 'city of forbidden shrines' and 'Origin myths' or even 'colour fragments' seem to be about challenging the traditional way we appreciate (ethnic) authenticity?

NMP. My struggle is not unique; so many of us come up against ideas of what it means to truly belong. My friend, who is also mixed, offered this phrase to me in a conversation the other day: 'catching up'. Growing up in a majority-white country, with mostly white friends, you just always feel like you're constantly trying to catch up when it comes to things like cultural festivals, recipes, languages, customs. I hope to bring this unsteady in-between space to the forefront in my writing. It's a space of insecurity, doubt and dislocation, but it's also a place of warmth and connection.

JW. You have written about your nostalgia for Asian food in your memoir and poetry. Why do you write about it or has relevance for you as a writer?

NMP. I write about food because I love to eat. I am always thinking about my next meal; it's always on my mind, so I always circle back to it in my writing. It has in my life also been a crucial point of connection to my Malaysian-Chinese heritage. I am interested in what it means to be a woman who writes about enjoying eating – what it means to take up space deliberately and extravagantly in that way, to not deny myself the pleasure of eating, as the world often expects us to.

On language

JW. Can you tell us about your relationship with language(s)? For example in Small Bodies of Water, *you offer such a fascinating account charting your experience of the Chinese language, and of your ways of breaking down the meaning of words.*

NMP. If you've done any learning of a pictorial language with characters instead of a phonetic alphabet, you know that rote learning is incredibly difficult. It comes down to repetition and muscle memory. It's been nearly five years now since I was engaged in full-time language study. So much has slipped away, but the places where it's stayed with me are in my fingers, hands, and my tongue and mouth. I am interested in the physical aspects of language learning and this slippage – you can constantly feel bits of the language slipping away, even as you acquire more of it. Some days you feel you might be 'fluent', but the next day, you feel like a child again. No writer has articulated this better to me than Polly Barton in her recent memoir Fifty Sounds, about living in Japan and learning Japanese. To me, language is fluid and physical and intimate.

On writing influences

JW. What writers do you like?

NMP. The writers who first taught me how to write were Anne Carson, Ocean Vuong and Katherine Mansfield. It's been unbelievably hard to read with sustained attention over the past two years but I've recently enjoyed several short memoirs and novellas, especially *Cold Enough for Snow* by Jessica Au, *Dear Memory* by Victoria Chang and *Luster* by Raven Leilani.

JW. How did you see your work as different from the mainstream poets?

NMP. I try to compare myself to others as little as possible, otherwise it would be paralysing! So I'm not sure – I'm also not sure where the 'mainstream' lies, or that poetry can ever be mainstream. I think that's what I like about it. I feel that in poetry I can hide away a little bit, and only reveal parts of myself as and when I choose. One point of difference I often think about is that I'm not a performer. So many poets are able to embody their work in physical performance and that is magical to me.

A conversation with Jennifer Lee Tsai
(4 April 2022)

On the meaning of home

JW. When did your family move to the UK? What did they do when they first arrived here?

JLT. As a second-generation British-born Chinese woman, the meaning of home has always opened itself up to imaginative and transcendent possibilities. I was born in Bebington, a town on the Wirral in Merseyside in the North West of England, to Chinese parents who emigrated to Liverpool in the 1960s with their respective parents. Like most Chinese immigrants of their generation, my parents and grandparents worked in the restaurant and catering business. I grew up in Liverpool, which has the oldest Chinese community in Europe.

By birth, I am British, specifically English. However, my identity and sense of home feel quite hybrid, complex and multi-layered, through the inescapable fact of my Chinese ancestry and ethnicity.

For me, metaphorically, home is not merely a fixed physical place or space in a geographical sense. I conceive of it as an ongoing quest for embodiment – rooted in the body, heart, mind, soul and spirit.

On identity as a writer

JW. How do you see yourself as a writer and who do you write for?

JLT. First and foremost, I see myself as being a writer. However, who am I writing for and why do I write? These are both crucial and complex questions to ask and to answer.

I could answer in a variety of ways; I write for myself, I write for my ancestors, for my parents who will never be able nor perhaps wish to read what I write for my family, for a future version of myself or someone like me, for a lover, a friend, a stranger, for you.

My connection to Hong Kong and China is felt through my family heritage, from my parents and grandparents on both my mother and father's side. My father originally came from Guangzhong in South China and my mother comes from the New Territories in Hong Kong. My paternal grandfather was a seaman on the Blue Funnel Line, which was a shipping company founded in 1865 by Alfred Holt and played an important part in Liverpool's maritime history and position as a port. It employed a large number of Chinese seafarers. The origins of Liverpool's China town and Chinese community are partly attributable to the Blue Funnel connection. My mother originates from the Hakka tribe, a Han-Chinese minority, reputed for their diasporic nature.

If I had to define myself as a writer in terms of nationality, I would describe myself as a British-Chinese writer. Questions of race and belonging or not belonging are ones that I explore in my work as well as concepts of Chineseness, and what it means to be second-generation British-born Chinese.

JW. Would you call yourself a feminist?

JLT. I would definitely describe myself as being feminist. In both my creative and critical work, I am inspired by and critically respond to the work of the so-called French feminists including Hélène Cixous, Julia Kristeva and Luce Irigaray.

I am interested in the interplay between historical fact, poetic truth and the imagination in my work, the impossibility or complexities of knowing or not knowing, and exploring those silences and omissions.

My work is written from my own unique perspective, of a British-born Chinese woman and explores questions of class, identity and race from that viewpoint.

On diasporic imagination and writing about the family

JW. How do you understand authenticity?

JLT. I am interested in questions of authenticity and exoticism in relation to identity and how the lyric can expand or transform to articulate and convey the complexities of a racialized subjectivity. I am fascinated by questions of authenticity, subjectivity and otherness from a psychoanalytic perspective.

On language

JW. Can you tell us more about your relationship with language(s)?

JLT. I grew up speaking two languages, English and Cantonese. Being British-born, and having lived in Britain all my life, English is very much my dominant language. I am interested in the ways that language shapes our identity and how that relates to poetry and poetic form.

With regard to language and my relationship to Cantonese, I am aware of the effects of language loss or disruption, how one's identity may be affected and enriched by the meeting or collision of two contrasting identities and conflicting cultures: the transformative and radical possibilities that might emerge from such hybridity.

On writing influences

JW. Who are your literary influences?

JLT. My literary influences are extremely eclectic and have developed over a long time. I like and admire the work of so many writers. At school, I loved poets such as Sylvia Plath, Emily Dickinson, Blake, Keats, Dylan Thomas, Shelley, Christina Rossetti but also Shakespeare, Thomas Hardy, the Brontës, George Eliot, Tolstoy. I studied Latin and Ancient Greek both at school and university so I also loved Homer, Virgil, Ovid, Sappho. I became interested in women's writing and spirituality when I did my first master's degree, which was called 'Women and the Word', where I studied a range of female writers and philosophers on questions of gender, spirituality and belief. For a few years, I immersed myself deeply in the works of Virginia Woolf, Anaïs Nin, Jean Rhys and psychoanalytic theory and philosophers such as Jung, Otto Rank, Luce Irigaray, Julia Kristeva, Hélène Cixous.

With regard to contemporary poetry and poets, I love the work of poets such as Audre Lorde, Theresa Hak Kyung Cha, Sandeep Parmar, Vahni Capildeo, Bhanu Kapil, Ocean Vuong, Nuar Alsadir, Ilya Kaminsky, Valzhyna Mort, Claudia Rankine, Emily Berry, Mei-mei Berssenbrugge, Denise Riley.

JW. Do you feel that you are more influenced by Chinese or English poetics (if we can approximate them as such)?

JLT. At school, I grew up mainly with the English poetic lyric tradition so to an extent, these poets are present within my imaginary but I seek to move beyond these influences. In recent years, I look towards the American lyric tradition, at ways that writing can innovate and create new forms.

My understanding of Chinese vs English poetics is guided by intuition and instinct, and what I know of their linguistic differences. I don't really see myself as being influenced by any Chinese poets specifically, although I sense the significance of a shared collective unconscious and a rich reservoir of imagery. I admire the work of Chinese poets such as Bei Dao, Wang Xiaoni and Zhai Yongming, as well as philosophical texts such as Lao Tzu's Tao-Te Ching and the I-Ching.

JW. What are you working on?

JLT. More recently, I am interested in exploring hybrid forms of writing, the lyric essay, the use of theory/philosophy, notebook fragments, memoir and autobiography in poetry.

JW. Would you say that your poetry breaks taboos by alluding to a woman's sexual desire/experiences and engages with the uneasy terrains of inequality in gender relationships?

JLT. As a British Chinese woman writer, I feel that my poetry does engage with and breaks certain cultural taboos that my parents' and grandparents' generations hold or held, in writing about difficult experiences to do with violence, lyric shame, abuse and childhood trauma as well as the complexities of desire.

JW. How much have your appreciation of the works by French feminists helped you reshape your language or to discover ways of writing difficult feelings and contesting gender positions (e.g. embarrassment, vulnerable feelings or traumatic memories)? E.g. in the uncomfortable intimacy in 'You Said' and 'Black Star'?

JLT. The work of the so-called French feminists has enabled me to explore and interrogate notions of otherness, spirituality and embodiment, to focus on the invitation to write the body, to embrace the idea of a feminine writing, the primacy of the unconscious.

Bibliography

Abbas, Ackbar, *Hong Kong: Culture and the Politics of Disappearance* (Minneapolis: University of Minnesota Press, 1997).

Altehenger, Jennifer and Denise Ho, *Material Contradictions in Mao's China* (Washington: University of Washington Press, 2022).

Ang, Ien, *On Not Speaking Chinese: Living between Asia and the West* (London and New York: Routledge, 2005).

Appadurai, Arjun and Carol Breckenridge, 'On Moving Targets', *Public Culture*, 2 (1989), i–v.

Ashcroft, Bill, 'Including China: Bei Dao, Resistance and the Imperial State', *Textual Practice*, 27.3 (2013), 357–77.

Aw, Tash, 'Fluidity and Resistance: Ideas of Belonging in a Fractured World', in *East Side Voices: Essays Celebrating East & Southeast Asian Identity in Britain*, edited by Helena Lee (London: Hodder & Stoughton, 2022).

Baraka, Amiri, *Digging: The African-American Soul of American Classical Music* (Berkeley and Los Angeles, CA: University of California Press, 2009), 23, 26.

Benton, Gregory, Huimei Zhang and Hong Liu (eds), *Chinese Migrants Write Home: A Dual Language Anthology of Twentieth-century Family Letters* (Singapore, Hackensack, New Jersey and London: World Scientific, 2020).

Bei, Dao, *Notes from the City of the Sun: Poems by Bei Dao*, edited and translated by Bonnie McDougall (Ithaca, NY: Cornell University, 1983).

Bei, Dao, 'Interview with Siobhan LaPiana', *The Journal of the International Institute*, 1.2 (1994), <http://quod.lib.umich.edu/j/jii/4750978.0002.102?view=text;rgn=main> [Accessed 10 May 2017].

Bei, Dao, 'Interview with Gabi Gleichmann', *Modern Chinese Literature*, 9 (1996), 387–93.

Bei, Dao, *Bei Dao's Poems* (Haikou: Nan Hai Publishing, 2003).

Bei, Dao, *The Rose of Time: New and Selected Poems*, edited by Eliot Weinberger, translated by Yanbing Chen, David Hinton, Chen Maiping, Iona Man-cheong, Bonnie S. McDougall and Eliot Weinberger (New York: New Directions, 2009).

Bei, Dao, 'Interview with Xiaodu Tang', *World Literature Today*, 82.6 (2008), 20–36.

Bei, Dao, *The Selected Works of Bei Dao* (Wuhan: Changjiang Literature and Art Press, 2012).

Benton, Gregor, 'Chinese Transnationalism in Britain: A Longer History', *Chinese Transnationalism in Britain: A Longer History, Identities: Global Studies in Power and Culture*, 10.3 (2003), 347–75.

Berger, Stefan, Linas Eriksonas and Andrew Mycock, *Narrating the Nation: Representations in History, Media and the Arts* (New York and Oxford: Berghahn Books, 2008).

Bhabha, Homi, *The Location of Culture* (London and New York: Routledge, 2004).

Boehmer, Elleke, *Postcolonial Poetics: 21st Century Critical Readings* (Basingstoke: Palgrave Macmillan, 2018).

Brady, Andrea, 'The White Privilege in Poetry Is Getting Worse', 8 October 2015, <https://theconversation.com/the-white-privilege-of-british-poetry-is-getting-worse-48516> [Accessed 2 April 2018].

Brah, Avtah, *Cartographies of Diaspora: Contesting Identities* (London and New York: Routledge, 2005).

Broughton, Trev Lynn and Linda R. Anderson, *Women's Lives/Women's Times: New Essays on Auto/Biography* (Albany: State University of New York Press, 1997).

Brown, Mark, 'T. S. Eliot Prize: Poet Sarah Howe Wins with "Amazing" Debut', *The Guardian* (2016), <https://www.theguardian.com/books/2016/jan/11/ts-eliot-prize-poet-sarah-howe-wins-with-amazing-debut> [Accessed 6 June 2016].

Bruno, Cosima, 'Writers in London: Home and Languaging in the Work of Poets of Chinese Descent', *Life Writing* 14.1 (2017), 37–55.

Craig-Norton, Jennifer, Christhard Hoffmann and Tony Kushner, *Histories and Historiographies: Essays in Honour of Colin Holmes* (London and New York: Routledge, 2018).

Bush, Katy Evans, 'Witnessing the Flow: On Hannah Lowe, Matreyabandu, Marianne Burton and Rebecca Goss, New Poets Immersed in the Stuff of Life', *Poetry Review*, 104.4 (2014), 77.

Butler, Judith, *Undoing Gender* (London and New York: Routledge, 2004).

Butler, Judith, *Gender Trouble: Feminism and the Subversion of Identity* (London and New York: Routledge, 2007).

Cashmore, Ellis et al., *Dictionary of Race and Ethnic Relations*, 2nd edition (London: Routledge, 1984).

Cashmore, Ellis, *Encyclopedia of Race and Ethnic Studies* (London: Routledge, 2008).

Chambers, Iain, *Migrancy, Culture and Identity* (London and New York: Routledge, 1994).

Chan, Mary Jean, 'Queerness as Translation: From Linear Time to Playtime', *Modern Poetry in Translation*, 2 (2018), <https://modernpoetryintranslation.com/queernessas-translation-from-linear-time-to-playtime/> [Accessed 2 April 2018].

Chan, Mary Jean, *Flèche* (London and New York: Faber & Faber, 2019).

Chan, Mary Jean, *A Hurry of English* (Oxford: ignitionpress, 2018).

Chan, Mary Jean, "Journeying is Hard': Difficulty, Race and Poetics in Sarah Howe's *Loop of Jade*", *Journal of British and Irish Innovative Poetry* 12(1) (2020), 1–22.

Chan, Sucheng, 'Asian American Historiography', *Pacific Historical Review*, 65.3 (1996), 371.

Chang, Chung-yuan, *Creativity and Taoism: A Study of Chinese Philosophy, Art, and Poetry* (London and Philadelphia: Singing Dragon, 2011).

Chang, Elizabeth, 'Britain's Chinese Eye: Literature, Empire, and Aesthetics in Nineteenth-century Britain', *Victorian Studies*, 53.4 (2011), 751–3.

Cheung, King-Kok, 'An Interethnic Companion to Asian American Literature' (1997).

Cheung, King-Kok, 'The Chinese American Writer as Migrant: Ha Jin's Restive Manifesto', *Amerasia*, 38.2 (2012), 2–12.

Cheung, King-Kok, 'Ethnic Ethic and Aesthetic: Russell C. Leong and Marilyn Chin', *Foreign Literature Studies*, 39.5 (2017), 9–25.

Cheung, King-Kok, 'Transpacific Poetics: Ideographic and Prosodic Transpositions in Li-Young Lee's "Persimmons" and Marilyn Chin's "Summer Sleep"', *University of Toronto Quarterly*, 82.2 (2019), 246–62.

Childers, Joseph and Gary Hentzi, *The Columbia Dictionary of Literary and Cultural Criticisms* (New York: Columbia University Press, 1995).

Chin, Marilyn, *Dwarf Bamboo* (New York: Greenfield Review Press, 1987).

Chin, Marilyn, Garrett Hongo, Li-Young Lee, David Mura and Mary Slowik, 'Beyond Lot's Wife: The Immigration Poems of Marilyn Chin, Garrett Hongo, Li-Young Lee, and David Mura', *MELUS*, 25.3/4 (2000), 221–42.

Chin, Marilyn, 'An Interview with Maxine Hong Kingston', *MELUS*, 16.4 (2002), 57–74.

Chin, Marilyn, *Rhapsody in Plain Yellow* (New York and London: W. W. Norton, 2002).

Chin, Marilyn, *Hard Love Province* (New York and London: W. W. Norton, 2014).

Chin, Marilyn, *Portrait of the Self as Nation: New and Selected Poems* (New York and London: W. W. Norton, 2018).

Chingonyi, Kayo, 'Worrying the [Blood]line of British Poetry: Notes on Inheritance and Alterity', < http://swimmers.london/swim_kayochingonyi_worryingthebloodline. pdf> [Accessed 2 April 2018].

Clifford, James, *Routes: Travel and Translation in the Late Twentieth Century* (Cambridge, MA: Harvard University Press, 1997), 257.

Clifford, James, 'Diasporas', *Cultural Anthropology*, 9.3 (1994), 302–38.

Chow, Rey, *Not Like a Native Speaker: On Languaging as a Postcolonial Experience* (Columbia: Columbia University Press, 2014).

Cooppan, Vilashini, 'World Literature and Global Theory: Comparative Literature for the New Millennium', *Symploke*, 9 (2001), 33.

Crucefix, Martyn, 'Forward First Collections Reviewed 5: Sarah Howe' (2015), <https:// martyncrucefix.com/2015/09/06/forward-first-collections-reviewed-5-sarah-howe/> [Accessed 6 June 2016].

Cua, Antonio, *Encyclopedia of Chinese Philosophy* (New York and London: Routledge, 2003).

Cushman, Stephen et al. (eds), *Princeton Encyclopaedia of Poetry and Poetics*, 4th edition (Princeton and Oxford: Princeton University Press, 2012).

Damrosch, David, *What Is World Literature?* (Princeton and Oxford: Princeton University Press, 2003).

Damrosch, David, 'World Literature, National Contexts', *Modern Philology*, 100.4 (2003), 527–8.

Damrosch, David, *How to Read World Literature* (New Malden, MA: Wiley-Blackwell, 2009).

Daniel, Roger, 'The Coming of the Chinese', in *Asian American: Chinese and Japanese in the United States since 1850* (Seattle: University of Washington Press, 1988).

Dowson, Jane, *The Cambridge Companion to Twentieth Century British and Irish Women's Poetry* (Cambridge: Cambridge University Press, 2011).

Du Bois, W. E. B., *The Souls of Black Folk* (London: Archibald Constable & Co., 1905).

Dufoix, Stéphane, *Dispersion: A History of the Word Diaspora* (Leiden: Brill, 2016).

Dung, Kai-Cheung, *Atlas: The Archaeology of an Imaginary City*, edited by Trs Dung Kai-cheung, Anders Hansson and Bonnie McDougall (New York: Columbia University Press, 2012).

Edmond, Jacob, *A Common Strangeness: Contemporary Poetry, Cross-cultural Encounter, Comparative Literature* (New York: Fordham University Press, 2012).

Erikson, Erik, *Identity: Youth and Crisis* (New York: W. W. Norton, 1968).

Evaristo, Bernadine and Daljit Nagra (eds), *Ten: New Poets from Spread the Word* (Tarset: Bloodaxe Books, 2010), <https://www.bloodaxebooks.com/ecs/product/ten-new-poets-from-spread-the-word-974> [Accessed 21 July 2020].

Fan, Kit, *As Slow as Possible* (Todmorden: Arc Publications, 2018).

Farris, S. Catherine, 'Gender and Grammar in Chinese: With Implications for Language Universals', *Modern China*, 14.3 (1988), 277–308.

Flowerdew, John, 'Discriminatory Discourse Directed towards Mainlanders', in *Critical Discourse Analysis in Historiography* (London: Palgrave Macmillan, 2012).

Fluharty, Matthew, 'An Interview with Li-Young Lee', *Missouri Review* Issue 23.1 (2000), 81–100.

Fox, 'A Conversation with Li-Young Lee', *Rattle* (2013), <https://www.rattle.com/a-conversation-with-li-young-lee/>, [Accessed 20 April 2018].

Friedman, Susan Stanford, *Mappings: Feminisms and the Cultural Geographies of Encounter* (Princeton: Princeton University Press, 1997).

Friedman, Susan Stanford, 'Bodies on the Move: A Poetics of Home and Diaspora', *Tulsa Studies in Women's Literature*, 23.2 (2004), 189–212.

Gao, Jay, *Imperium* (Manchester: Carcanet, 2022).

Gao, Jay, 'Jay Gao on *Imperium*', *The London Magazine* (2022) [Accessed 22 September 2022].

Garber, Linda, *Identity Politics: Race, Class, and the Lesbian-feminist Roots of Queer Theory* (New York: Columbia University Press, 2001).

Geoghegan, Vincent, 'Remembering the Future', *Journal of the Society for Utopian Studies*, 1.2 (1990), 67.

Gilroy, Paul, *There Ain't No Black in the Union Jack: The Cultural Politics of Race and Nation* (Abingdon and Oxfordshire and New York: Routledge, 1987).

Gilroy, Paul, *The Black Atlantic: Modernity and Double Consciousness* (London and New York: Verso Books, 1993).

Gleason, Philip, 'Identifying Identity: A Semantic History', *The Journal of American History*, 69.4 (1983), 910–31.

Goh, Robbie, 'Imagining the Nation: The Role of Singapore Poetry in English in Emergent Nationalism', *Journal of Commonwealth Literature*, 41.2 (2006), 21.

Goya, Yogita, *The Cambridge Companion to Transnational American Literature* (Cambridge: Cambridge University Press, 2017).

Gustafsson, Lars, '"The Utopia of the Moment": The Poetry of Tomas Transtromer', *World Literature Today*, 64.4 (1990), 596–7.

Guthrie, Andrew, 'Hong Kong Poet Tammy Ho: Art in Politics or Politics in Art?' *Hong Kong Free Press* (2016), <https://hongkongfp.com/2016/10/24/hong-kong-poet-tammy-ho-art-politics-politics-art/> [Accessed 5 May 2021].

Hall, Stuart, 'Cultural Identity and Diaspora', in *Identity, Community, Culture, Difference*, edited by Jonathan Rutherford (London: Lawrence & Wishart, 1990).

Haralson, Eric (ed.), *The Encyclopedia of American Poetry: The Twentieth Century* (New York and Oxford: Fitzroy Dearborn Publishers, 2001).

Harris, Will, *Mixed-race Superman* (London: Peninsula Press, 2018).

Harris, *RENDANG* (London: Granta, 2020).

Hena, Omaar, 'Multi-ethnic British Poetries', in *The Oxford Handbook of Contemporary British and Irish Poetry*, edited by Peter Robinson (Oxford: Oxford University Press, 2013).

Hillenbrand, Margaret, 'Communitarianism, or, How to Build East Asian Theory', *Postcolonial Studies*, 13.4 (2010), 317–34.

Hillenbrand, Margaret, *Negative Exposures: Knowing What Not to Know in Contemporary China* (Durham: Duke University Press, 2020).

Hong, Cathy Park, *Minor Feelings: A Reckoning on Race and the Asian Condition* (London: Profile Books, 2020).

Hong, Zicheng, 'The Early Poems of Bei Dao', *Journal of Hainan Normal University*, 18.1 (2005), 4–10.

Hong, Zicheng, *A History of Contemporary Chinese Literature* (Leiden and Boston: Brill, 2007).

Ho, Tammy, *Hula-hooping* (Hong Kong: Chameleon Press, 2015).

Ho, Tammy, 'Can We Say Hong Kong?' *The Offing* (17 January 2017), <https://theoffingmag.com/enumerate/can-say-hong-kong/> [Accessed 21 January 2022].

Ho, Tammy, *Too Too Too Too* (Singapore: Math Paper Press, 2018).

Ho, Tammy and Jason Eng Hun Lee, 'Anglophone City Poetics and the Asian Experience: A Conversation with Grace Chia', *World Literature Today*, 93.1 (2018), 34–8.

Howe, Sarah, *A Certain Chinese Encyclopedia* (Luton: tall-lighthouse, 2009).

Howe, Sarah, *Loop of Jade* (London: Chatto & Windus, 2015).

Howe, Sarah, 'To China: That Blue Flower on the Map', *The Best American Poetry Blog* (2016), <http://blog.bestamericanpoetry.com/the_best_american_poetry/2016/02/i-to-china-that-blue-flower-on-the-map-by-sarah-howe.html> [Accessed 6 June 2016].

Howe, Sarah, 'Sarah Howe in Conversation with Nicholas Wong', *Wasafiri*, 32.3 (2017), 32–7.

Hsiao, Irene, 'Broken Chord: Sounding Out the Ideogram in Marilyn Chin's Rhapsody in Plain Yellow', *MELUS*, 37.3 (2012), 189–214.

Hsu, Madeline Yuan-yin, *Dreaming of Gold, Dreaming of Home: Transnationalism and Migration between the United States and South China, 1882–1943* (Stanford, CA: Stanford University Press, 2000).

Hua, Anh, 'Diaspora and Cultural Memory', in *Diaspora, Memory, and Identity: A Search for Home*, edited by Vijay Agnew (Toronto: University of Toronto Press, 2005).

Huen, 'The "Old Hong Kong" and "A Gold-Sifting Bird": Hong Kong and Chinese Ekphrasis in Contemporary British Poetry', *Wasafiri*, 37.1 (2022), 13–21.

Innes, C. L., *A History of Black and Asian Writing in Britain* (Cambridge, UK and New York: Cambridge University Press, 2008).

Ingersoll, Earl, *Breaking the Alabaster Jar: Conversations with Li-Young Lee* (New York: BOA Editions, 2006).

Ingham, Michael Anthony and Xu Xi, *City Voices: An Anthology of Hong Kong Writing in English: 1945 to the Present* (Hong Kong: Hong Kong University Press, 2003).

Jin, Ha (Jin Xue Fei), *The Writer as Migrant* (Chicago, IL: University of Chicago Press, 2008).

Kangxi Dictionary, <http://www.zdic.net/z/18/xs/5BB6.htm> [Accessed 7 May 2017].

Katrin, Kohl, Rajinder Dudrah, Andrew Gosler, Suzanne Graham, Martin Maiden, Wen-chin Ouyang and Matthew Reynolds (eds), *Creative Multilingualism: A Manifesto* (Cambridge: Open Book Publishers, 2020).

Kerr, Douglas, 'Afterword', in *Incense Tree: The Collected Poems of Louise Ho*, edited by Louise Ho (Hong Kong: Hong Kong University Press, 2009), 155–62.

Kinnahan, Linda, *Lyric Interventions: Feminism, Experimental Poetry, and Contemporary Discourse* (Iowa City: University of Iowa Press, 2004).

Kington, Maxine Hong, *PBS Newshour* (2019), <https://www.youtube.com/watch?v=B6pYuYCOgC4> [Accessed 9 May 2021].

Lam, Agnes, *Becoming Poets: The Asian English Experience* (Bern: Peter Lang, 2014).

Larrissy, Edward, *The Cambridge Companion to British Poetry, 1945–2010* (New York: Cambridge University Press, 2016).

Lazarus, Neil, *The Postcolonial Unconscious* (New York: Cambridge University Press, 2011).

Lavie, Smadar and Ted Swedenburg (eds), *Displacement, Diaspora, and Geographies of Identity* (Durham and London: Duke University Press, 1996).

Lee, Li-Young, *The City in Which I Love You* (New York: BOA Editions, 1990).

Lee, Li-Young, *The Rose* (New York: BOA Editions, 1986).

Lee, Li-Young, *From Blossoms: Selected Poems* (Tarset: Bloodaxe Books, 1986).

Lee, Li-Young, *The Undressing* (London and New York: W. W. Norton, 2018).

Lee, Erika and Judy Yung, *Angel Island: Immigrant Gateway to America* (Oxford: Oxford University Press, 2012).

Lee, Gregory, *China Imagined: From European Fantasy to Spectacular Power* (London: Hurst & Co, 2018).

Lee, Gregory, 'An English poet from the Liverpool Cantonese borderlands – Lee Tsai, Jennifer, Kismet (ignitionpress, 2019).

Lee, Jason EH and Iyer, Sreedhavi, 'On not writing back: Cosmopolitan paradoxes in new diasporic Malaysian writing today', *Journal of Postcolonial Writing* 57.1(2021), 1–15.

Lee, Laura Jane, *Flinch & Air* (London: Outspoken Press, 2021).

Leung, Ping-kwan, *City at the End of Time: Poems by Leung Ping-kwan*, edited by Esther M. K. Cheung, translated by Gordon T. Osing and Leung Ping-kwan (Hong Kong: Hong Kong University Press, 2012).

Leung, Rachel Ka Yun and Silvia Suk Yi Tse (eds), *People, Pandemic and #######: The Kongpowrimo 2020 Anthology* (Birmingham: Verve Poetry Press, 2020).

Li, Chen-yang, *The Confucian Philosophy of Harmony* (London and New York: Routledge, 2014).

Li, Dian, 'Ideology and Conflicts', *Modern Chinese Literature*, 9.2 (1996), 372.

Li, Dian, *The Chinese Poetry of Bei Dao 1978–2000* (New York: Edwin Mellen Press, 2006).

Lim, Geok-lin, Shirley, 'Feminist and Ethnic Literary Theories in Asian American Literature', *Feminist Studies*, 19.3 (1993), 570–95.

Lim, Shirley Geok-lin and Mayumi Tsutakawa (eds), *The Forbidden Stitch. An Asian American Women's Anthology* (Corvallis: Calyx, 1989).

Lim, Shirley, John Geok-lin, Stephen Sohn and Gina Valentino, *Transnational Asian American Literature: Sites and Transits* (Philadelphia: Temple Press, 2006).

Lim, Shirley, John Gamber Geok-lin, Stephen Sohn and Gina Valentino, *Walking Backwards* (Alberqueque: West End Press, 2010).

Lim, Shirley, John Gamber Geok-lin, Stephen Sohn and Gina Valentino, *Embracing the Angel: Hong Kong Poems* (Hong Kong: City University of Hong Kong Press, 2014).

Lim, Shirley, John Gamber Geok-lin, Stephen Sohn and Gina Valentino, *Do You Live In?* (Singapore: Ethos Books, 2015).

Lim, Shirley, John Gamber Geok-lin, Stephen Sohn and Gina Valentino, *In Praise of Limes* (Santa Barbara: Sungold Editions, 2015).

Lim, Walter S. H., *Narrative of Diaspora*: *Representations of Asia in Chinese American Literature* (London: Palgrave Macmillan, 2013).

Liew, Walter, *Premonitions: The Kaya Anthology of New Asian North American Poetry* (New York: Kaya Productions, 1995).

Ling, Amy, *Between Worlds. Women Writers of Chinese Ancestry* (New York: Pergamon Press, 1990).

Ling, Huping, *Surviving on the Gold Mountain: A History of Chinese American Women and Their Lives* (Albany, NY: SUNY Press, 1998).

Liu, Shuang, *Identity, Hybridity and Cultural Home: Chinese Migrants and Diaspora in Multicultural Societies* (London and New York: Rowman & Littlefield International, 2015).

Liu, Shu-hsien and Kwong-loi Shun, 'Some Reflections on Mencius's Views of Mind-Heart and Human Nature', *Philosophy East and West*, 46.2 (2006), 147.

Loh, Lucienne, *Postcolonial Literature and Challenges for the New Millennium* (London and New York: Routledge, 2015).

Lowe, Hannah, *Chick* (Tarset: Bloodaxe Books, 2013).

Lowe, Hannah, *Ormonde* (London: Hercules Editions, 2014).

Lowe, Hannah, *Chan* (Tarset: Bloodaxe Books, 2016).

Lowe, Hannah, 'Writing the *Empire Windrush* and *Chan'* (Doctoral thesis, Newcastle University, 2016).

Lowe, Hannah, *Old Friends* (London: Hercules Edition, 2022).

Ma, Sheng-mei, 'Orientalism in Chinese American Discourse: Body and Pidgin', *Modern Language Studies*, 23.4 (1993), 105.

Madsen, Deborah, *Feminist Theory and Literary Practice* (London: Pluto Press, 2000).

Manley, Lawrence, *The Cambridge Companion to the Literature of London* (Cambridge: Cambridge University Press, 2011).

Mao, Sally Wen, 'Interview: A Conversation with Marilyn Chin' (2020), <https://www.poetryfoundation.org/articles/153560/wild-girl-poet> [Accessed 20 July 2021].

Marshall, Tod and Li-Young Lee, 'To Witness the Invisible: A Talk with Li-Young Lee', *Kenyon Review*, 22.1 (2000), 132.

McCarthy Woolf, Karen (ed.), *Ten: The New Wave* (Tarset: Bloodaxe Books, 2014).

McDougall, Bonnie, 'Problems and Possibilities in Translating Contemporary Chinese Literature', *The Australian Journal of Chinese Affairs*, 25 (1991), 45, 49.

McKirdy, David, *Ancestral Worship* (Hong Kong: Chameleon Press, 2014).

Meyer, Jean-Baptiste, 'Diaspora', *Encyclopaedia Britannica* (2014), <https://www.britannica.com/topic/diaspora-social-science> [Accessed 5 May 2017].

Mills, C. Wright, *Sociological Imagination* (London: Penguin, 1970).

Miller, Cynthia, *Honorifics* (Rugby: Nine Arches Press, 2021).

Milosz, Czeslow, 'Notes on Exile', *Books Abroad*, 50.2 (1976), 281–4.

Morley, David, *Home Territories: Media, Mobility and Identity* (London and New York: Routledge, 2000).

Morley, David and Kuan-Hsing Chen, *Stuart Hall: Critical Dialogues in Cultural Studies* (London and New York: Routledge, 1996).

Mu, Michael Guanglun and Bonnie Pang, *Interpreting the Chinese Diaspora: Identity, Socialisation and Resilience According to Pierrre Bourdieu* (London and New York: Routledge, 2019).

Mura, David, 'The Margins at the Center, the Center at the Margins: Acknowledging the Diversity of Asian American Poetry', in *Reviewing Asian America: Locating Diversity*, edited by Wendy Ng (Washington: Washington University Press, 1995), 171–84.

Naradan, Saad Nawras, *Orientalism: On the Problem of Speaking for the Orient*. Diss. Colorado State University, 2015, Web [Accessed 5 September 2016].

Nasta, Susheila, *Writing Across Worlds: Contemporary Writers Talk* (London and New York: Routledge, 2004).

Nasta, Susheila, *The Cambridge History of Black and Asian British Writing* (Cambridge: Cambridge University Press, 2019).

Nayar, Pramod, *The Postcolonial Studies Dictionary* (Chichester: John Wiley & Sons, 2015).

Neigh, Janet, 'Ramazani's Global Vocabulary for Poetry', *Journal of Modern Literature*, 34.3 (2011), 199–202.

NeuJournal, 'Interview by NeueJournal' (2016), <http://neuejournal.com/sarah-howe/> [Accessed 6 June 2016].

Ng, Franklin, *Asian Americans: Re-conceptualising Culture, History, Politics* (New York and London: Garland Publishing, 1997).

O'Neill, Mark, *The Chinese Labour Corps: The Forgotten Chinese Labourers of the First World War* (Melbourne, VIC: Penguin Group Australia, 2014).

Ortmann, Stephan, 'Singapore: The Politics of Inventing National Identity', *Journal of Current Southeast Asian Affairs*, 28.4 (2009), 23–46.

Osborne, Deirdre (ed.), *The Cambridge Companion to British Black and Asian Literature* (Cambridge: Cambridge University Press, 2016).

Owen, Stephen, 'Stepping Forward and Back: Issues and Possibilities for "World" Poetry', *Modern Philology*, 100.4 (2003), 532–48.

Parmar, Nissa, '"Double Happiness": An interview with Marilyn Chin', *Contemporary Women's Writing*, 8.3 (2014), 251–61.

Parmar, Sandeep, 'Not a British Subject: Race and Poetry in the UK', *LA Review of Books* (2015), < https://lareviewofbooks.org/article/not-a-british-subject-race-and-poetry-in-the-uk/> [Accessed 2 April 2018].

Parmar, Sandeep, 'The I, Lyric Time and Slant', *Poetry London*, 88 (2017), 40–3.

Patke, Ranjeev, *Postcolonial Poetry in English* (London and New York: Oxford University Press, 2006).

Petit, Pascale, 'Chair of Judges 2015 T S Eliot Prize-giving Speech', *Poetry Book Society*, <http://www.poetrybooks.co.uk/projects/47> [Accessed 6 August 2016].

Poetics of Home Chinese Diaspora Poetry Festival (2021), <https://www.youtube.com/channel/UCNhG-SgDJcBtl7-BJ_NlJ7Q> [Accessed 6 August 2016].

Polly, Jason S., Vinton Wing Kin Poon and Lian-Hee Wee (eds), *The Cultural Conflict in Hong Kong* (Singapore: Palgrave, 2018).

Porter, David, *The Chinese Taste in Eighteenth-century England* (Cambridge: Cambridge University Press, 2010).

Powles, Nina Mingya, *Tiny Moons: A Year of Eating in Shanghai* (London: The Emma Press, 2019).

Powles, Nina Mingya, *Magnolia*, 木蘭 (Rugby: Nine Arches Press, 2020).

Price, Barclay, *The Chinese in Britain: A History of Visitors and Settlers* (Stroud: Amberley Publishing, 2019).

Quayum, Mohammed A. and Shirley Geok-lin Lim, 'Shirley Geok-lin Lim: An Interview', *MELUS*, 28.4 (2003), 83–100.

Ramazani, Jahan, 'A Transnational Poetics', *American Literary History*, 18.2 (2006), 332–59.

Ramazani, Jahan, *A Transnational Poetics* (Chicago and London: University of Chicago, 2009).

Ratiner, Steven, *Giving Their Word: Conversations with Contemporary Poets* (Amherst: University of Massachusetts Press, 2004).

Reynolds, Matthew, *Prismatic Translation* (Cambridge: Modern Humanities Research Association, 2021).

Riemenschnitter, Andreaa and Deborah L. Madsen, *Diasporic Histories: Cultural Archives of Chinese Transnationalism* (Hong Kong: Hong Kong University Press, 2009).

Rosemont, Henry and Roger T. Ames (eds), *The Chinese Classic of Family Reverence: A Philosophical Translation of the Xiaojing* (Hawaii: University of Hawaii Press, 2009).

Rushdie, Salman, *Imaginary Homelands: Essays and Criticisms 1981–1991* (London: Granta Books, 1991).

Rushdie, Salman, *Step across This Line: Collected Non-fiction 1992–2002* (Toronto: Alfred A. Knopf).

Said, Edward, *Edward Said and Critical Decolonization*, edited by Ferial J. Ghazoul (Cairo: American University in Cairo Press, 2000).

Said, Edward, *Reflections on Exile and Other Essays* (London: Grants Books, 2002).

Said, Edward, *Orientalism* (London and New York: Penguin, 2003).

Sean, Wai-keung, *Sikfan Glaschhu* (Birmingham: Verve Poetry Press, 2021).

Shih, Shu-mei, 'Global Literature and the Technologies of Recognition', *PMLA*, 119.1 (2004), 16–30.

Shih, Shu-mei, 'Against Diaspora: The Sinophone as Places of Cultural Production', in David Der-wei Wang's *Global Chinese Literature: Critical Essays* (Leiden: Brill, 2010).

Siu, Paul, *The Chinese Laundryman* (New York and London: New York University Press 1987).

Sleigh, Tom, *Interview with a Ghost: Essays* (Minnesota: Graywolf Press, 2006).

Slowik, Mary, 'Beyond Lot's Wife: The Immigration Poems of Marilyn Chin, Garrett Hongo, Li-Young Lee and David Mura', *MELUS*, 25 (2000), 221–42.

Smadar, Lavie and Ted Swedenburg (eds), *Displacement, Diaspora, and Geographies of Identity* (Durham and London: Duke University Press, 1996).

Sollors, Werner, *Beyond Ethnicity: Consent and Descent in American Culture* (New York: Oxford University Press, 1986).

Stearns, Peter N., 'Chinese Overseas', in *The Oxford Encyclopedia of the Modern World* (Oxford: Oxford University Press, 2008).

Sun, Wenbo, *Writing in Relativity (Zhai Xiang Dui Xing Zhong Xie Zuo)* (Beijing: Peking University Press, 2010).

Schwartz, Catherine et al. (eds), *The Chambers Dictionary*, 7th edition (Edinburgh: Chambers Harrap Publishers, 1988).

Stevenson, Angus (ed.), *Oxford Dictionary of English*, 3rd edition (Oxford: Oxford University Press, 2010).

Tan, Chee-Beng, *The Routledge Handbook of the Chinese Diaspora* (London and New York: Routledge, 2013).

Tan, Chee Lay, *Constructing a System of Irregularities: The Poetry of Bei Dao, Yang Lian, and Duoduo* (Newcastle upon Tyne: Cambridge Scholars Publishing, 2016).

Tay, Eddie, *The Mental Life of Cities* (Hong Kong: Chameleon Press, 2010).

Tay, Eddie, *Colony, Nation, and Globalisation: Not at Home in Singaporean and Malaysian Literature* (Hong Kong: Hong Kong University Press, 2010).

Tay, Eddie, *Dreaming Cities* (Singapore: Math Paper Press, 2016).

Tay, Eddie, *Anything You Can Get Away with: Creative Practices* (Singapore: Delere Press, 2018).

Tay, Eddie, *Anything You Can Get Away with: Creative Practices* (Hong Kong: Delere Press, 2018).

Thurston, Michael and Nigel Alderman, *Reading Postwar British and Irish Poetry* (New Jersey: Wiley-Blackwell, 2014).

Tölölyan, Khachig, 'The Nation-State and Its Others: In Lieu of a Preface', *Diaspora: A Journal of Transnational Studies*, 1.1 (1991).

Tu, Weiming, *The Living Tree: The Changing Meaning of Being Chinese Today* (Stanford, CA: Stanford University Press, 1994).

Van Crevel, Maghiel, *Chinese Poetry in Times of Mind, Mayhem and Money* (Leiden: Brill, 2008).

Vertovec, Stephen, 'Three Meanings of Diaspora, Exemplified among South Asian Religions', *Diaspora*, 6.3 (1997), 277–99.

Vertovec, Stephen, 'Migrant Transnationalism and Modes of Transformation', *International Migration Review*, 38.3 (2004), 970–1001.

Vertovec, Stephen, *Transnationalism* (London and New York: Routledge, 2009).

Vixram, Rozina, 'History of Asians in Britain 1600–1950', in *Migrant Britain* (London and New York: Routledge, 2018).

Wade, Peter, 'Hybridity Theory and Kinship Thinking', *Cultural Studies*, 19.5 (2005), 602–21.

Wager, Jason, 'Marilyn Chin', in *The Chronicle* (Durham: Duke University Press, 1998).

Wai-Lim, Yip, *Diffusion of Distances: Dialogues between Chinese and Western Poetics* (Oxford: University of California Press, 1993).

Wang Der Wei, David and Jing Tsu, *Global Chinese Literature: Selected Essays* (Leiden: Brill, 2010).

Wang, Dorothy, *Thinking Its Presence: Form, Race, and Subjectivity in Contemporary Asian American Poetry* (Stanford, CA: Stanford University Press, 2013).

Wang, Gungwu, 'A Single Chinese Diaspora?' in *Diasporic Chinese Ventures: The Life and Work of Wang Gungwu*, edited by Gregor Benton and Hong Liu (London and New York: Routledge, 2004), 157–8.

Wang, Gungwu, *Nanyang: Essays on Heritage* (Singapore: Yusof Ishak Institute ISEAS, 2018).

Wang, Gungwu, *Home Is Not Here* (National University of Singapore Press, 2018).

Wang, L. Ling-chi and Gungwu Wang, *The Chinese Diaspora: Selected Essays* (Singapore: Times Academic Press, 1998).

Weisner, Ken, 'Interview with Marilyn Chin', *MELUS*, 37.3 (2012), 215–26.

White, Hayden, 'The Value of Narrativity in the Representation of Reality', *Critical Inquiry*, 7.1 (Autumn 1980), 5–27.

Wilson, Rob and Wimal Dissanayake, *Global/Local: Cultural Production and the Transnational Imaginary* (Durham and London: Duke University Press, 1996).

Witchard, Anne (ed.), *British Modernism and Chinoiserie* (Edinburgh: Edinburgh University Press, 2015).

Wong, Jennifer, 'An interview with Eleanor Goodman' (2015), unpublished manuscript.

Wong, Jennifer, 'Walking to Jupiter: The Place of the Personal for Chinese Women', *Poetry London*, 83 (2016), 54, 55.

Wong, Jennifer, 'Redeeming Desire: A Conversation with Li-Young Lee', *World Literature Today*, 92.1 (2018), <https://www.worldliteraturetoday.org/2018/january/redeeming-desire-conversation-li-young-lee-jennifer-wong> [Accessed 20 April 2018].

Wong, Jennifer, 'On Home, Belongingness, and Multicultural Britain: A Conversation with Hannah Lowe', *World Literature Today*, 92.2 (2018), <https://www.worldliteraturetoday.org/2018/march/home-belongingness-and-multicultural-britain-conversation-hannah-lowe-jennifer-wong> [Accessed 20 April 2018].

Wong, Jennifer, 'A conversation with Nina Mingya Powles' (2021), mss.

Wong, Nicholas, *Crevasse* (LA: Kaya Press, 2015).

Wong, Nicholas, *Besiege Me* (New Mexico: Noemi Press, 2021).

Wong, Nicolette (ed.), *Looking Back at Hong Kong: An Anthology of Writing and Art* (Hong Kong: Cart Noodle Press, Chinese University of Hong Kong, 2021).

Wootten, William, 'On Jack Underwood and Sarah Howe', *Poetry Review*, 105.3 (2015), 89.

Worra, Bryan Thao, 'Interview with Marilyn Chin' (2008), <http://thaoworra.blogspot.co.uk/2008/03/2003-interview-with-marilyn-chin.html> [Accessed 9 May 2017].

Xu, Wenying, *Eating Identities. Reading Food in Asian American Literature* (Honolulu: University of Hawai'i Press, 2008).

Yao, Steven, *Foreign Accents: Chinese American Verse from Exclusion to Postethnicity* (Oxford and New York: Oxford University Press, 2010).

Ying, Li-hua, *Historical Dictionary of Modern Chinese Literature* (Lanham: Scarecrow Press, 2010).

Young, Robert C., *Colonial Desire: Hybridity in Theory, Culture and Race* (London: Routledge, 2005).

Yu, Shi, 'Identity Construction of the Chinese Diaspora, Ethnic Media Use, Community Formation, and the Possibility of Social Activism', *Continuum*, 19.1 (2005), 55–72.

Yu, Timothy, *Race and the Avant-garde: Experimental and Asian American Poetry since 1965* (Stanford, CA: Stanford University Press, 2009).

Yu, Timothy, *Diaspora Poetics: Asian Writing in the United States, Canada, and Australia* (Oxford University Press), 2021.

Zhang, Benzi, 'Of Nonlimited Locality/Identity: Chinese Diaspora Poetry in America', *Journal of American Studies*, 40.1 (2006), 134–6.

Zhang, Benzi, *Asian Diaspora Poetry in North America* (London and New York: Routledge, 2008).

Zhou, Min, *Contemporary Chinese Diasporas* (Singapore: Palgrave Macmillan, 2017).

Zhou, Xiaojing, *The Ethics and Poetics of Alterity in Asian American Poetry* (Iowa: Iowa University Press, 2006).

Zhu, Xiaowen Zhu, *Oriental Silk* (Berlin: Hatje Cantz, 2020).

Index

Milton Keynes UK
Ingram Content Group UK Ltd.
UKHW011456010224
437107UK00002B/4